Stock Market Investing for Beginners

The Complete Guide to Forex Trading and Stock Investments. Earn with Swing and Day Trading Techniques to Create a Passive Income.

Martha Guertin

Table of Contents

Options Trading

Beginner's Guide to Forex Market Tools and Tactics, Volume Price Analysis (VPA) and Swing Trading Investments. Risk and money management in the stock market to create passive income.

Martha Guertin

Options Trading Part 1

Introduction Part 1

Congratulations on purchasing *Options Trading* and thank you for doing so.

The following chapters will discuss various topics that are crucial to trading options. If you have ever wanted to learn about options, then this is the perfect book for you. We introduce you to options in a simple yet effective way so that you get to understand the basics as well as essential details for successful trading.

The book not only introduces you to some basic techniques but also introduces you to other crucial topics including technical analysis, options chains, about brokers and brokerage firms, and even risk management. This way, you will not just learn how to trade options but also how to safeguard your trading capital and profits as well.

There are plenty of books on this subject on the market, thanks again for choosing this one! Every effort was made to ensure it is full of as much useful information as possible, please enjoy it!

Chapter 1: An Introduction to Options Trading

What is Options Trading?

There are numerous ways of creating wealth but trading the markets is among the most popular. Trading is known to generate high returns whether it is active or passive. The most lucrative form of trading involves trading options. Any trader that wants to grow their wealth should move away from traditional investments and move to more lucrative stock market instruments. For instance, traders should invest their funds in options to grow wealth much faster and in significant amounts.

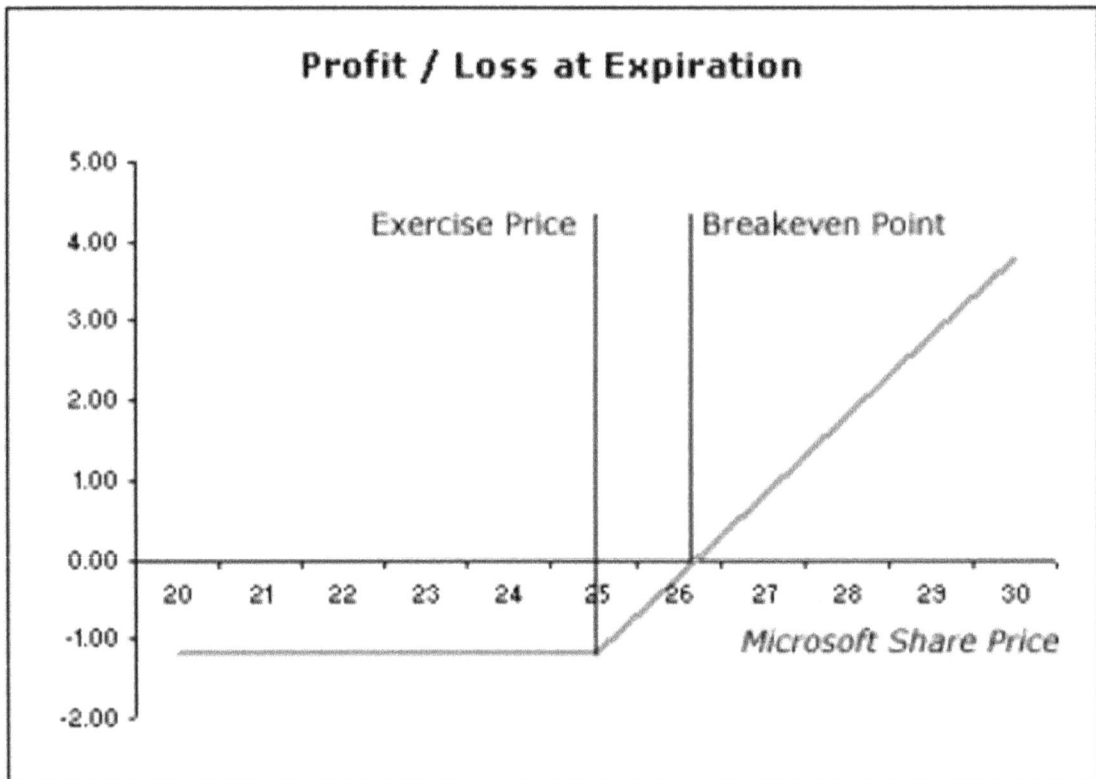

Profit / Loss at Expiration

5.00	
4.00	Exercise Price Breakeven Point
3.00	
2.00	
1.00	
0.00	

Microsoft Share Price

What are Options?

Options are a type of financial security that is traded at the financial markets. This means you can buy and sell options and make a profit in the process. However, they are not a direct security but a derivative. This implies that options are a kind of derivative or a security whose value is *derived* from that of an underlying security.

An option contract is defined as a contract agreed between two individuals. These are the seller and the buyer. The option contract awards the buyer a right to sell the underlying asset at a certain price and a particular date. However, there is no obligation on the buyer's part. On the other hand, the seller is obligated to sell the underlying stock should the buyer choose to exercise the option.

You can buy and sell options at the markets just like you do with other securities like shares and so on. Only that options are derivates and therefore they are traded a little differently than other securities. Derivatives obtain their value from an underlying or other asset. This asset can be a stock, shares, commodities, currencies, and so on. As the price of the underlying asset rises and falls, that of the option is also affected.

When it comes to trading the markets, we know that we are supposed to buy when prices are low and then sell when prices are high. This is simple enough to understand. However, options trading is not necessarily that simple. It is a little more complex in comparison. If you take time to understand the underlying principles and how different strategies work, then you will get a better understanding of options.

Options Carry a Higher Risk

Options do carry a higher than average risk because of various factors. They are known to be risky and complicated with some traders losing all their money and in some cases exposure to unlimited losses. However, these risks become a threat when you do not properly understand how options work and how to trade in them.

If you learn the right way and take the time to learn all about them, then options should be pretty easy to understand and much less complicated.

The fact is that options traders assume much larger risks than the ordinary trader. There are a couple of factors that come to play when dealing options. These include time decay and implied volatility. Time decay is crucial because all options contracts are time-bound. A contract loses its value with time. It has premium value once it is written and sold. From there onwards, the value will keep depreciating.

Different traders use options for various purposes. There are those who use options to hedge against risks. Others use options to protect against future price hikes. However, the majority of options traders are in it to make huge profits which are possible using this strategy.

Understanding the Principles behind Options

An option is actually a contract that allows you the opportunity to sell or buy 100 shares of a particular stock, at an agreed price and a set date. Options grant you the right to buy or sell the stock but you are never obligated to do so.

There are call options and put options. A put option is an option that grants you the rights to sell an underlying security while a call option awards you the right to buy an underlying security.

If you choose to exercise your right to buy or sell an underlying security, then you will have to do so within the stipulated time period and at the set price. If you wish, then you can forego the right and the option will expire. At the very least, you will only have lost the cost of setting it up.

Options may sound complex but are pretty easy to understand if you pay keen attention. You will come across numerous traders' profiles with different security types including bonds, stocks, mutual funds, ETFs and even options.

Options are another asset class. If applied correctly, they will offer numerous benefits that all other assets on their own cannot. For instance, you can use options to hedge against negative outcomes like a declining stock market or falling oil prices. You can use options to generate recurrent income and for speculative purposes like wagering on the movement of a stock.

When to use Options

As an investor, you will have a number of opportunities to use options. However, there are a number that are truly beneficial. Here is a brief look at them.

- Options buy you time if you need to sit back and watch things develop
- You require very little funds to invest in options compared to buying shares
- Options will offer you protection from losses because they lock in price but without the obligation to buy

Always keep in mind that options offer no free ride or a free lunch. Trading in options carries some risks due to their predictive nature. Any prediction will turn out one way or another. The good news here is that any losses that you incur will only be equivalent to the cost of setting up the option. This cost is significantly lower than buying the underlying security.

Different Kinds of Options Contracts

A lot of the time, people hear of options and think of stock options. However, options can be written on just about all kinds of financial products. These include commodities, currencies, bonds, stock indices, futures contracts, and much more.

When it comes to stock options, there are only certain types that are accepted for options trading and not all. For a company's stock to qualify, then it must meet certain qualifying criteria. The criterion is set by the exchange where the stock is traded. As long as the criterion is set, then the stock will be eligible. However, when it fails, then it gets disqualified.

Different Types of Options

- The Protective Put- Stock Options
- Weekly Options- Mini Options
- Index Options - Mini Index Options
- Futures Options- ES Weekly Options
- Binary Options- E-Mini Options
- IRA Accounts- ETF Options
- Near month in-the-money options

1. Near Month In-the-Money Options

Some options are best suited for day trading. One such example is the near month in-the-month option. This option basically refers to options contracts that are set to expire at the close of the next month. Such options are usually past their strike price so investors are free to exercise them.

The inherent value of this options contract is one of the determining factors of the premium especially when it nears its expiration date. Such options are often traded in large volumes and this causes a smaller gap between the asking and bidding prices. As the option nears its expiration date, its time value diminishes.

2. Protective Put Option

The protective put is an option that is used by traders who wish to purchase both an option and its underlying securities. This is the preferred strategy anytime that the underlying stock is expected to undergo periods of high volatility.

There are instances when day traders will continually buy and sell the same stock option for a long time, maybe a couple of months, in order to benefit from a short-term upward trend. At other times, day traders make use of a strategy of purchasing put options on the same underlying security just so they insure themselves against any sharp losses in the stock's price. This is considered as a risk management technique. While there are certain small loses paid in order to protect the share, the opportunity to minimize losses on a downward trend is absolutely invaluable.

3. Stock Options

Traders acquire a way to increase their profits through straightforward stock options by simply purchasing or shorting shares at a certain set price at a set date at the options market. Day traders have certain advantages when it comes to stock options because the parameters are applied to stock options. Since both stock options and stocks are traded on an exchange, the market will have the same liquidity and will enable the fast execution of orders. Sophisticated investors can use options as an effective hedge against risks.

Stock options have the potential to cost you 100% of your funds. Brokers only permit sophisticated traders to deal with complex options systems like stock options. You can be exposed to enormous amounts of risk and it is crucial that you avoid strategies that require substantial experience. But it's good to note that day traders rarely sell options.

4. Weekly Options

Weekly options are also popularly referred to as weeklies. Such options are generally listed with only one week left to expiration. Most options often have several months and sometimes even years to expiration. However, weeklies are generally available to day traders. They are found on ETNs or exchange-traded notes, broad-market indices in the US, and ETFs or exchange-traded funds.

A lot of traders view traditional options are a huge setback largely because of the long-time duration. These traders very much prefer weeklies and view them as major game-changers. They get to apply leverage of options even as they engage in more short-term strategies.

Created on Thursdays

Weekly contracts are usually created once each week on a Thursday. They remain valid until the following Friday for ETNs, ETFs, and equities. Weekly index options, however, often close their final trading sessions on Fridays or Thursdays depending on the index. These basically have a total lifetime of seven trading days or one week.

As a day trader, you can benefit hugely if you take advantage of the increased volatility that comes with the time decay and expiration that is associated with options. Weekly options have 52 expiration periods throughout the year and this increases your chances of benefiting from expiring options.

While weeklies provide a couple of advantages to day traders, they have some possible disadvantages especially due to time factors. Option buyers generally pay a lower price for the cost of a weekly option compared to regular options they usually experience a hugely limited opportunity window especially when trades move in the opposite of the intended direction. There is generally very limited opportunity for price recover and it is hard to fix a trade through strike adjustments.

5. Mini Options

Mini options are actually options that let traders and investors trade-in options that are based on 10-share sets rather than the standard 100-share sets. Mini options have expiration dates that are similar in nature to regular expiration dates. This expiration date is also similar to quarterlies and weeklies.

Other features like the bids, strike price, and offers are also similar and correspond to features of regular options. However, they do offer certain benefits. As a trader, you stand to enjoy the following benefits by simply trading in mini options.

Benefits of mini options

- You are able to hedge a position for very little money
- Mini options are more affordable per transaction
- They can be exercised on any business day as long as they are not expired because they are American style in nature

Sadly, they also have some drawbacks. For instance;

- Mini options are available for only limited securities
- They have much lower liquidity
- The bid-ask spreads are much wider
- They charge a higher commission based on percentages

In general, mini options act as a great tool for hedging highly valued securities and for day trading. However, their use in day trading is limited unless they are available on a bigger variety of ETFs and stocks.

6. Index Options

We also have another type of options contract which is known as the index option. These options let you make use of put or call options to speculate on the movements of a whole stock market index like the S&P 500 or the Dow Jones instead of individual stocks and shares.

A trader who trades index options can capitalize on their predictions based on volatility or direction of an entire market without any need to trade options based on individual stocks. One of the main challenges that traders encounter when pricing index options is accurately calculating dividend estimates.

Features of index options

- Basically, index options are less vulnerable to volatility compared to stocks in general that constitute an index
- Index options are well able to handle fluctuations that individual stocks could be exposed to and as such, they tend to be more stable compared to other kinds of options
- A lot of index options are exercised in a European style. This is because they cannot be traded until they expire. However, the trader or investor will not necessarily be stuck with them as they can be sold or bought as long as they haven't expired
- Index options often trade in large volumes because they are largely traded by investment firms, hedge funds, and individual traders
- Unfortunately for day traders, large volumes minimize the spreads quoted at the markets

7. Mini Index Options

The mini index options happen to be quite similar to ordinary index options. However, they cost 10% less and are only 10% of the normal contract size. Traders and investors with limited capital are easily able to trade this option type and benefit from trading on the general market. Day traders benefit from this option type as they are able to have a wider strategy scope.

There are certain benefits or advantages of the mini index options. Here is a look at some of these benefits.

- They are a lot cheaper compared to ordinary index options
- They resemble the underlying index perfectly
- They generally offer a partial hedge against ordinary index options

There are some disadvantages as well. Some of these disadvantages include;

- Mini index options have a large bid-ask spread
- They usually have a higher extrinsic value due to lower liquidity
- Are a lot more expensive

8. Binary Options

Binary options are among the most commonly traded options. They are known by different names depending on the platform where they are trading. For instance, binary options are referred to as FROs or fixed return options when traded on the American Stock Exchange. On the Forex markets, they are referred to as digital options and sometimes as all-or-nothing options on the ASE or American Stock Exchange.

The reason why they are known as binary is because this option class offers returns or profits in two outcomes. This means you get something or nothing. In this instance where you have binary options, the profitability is usually a pre-set amount such as $100. There are certain assets that can be traded as binary options. These assets include;

- Stocks
- Commodities
- Currencies
- Stock indices

While there are plenty of different types of binary options, only two are commonly used by day traders. These popular binary options are;

- Asset or nothing binary options
- Cash or nothing binary options

The asset or nothing binary option pays the entire value of the underlying security. The cash or nothing binary option pays an investor a set amount of money should the option be in-the-money upon expiry. This is the reason why this type of option is referred to as binary. You can expect to receive only one of two outcomes investing in this particular options class.

The reasoning behind binary options day trading is pretty simple. As a trader, the aim is to enter a trade position and exit before the close of the trading day. All binary options contracts come with expiry times and dates. This means that most binary options contracts have a set expiry date except on trading platforms where traders have variable expiry on options.

As a day trader, you should identify expiry dates that will conclude trades within the same day. This is because once you enter a trade that has an expiry date, you will not be able to exit manually the same way that you do with all other options trades.

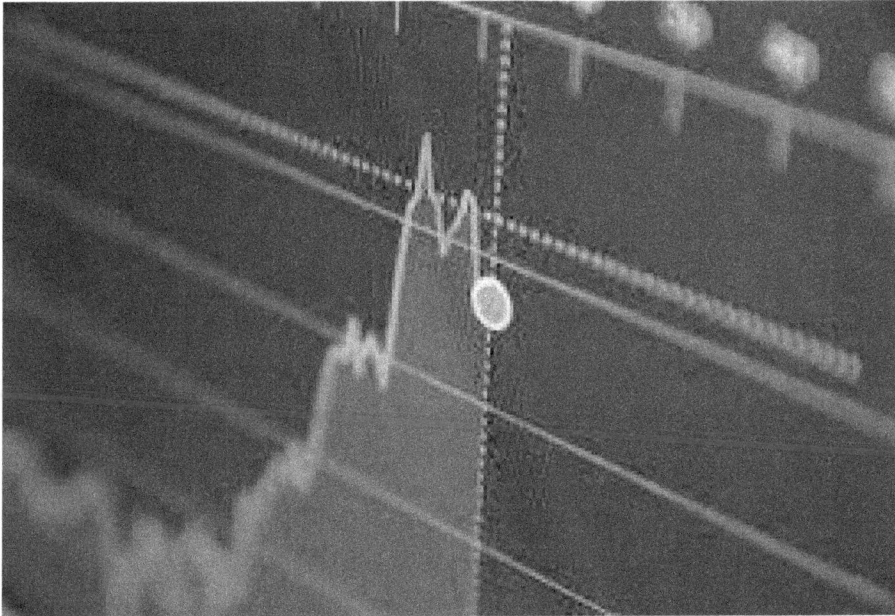

Options are Derivatives

Options are a kind of derivative. Investors are often talking about different derivatives. Options derive their value from an underlying stock or security. In fact, options belong to the class of securities known as derivatives. For a long time, people associated derivatives with high-risk investments. This notion is not really true.

Derivatives obtain their value from an underlying security. Think about wine, for instance. Wine is produced from grapes. We also have ketchup which is derived from tomatoes. This is basically how derivatives function.

An Example of How Options Work

There are plenty of real-life examples of how options apply in our lives. It is possible that you have seen them in action or maybe even used options in your business or life. For instance, if you have ever bought insurance such as home insurance or health and car insurance, you have applied principles similar to those that apply to options trading.

Auto Insurance

Take auto insurance for instance. If you buy a brand new car, or just a really good vehicle, you will not want to risk driving it without insurance cover. Doing so is risky because anything could happen and you risk suffering serious losses. This is the main reason why people take insurance.

Now when you take out insurance for your automobile or any other insurance, you pay a monthly or annual fee for the cover provided by the insurance company. The benefit you stand to get from the cover is much greater than what you pay for it.

Even if you do not get into an accident, the price you will have paid is in actual sense a tiny amount yet you had the car all this time and drove it with peace of mind. This amount that you paid for the insurance can be referred to as premium.

Same Principle Applies to Options

This principle applies in much the same manner when it comes to options. However, instead of investing in a car, your money will go to your favorite stocks. Let's say you put your money on stock ABC which is trading at $20 a share and you think this price will rise to $30 in the coming months.

The problem here is that you do not have sufficient funds to purchase the share. You can instead purchase an options contract which you can afford. For instance, you can buy an options contract for 100 shares at only $1.00 so only $1.00 of your money would get tied up instead of $2,000 which would be required to buy the actual shares.

Basics of Options Contracts

Anytime that you trade an option you are in real sense selling or buying an options contract. A single options contract is equivalent to 100 shares of the underlying security. For instance, if you wish to purchase 100 shares of company ABC at $20, you would spend $2,000. However, with a call option, you can control the same amount of shares at only $1.50 per 100 shares which would total to $150. Therefore, the contract would cost you $150 while buying the shares would cost $2,000. A single options contract controls 100 shares. Two contracts refer to 200 shares and so on.

Anytime that you purchase options, you will receive a price quote that refers to the share price and not contract price. For instance, an option that costs $1.50 means that a single share will cost you $1.50. In this case, a contract of 100 shares will cost you $150.

Options Premium

Options are not free and traders have to part with funds in order to purchase an options contract. The money paid is referred to as a premium. This money, once paid, is not refundable regardless of how a trade works out. For this small fee, you get to control shares and benefit from them in the same way the owner would. The investment is very little but the potential gain is significantly huge.

Buying options is often a cheaper way of investing in the stock market yet it offers the chance of benefiting just as much as a stock investor and most of the time even more. With just a small amount of money, you can make a small initial investment with the potential return that can easily surpass what the traditional stock investor might achieve on a percentage basis. Individuals with little capital can access a wider variety of ETFs and equities via options. This would otherwise not have been possible except for the options.

Power of Options

Options are quite powerful. This is because they can enhance your portfolio and also earn you serious profits. They also provide added leverage as well as protection against shocks and losses. Traders and investors are often facing different challenges in the course of trading the markets. Depending on the situation, there is always an options contract that can be used to provide relief.

You need to understand that just like with stocks and bonds, there is no free lunch associated with options. There are risks involved so you need to learn about risk management. However, apart from risk management, you also need to learn about risk management among other things. You will also note that most brokers issue a disclaimer simply because of the high risks involved. Fortunately, these can be avoided most of the time with consistency and time.

Characteristics of Options Contracts

Options are generally a lot different compared to most other financial securities like stocks, commodities, bonds, and currencies. The value of an options contract depends upon the value of the underlying asset. As such, options are ideally contracts permitting future transactions based on the underlying security. The contract is entered by two parties consisting of a buyer and a seller.

The contracts come with terms relevant to future transactions. For instance, there is always a definition of the underlying asset and its properties. For instance, the contract will define the underlying security, the price, expiration date, and if it can be sold or purchased.

Details of Options Trading

There are numerous ways to trade securities at the markets. Traders and investors have a wide choice of securities to choose from. The characteristics of options are rather unique and different from all other instruments. While it is more complex and complicated than all the others, its most basic tenets are very similar to that of other securities.

The basics here are as simple as buying and selling securities. Traders deal in options in order to make profits. The crucial point to note in this instance is that when it is profitable, it is extremely profitable. Traders occasionally make profits of 300% and even higher when they get things right. This is very possible as options are potentially highly profitable. Even the complex options are contracts that are similarly designed to generate profits for the trader.

Options offer numerous ways of making profits. Traders can profit from the price movements of various items such as currencies, stocks, indexes, and even bonds. There are opportunities to make money when prices go up when prices fall, and even when prices make sideways movements only. However, they are not always straightforward which means traders have to be extremely keen and sharp at all times.

Pros of Trading Options

There is often confusion about why traders choose options when stocks and bonds do just fine. What some tend to miss out is the vast difference in the earnings potential. Stocks generally return a profit of 8% - 12% per annum which is pretty impressive in and of itself. However, options are a lot more lucrative with much larger potential.

There are options trades that typically generate profits upwards of 50%. Making 100% profits within a short period of time and even more, is not unheard of. This is why a lot of experienced traders choose options. They are extremely lucrative and highly profitable. It is also possible to make money trading options in any market conditions. Traders can make money when the market is bullish, bearish, and even when it is stagnant. As such, you do not need specific market conditions and hence profitability throughout the year is very possible.

Experts agree that trading options offer plenty of benefits that are not offered by other types of securities. While not all traders may want to engage in options trading, there are certain aspects of it that other traders find attractive.

1. Potential for Astronomical Profits

One of the main reasons for trading options is the opportunity of making significantly large profits compared to all other forms of trade in the markets. This is possible even without large sums of money. The principle behind this approach is leverage. A trader needs not have large amounts of funds to earn huge profits. For instance, with as little as $10,000, it is possible to earn amounts such as $300,000 or even $800,000 simply by using leverage.

Take the example of a trader whose trading fund is $10,000. The trader wishes to invest this amount in Company ABC. Now the current stock price is $20 though this price is expected to rise. The trader could use the funds to directly purchase the shares and receive a total of 500 shares for his money. If the stock price was to rise to $25 within a month, the trader will have made $5 per share or a total of $2,500 in profits.

Alternatively, the trader could purchase call options of XYZ stocks with the same amount of money. The options allow the trader to purchase back the underlying stocks within a certain period of time. Now, options contracts cost between $1 and $4 depending on certain factors such as the value of the underlying security. In our example, one call options costs $2 so for the $10,000, the trader receives 5,000 options contracts.

If the trader chooses to exercise the right to sell the underlying shares in the next month, then he stands to make a profit of $5 per share. Remember that he has a right to a total of 5,000 shares for a total profit of $25,000. This clearly demonstrates the capacity and power of options as well as how profitable this kind of trade can be.

2. Great Risk vs. Reward Consideration

Like all good traders, it is essential to weight the risk posed by a certain trade compared to the possible rewards. When trading using options, then the style adapted will indicate the type of risk inherent in the trade. The above example clearly shows how profitable options trading process is. If a loss was to be incurred in the above instance, then the total loss would have been the cost of the options.

In this instance, the risk is well worth the reward because the amount set to be lost is insignificant compared to the amount of profit to be made. In general, the higher the risk than the higher the potential return. Any time that a trader considers a trade, then the risk versus reward ratio should be taken into consideration.

As an options trader, you should learn how to benefit from volatility. Volatility needs to be your friend and partner as you can benefit from sharp and sudden movements in the markets. Options are mostly affected by implied volatility which is essentially the most crucial factor affecting options prices. You need to learn to be on the lookout for implied volatility and determine whether it is low or high. This way, you will easily be able to get a sense of direction regarding the type of options to engage with.

3. Versatility and Flexibility

Another extremely appealing benefit of trading in options is the inherent flexibility. Options offer lots of flexibility with dozens of different strategies to pursue. This compares really well with numerous other trade and investment options out there.

Most of these do not offer as much flexibility as options do. Also, most other securities have limited strategies and this tends to limit the flexibility that a trader has on that security.

Take stocks for instance. Even stock traders encounter certain limitations that are not inherent in options trading. There are plenty of strategies ranging from simple to compound to complex strategies. Stock traders generally buy, hold, or sell stocks. There isn't much else that they can do. This contrasts greatly with options because of the tens of strategies available to them. The versatility and flexibility inherent in options trading far surpasses that of most other securities.

Firstly, options' flexibility allows them to be traded based on a wide variety of underlying securities. The variety and range of options strategies are massive. Also, the spreads provide real flexibility in the manner in which they can be traded. Traders have flexibility and versatility when it comes to limiting risks of assuming market positions when it comes to hedging, and even simply trying to benefit from stock movements, there are numerous opportunities available.

Downsides of Options Trading

While options trading can be extremely profitable, it can also be extremely disastrous. This is why beginners need to stick to the basic strategies until they acquire sufficient knowledge, understanding, and experience. After a while, it will be possible to apply more advanced and even complex strategies that are very likely to make a profit regardless of market conditions. Risks remain though so it is always better to be cautious at the onset.

It is crucial that traders understand the risks and cons associated with trading options. The numerous benefits have seen more and more traders, including amateurs and pros, venture into the world of options in the hope of cashing in on this lucrative trade.

Not an Easy Task

First of all, it is advisable to note that trading options is not as simple as it sounds. Options are complex securities. They are actually contracts that come with certain terms. These terms need to be clearly understood and taken into consideration at all times. Part of the options contracts has to do with time. Unlike stocks and other securities, options have a time limit. This time decay factor makes them extremely short-lived. If a trading strategy does not work out, then the options could expire worthless.

One of the most prohibitive factors about trading options is its complex nature. Numerous numbers of traders avoid options because they are difficult to master. The basics are quite okay and relatively simple to comprehend. However, they have a limited scope as well as limited profitability. Real profitability lies in the compounded strategies which can be quite complex.

Traders can lose a lot of funds if they do not master options correctly. It is possible to even lose more money that invested because trading options are a complex affair. Trading can, therefore, be an ominous and intimidating task. More traders lose money that those who do make money. The main challenge is in understanding the complex nature of options. Learning how to trade options is possible but it is a process that takes both commitment and time. Only traders who are dedicated and invest their time and effort will be rewarded with success.

Trading Options is a Risky Venture

Options trading process is considered an extremely risky affair. Basically, all investment opportunities and even trading ventures carry a certain element of risk. The traders most at risk are beginners and novices. These groups are generally not as well versed or sufficiently experienced to deal with options. Knowledge is crucial in options trade but experience is absolutely essential. Rather than hemorrhage money, traders prefer to avoid options trading altogether.

Yet the options trading process has been popularly utilized in the management of risks. Traders with stocks and other securities often buy options in order to protect themselves from inherent losses. Let us say a trader is holding stock ABC and predicts that its value will fall by 30% in the next one month. This trader has two options in this case. The first one is to sell the stock and hope to attract a great price. The other is to purchase a call option as a form of hedging against any market risks.

Trading options is a highly risky venture. Even seasoned traders sometimes lose money. Chances of making huge profits exist but chances of losing large amounts also exist. It all depends on the strategies applied, a trader's experience, and amounts involved. Trading options can be a highly risky venture mostly for inexperienced persons.

The best advice is to learn as much about trading options as possible and understanding the basics as clearly as possible. Plenty of practice also helps. Traders with little or no experience need to put their skills to practice as often as possible. There are plenty of platforms that provide dummy trading platforms where prospective traders can try out different strategies.

There are also plenty of tools and solutions that make options trading easier. All these when applied to different strategies can result in better performance at the markets. Once the basic strategies are well understood and practiced sufficiently, a trader can then proceed to implement and finesse them until the confidently execute them flawlessly. This is how a trader goes from beginner to novice, to advanced, and eventually professional trading levels.

One of the most prohibitive factors about trading options is its complex nature. Numerous numbers of traders avoid options because they are difficult to master. The basics are quite okay and relatively simple to comprehend. However, they have a limited scope as well as limited profitability.

Real profitability lies in the compounded strategies which can be quite complex. This is why learning as much as possible about options can be really profitable. Plenty of excellent traders have seen their fortunes turn around by simply applying these strategies after taking months and sometimes years to perfect them.

Chapter 2: The Basics of Trading Options

It has already been determined, in the previous chapter, that options are bought and sold just like other financial commodities. Options are contracts that are entered into between a buyer and a seller. As a trader, you can buy options at the options market through a broker. You can also approach writers and request options be written in respect of an underlying stock that you are interested in.

The contracts entered into have a predetermined price as well as an expiration period. This time period ranges from 3 months to about a year though this varies for various reasons. Therefore, a seller and buyer will agree on the terms of an options contract before entering into one.

The Options Markets

There are different options markets available. Basically, options can be based on a variety of securities. These range from commodities like gold or grain to stocks such as Bank of America shares and even currencies like the US dollar and the British Pound. Different traders have different needs and hence the variations when it comes to options contracts.

Reasons Why Traders Choose Options

There are also different reasons why traders, and others, choose to deal in options rather than other financial instruments. For starters, options can be used for hedging purposes. For instance, a person may survey the market or receive information that his or her stocks will plummet in the coming months. Now, if the person holds substantial amounts of stock, then the losses could be significant. But hedging provides a form of security.

Another reason why traders prefer trading options is because of the huge profit possibilities. Compared to other securities, options can be a source of huge wealth. There are a number of billionaires who've made their fortunes trading options. There are also numerous multi-millionaires and other superbly wealthy individuals whose fortunes were all made trading options. This is why more and more traders are opting for this approach. You also get to profit from options regardless of the market trends. This means you can make money when the markets are trending upwards, when there is a decline and even when there is zero movement.

Options Fundamentals

Options type: There are generally two types of options that you can sell or buy. These are call options and put options.

Strike Price: The strike price is also known as the exercise price. This is the price that you will sell or buy the underlying stock should you choose to exercise your options.

Expiration Date: The options contract is not indefinite and has an expiration date. The expiration date refers to the date when the contract entered into becomes void or expires.

Premium: This term refers to the price you pay for the option. This price is charged per share which means it will depend on the number of shares you sign up to. Premium has different components to it. These are the intrinsic value and time value of an option.

Intrinsic Value: This is the value of an option and refers to the difference between the underlying stock's strike price and its current market price.

Time value: The time value of a share refers to the amount of time that is available before an options contract expires. The time value decreases as the expiry date approaches.

Time decay is the term used to express the approach of the expiration date. As this time decay progresses, the time value of an option decreases. Time decay is also commonly referred to as "theta". This time is derived from the pricing model that was used to calculate it. Time is very valuable to investors hence the importance of time decay.

Other Terminology used in Options Trading

Listed options: A listed option is an option that qualifies for trading at a national trading platform like the Chicago Board Options Exchange, CBOE. A listed option generally represents 100 shares of a particular stock. Such an option with 100 shares is also referred to as 1 contract. Each contract has fixed expiration dates and strike prices.

In-the-money: A call option is said to be in-the-money when the share price exceeds the strike price. On the other hand, a put option is said to be in-the-money anytime the share price falls below the strike price.

The price, or total cost, of any option is referred to as the premium. It is affected by a number of factors including volatility, time value, strike price, and stock price.

Contract names: Options contracts do have names or options symbols similar to ticker symbols for stocks.

Ask price: This is the asking price that a seller will accept to trade the option. Basically, should you wish to purchase options, then this would be the premium that you would pay.

Volume: This refers to the total number of contracts that get traded in one day

Change: This refers to the difference in price from the previous to the current trading period. Sometimes change is expressed in terms of percentage.

Volatility: Volatility is simply the measure of a stock's price swing measured between the low and high prices of each day. For a long time, volatility has been measured using past data.

IV, also known as implied volatility, measures the likelihood that a market considers a stock will experience significant price swing. There are certain tools that are used to measure some of these parameters. One of these is Vega. Vega is a pricing model that calculates the theoretical effect of a single point change in implied volatility.

When the implied volatility is high, it means options prices will be high due to the potential upside for the options contract. It is good to keep in mind that volatility measurements are only estimates and never accurate. They are mostly predictions on the expected change of an option's price.

Employee stock option: While these are not readily available for all traders, they are a type of call option. Plenty of listed companies offer stock options to their treasured and talented staff members, especially management, in order to retain them for a long period of time.

Employee stock options are very similar to ordinary stock options as a holder receives the right, but not obligation, to purchase stocks at a certain price and within a stipulated time period. However, the contract only exists between the company owners or board and an employee. Others cannot trade or exchange it at the options stock markets.

This is different however if the options are listed. A listed option represents a contract between two different parties. This contract is completely unrelated to the company and easily be traded at the markets.

Terms Describing an Option's Value

We do not describe an option's performance as up, down, or level. This kind of description is not sufficient. Instead, we can definite performance in one of three distinct ways.

In the money: An option that has intrinsic value is said to be in-the-money. Basically, anytime that a stock's price in the stock market and the strike price both favor the contract owner, then the option contract is said to be in the money. Essentially, it is beneficial to the call option owner when the stock price is greater than the strike price. On the other hand, a put option is said to be in the money when the price of the stock is less than the strike price.

Out of the money: An option is said to be out of the money when there is absolutely no monetary gain expected in exercising it. This means it is a lot less lucrative or financially viable to sell stocks and shares at the strike price than it would in the general securities market. Therefore, we say that a call option is out of the money is the strike price is higher than the stock price. A put option, on the other hand, is said to be out of the money anytime that the stock price is high than the strike price.

At the money: Sometimes the strike price is just about equal to the stock price. In such a situation, we say that the option is at the money.

Options Seller and Buyer Terms

There are special terms used to refer to options traders. In other situations, we'd refer to the traders as buyers and sellers. However, when it comes to options trading, a more technical term is used.

Writer: The term writer refers to an investor who holds an options contract and is selling it. When the writer sells the option, they will receive a premium from the buyer. The buyer will be buying the right to buy a specific amount of shares at a strike price.

Holder: A holder is basically an investor seeking to purchase an options contract. A call options holder will buy an options contract and gain the right to purchase the underlying stock under stipulated terms. A put holder possesses all the rights to sell the underlying stock.

A holder and a writer are generally on opposite sides of an options transaction. One writes an option while the other signs up to it. However, the main difference between these two is the kind of losses they are exposed to.

Holders sign up to get the right to purchase or sell shares but without the obligation. The contract that they sign up to grants them the choice of if and when to exercise their rights. If the option, over time, becomes out-of-the-money, then they have the freedom to abandon the contract and let it expire. In such an instance, they will only lose the premium paid to set up the options contract.

On the other hand, things are a little different. For instance, writers lack this kind of flexibility. If a call options holder decides to exercise their right, then the writer is obligated to accept the order and execute it by selling the stock at the current strike price. Should the writer not be in possession of all the shares in a contract, then he or she will have to purchase these at current market rates and sell to the holder at the strike price. If there are any losses to be incurred, the writer is obligated to take on them.

Since the risks are pretty high for writers, it is recommended that beginners confine themselves to only buy stock options until they gather sufficient experience over the years.

Options are another asset class. If applied correctly, they will offer numerous benefits that all other assets on their own cannot. For instance, you can use options to hedge against negative outcomes like a declining stock market or falling oil prices. You can use options to generate recurrent income and for speculative purposes like wagering on the movement of a stock.

That's the stock that the option is based on. Not an indication your fly is down. It usually represents 100 shares.

That's the "strike price" for the stock. So the stock will change hands at $70 if the option is exercised.

That's the "premium" or per-share cost of the option. Option contracts usually represent 100 shares of the underlying stock, so you'll actually pay $310 plus commission for this contract. ($3.10 x 100 = $310)

XYZ DECEMBER 17, 2011 70 CALL AT $3.10

That's the date the option expires. The last day to trade this option is usually the third Friday of this month.

That's the type of option. There are two kinds of options: calls and puts. They're defined below.

Two Basic Types of Options

There are two basic types of options. These two are the most basic forms that you will ever encounter. Any other options strategy is derived from either one or both these basic types. With time you will come across numerous and complex options strategies. When you closely examine them, you will notice call or put options.

Put Options

Put options are option contracts that award you the right to sell the underlying stock. When you own a put option contract, then you are able to sell the underlying security at a specific price within a specified period of time. Put buyers or holders are generally bearish on the stock price and the markets in general. This means you expect the markets to fall together with the share price and you have a strategy to profit from this price downturn.

Example

Here is an example of how options operate in real life. You can compare it to an insurance policy. Let us say you own a home so you get a homeowner's cover. This policy is designed to protect your home from damage. You then pay an amount each month or perhaps annually towards the cover. This amount is the premium.

Now instead of your home, let's imagine a stock investment. If you own stocks or shares, then you can purchase a put option to protect your investment. Assume that you own 1000 shares of company ABC which are valued at $20 per share. However, you believe that the share price will drop in the coming months by $5 and you wish to protect yourself from any inherent losses.

You will then purchase put options at $1.50 per 100 shares which will cost you $15. The put option will protect you in case the price falls drastically. Suppose in 3 months the share price of ABC stock falls to $15. You will have the right to sell your shares at a previously agreed price, usually the price at the put creation stage. At the time the price was $20 so you will be able to save over $5 * 1000 = $5,000 in losses. This is very similar to an insurance policy that restores you back to your initial position after adversity.

Call Options

A call option is an options contract that grants you the right to buy an underlying security. It simply means that you have the right to "call" a security away from its owner. However, you have no obligation to do so.

As an investor, you should look to purchase call options only when you are bullish about the prices. You should also buy call options when you are positive about the market's direction in general.

Example

A call option can be viewed as a down payment for a future purpose. Let us assume that you wish to purchase a home in the future. You notice an upcoming development and become interested in buying property but only under certain terms and conditions.

For instance, you may only want to buy property in this new development if they put up certain amenities such as schools and parks. However, your interest will end should there be plans to put up a garbage dump or a processing plant.

To achieve your aim, you will have to set up and option so that you have the option to buy the property or not. You can buy a call option from the property developer any time in the next three years for a price of $450,000. This option will cost you some money. This cost is referred to as the premium.

The premium you pay for an option is non-refundable. It can be seen as the price you pay to earn the right extended to you as an option holder. In our case, the premium is $25,000. This amount goes to the property developer who agrees to sell the option. Now in three years' time, the property will sell for about $800,000. However, your buying price will be locked in at $400,000 and that is the price that you will pay for your home.

Options Contracts

Anytime that you trade an option you are in real sense selling or buying an options contract. A single options contract is equivalent to 100 shares of the underlying security. For instance, if you wish to purchase 100 shares of company ABC at $20, you would spend $2,000. However, with a call option, you can control the same amount of shares at only $1.50 per 100 shares which would total to $150. Therefore, the contract would cost you $150 while buying the shares would cost $2,000. A single options contract controls 100 shares. Two contracts refer to 200 shares and so on.

Anytime that you purchase options, you will receive a price quote that refers to the share price and not contract price. For instance, an option that costs $1.50 means that a single share will cost you $1.50. In this case, a contract of 100 shares will cost you $150.

Options Premium

You will have to pay some money in order to acquire an options contract. The money that you pay is referred to as a premium. This money, once paid, is not refundable regardless of how a trade works out. For this small fee, you get to control shares and benefit from them in the same way the owner would. The investment is very little but the potential gain is significantly huge.

Buying options is often a cheaper way of investing in the stock market yet it offers the chance of benefiting just as much as a stock investor and most of the time even more. With just a small amount of money, you can make a small initial investment with the potential return that can easily surpass what the traditional stock investor might achieve on a percentage basis. Individuals with little capital can access a wider variety of ETFs and equities via options. This would otherwise not have been possible except for the options.

A Look at Options Trading

Options generally offer investors a chance to participate in future price movements. For instance, if you invest in call options, then you will earn an opportunity to participate in the price increase of a stock without the need to own the stock. This security gives you an option to participate in the stock's uptrend.

It is crucial that you price options appropriately in order to enjoy maximum benefit. The pricing is a major factor in your ability to determine the probability of future price events. Ideally, the more likely that an event is to occur, then the costlier an option would be. For example, the value of a call option rises as the underlying stock's value goes up. Understanding this principle is crucial to understanding the relative value of options.

An example

Let us examine the call option of IBM, International Business Machines. In our example, IBM has a strike price of $200 which expires after 3 months. On the other hand, the IBM shares are trading at $175 at the stock market. Keep in mind that owning these call options gives you the right, at any time, to buy 100 IBM shares at a price of $200 anytime in the next three months.

Should the IBM stock price rise above $200 within the next three months, then the option will be said to be in-the-money. The value of an option decreases as it approaches expiry. The reason for this is that the opportunities for a price move decreases as the expiry date approaches. This is the reason why options are also referred to as wasting assets.

Let us say you purchase an option that is about one month old and is out of the money. In such a case, your option will lose value with each passing day. A three-month option is more valuable than a one-month option because time is a component of options. When more time is available, the chances of a favorable price move are higher. In the same manner, an option that expires in one year will be a lot more expensive than one that expires in three months' time.

Time factor

In our example above, IBM stock is worth $175 at the stock market. As the price approaches $200, then the value of the call option increases. In general, as the price of the underlying security rises, the higher the likelihood of the option to expire in-the-money.

Alternatively, as the price falls, the option will keep dropping its value. The gap between the underlying asset and strike price will also widen. If the price of IBM shares remains steady at $175, then the $185 strike call will be much more valuable than a $200 strike call. This is because the chances of the share price rising to $185 are much higher than $200.

Volatility

The price of an option will increase if there is volatility in the markets. The reason is that uncertainty tends to increase the odds of an outcome. Should the volatility of the underlying asset increase, then the possibilities of larger price swings will raise the possibility of significant price moves either way. Due to this reason, greater price swing will increase the likelihood of a price rise. This is why volatility tends to increase the price of an option. Large price swings tend to increase the likelihood of an event happening. This affects the price of an option. Increased volatility means increased options value.

Right to buy or sell the underlying stock

Options will grant you the right to buy or sell an underlying security. However, in most instances, this right is rarely, if ever, exercised. Options holders prefer to trade out or close their positions and take profits. They sell their options in the market which are then purchased by writers who proceed to close these positions. According to the Chicago Board of Options Exchange, 60% are closed or traded out and only about 10% of options are actualized. About 30% of options usually expire absolutely worthless.

Options generally offer investors a chance to participate in future price movements. For instance, if you invest in call options, then you will earn an opportunity to participate in the price increase of a stock without the need to own the stock. This security gives you an option to participate in the stock's uptrend.

It is crucial that you price options appropriately in order to enjoy maximum benefit. The pricing is a major factor in your ability to determine the probability of future price events. Ideally, the more likely that an event is to occur, then the costlier an option would be. For example, the value of a call option rises as the underlying stock's value goes up. Understanding this principle is crucial to understanding the relative value of options.

An example

Let us examine the call option of IBM, International Business Machines. In our example, IBM has a strike price of $200 which expires after 3 months. On the other hand, the IBM shares are trading at $175 at the stock market. Keep in mind that owning these call options gives you the right, at any time, to buy 100 IBM shares at a price of $200 anytime in the next three months.

Should the IBM stock price rise above $200 within the next three months, then the option will be said to be in-the-money. The value of an option decreases as it approaches expiry. The reason for this is that the opportunities for a price move decreases as the expiry date approaches. This is the reason why options are also referred to as wasting assets.

Let us say you purchase an option that is about one month old and is out of the money. In such a case, your option will lose value with each passing day. A three-month option is more valuable than a one-month option because time is a component of options. When more time is available, the chances of a favorable price move are higher. In the same manner, an option that expires in one year will be a lot more expensive than one that expires in three months' time.

Time factor

In our example above, IBM stock is worth $175 at the stock market. As the price approaches $200, then the value of the call option increases. In general, as the price of the underlying security rises, the higher the likelihood of the option to expire in-the-money.

Alternatively, as the price falls, the option will keep dropping its value. The gap between the underlying asset and strike price will also widen. If the price of IBM shares remains steady at $175, then the $185 strike call will be much more valuable than a $200 strike call. This is because the chances of the share price rising to $185 are much higher than $200.

Volatility

The price of an option will increase if there is volatility in the markets. The reason is that uncertainty tends to increase the odds of an outcome. Should the volatility of the underlying asset increase, then the possibilities of larger price swings will raise the possibility of significant price moves either way. Due to this reason, greater price swing will increase the likelihood of a price rise. This is why volatility tends to increase the price of an option. Large price swings tend to increase the likelihood of an event happening. This affects the price of an option. Increased volatility means increased options value.

Right to Buy or Sell the Underlying Stock

Options will grant you the right to buy or sell an underlying security. However, in most instances, this right is rarely, if ever, exercised. Options holders prefer to trade out or close their positions and take profits. They sell their options in the market which are then purchased by writers who proceed to close these positions. According to the Chicago Board of Options Exchange, 60% are closed or traded out and only about 10% of options are actualized. About 30% of options usually expire absolutely worthless.

Options Tables

It is accurate to state that options have a language of their own. This is why most novice traders find the information to be pretty challenging and a little overwhelming at first. The charts appear to be an entire string of numbers and rows of digits from top to bottom. However, these are options charts and they do provide plenty of useful information.

Option chains, also known as an options table, are listings that consist of all options contracts available. The chains display all call options, put options and strike prices. The listings include price information of the underlying assets as well as the included maturity period.

You can find real-time options chains across numerous websites and financial magazines including The Wall Street Journal, Yahoo! Finance, Google Finance, and so on. Basically, you will find an options chain anywhere you see a chart of the underlying stocks.

Options chains are split into two general categories. These are call options section and pull options section. Call options are often listed first. Both call and put options come with an expiry date. This date varies and will be indicated on the charts.

We also have the strike price indicated on the charts. This is the price at which a buyer buys call options or seller sells put options. Call options are less costly when they feature higher strike prices compared to those with a lower one. The reverse applies to put options. Higher option prices are experienced with low strike prices. For sellers, and also buyers, the market price of options needs to be higher than the strike price in order to realize a profit.

Understanding Option Chains

Options chains are viewed as the most appropriate platforms for presenting investors, both retail and institutional, with the information that they need about available options. To identify an option premium, traders like you need to follow the appropriate strike prices and maturity dates listed on the options chain.
Most of the stock trading platforms and online brokers display options information and data in real-time. It is easy for a trader to scan the charts and identify any price changes, open interest or simply interesting activity. This information enables traders to make decisions easily regarding any options they may be interested in.

Finding an asset is a simple process that includes identifying volume trading, frequency, and maturity months as well as strike price. Each option on the table contains its own symbol similar to the way underlying stocks do. Different options contracts come with different options symbols. The ask-and-bid prices generally indicate the prices at which sellers and buyers are willing to accept at that particular moment.

Option trading operates very similar to an auction house. The prices that prevail are only those that both sellers and buyers are willing to accept. Traders negotiate the prices and bargain until they come to an agreement. In the end, the buyers will purchase only at an agreed price and sellers at the best price.

In Conclusion

An option chain is also referred to as an option matrix. It is a display of listing of all available contracts relating to both put and call options. The chain provides information pertaining to a given security. Such a matrix is basically ideal for use the following morning. With this information, you are able to head to the markets and begin the process of either selling or buying stocks. Traders, on the other hand, tend to focus on crucial numbers including bid and ask prices as well as the net change and last prices.

Chapter 3: Swing Trading with Options

There are numerous ways of trading financial assets or securities. One of the best strategies for retail investors is swing trading. Swing trading is a trading style or strategy where a trader enters a position and will exit this position within a period of a single trading day up to a couple of months. The average time period is usually two days to about two weeks.

Swing trading is a favorite strategy for most retail traders. They love this trading style because it allows time for life. You are able to trade and make money while going about your daily routine. You can still go to work, take care of your family, study or play, and still make money on the side.

If you want to trade and be profitable whilst still doing everything that you like, then you should learn how to swing trade. A lot of very successful traders actually are swing traders. One of the best known of them is Warren Buffet. You will, therefore, be in great company. This chapter will take a close look at swing trading and examine how it applies to options. But first, let us take a look at some of the characteristics of options.

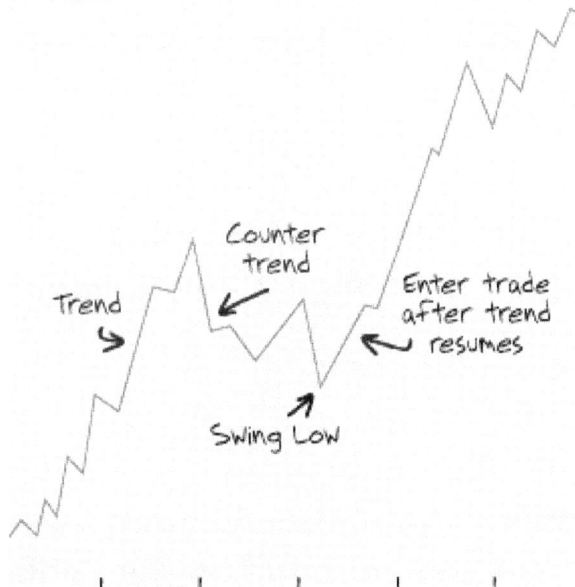

5 Main Characteristics of Options

1. Underlying Asset

One of the major characteristics of options is the underlying asset. An option is always based on financial security such as a stock. It can also be based on an asset or commodity like gold. The price of the stock is determined by the price of the underlying asset. The reason is that options contracts are derivatives. A derivative is anything whose price is derived from that of another asset. The most popular assets used with options are stocks. Others include indices, currencies, bonds, and so on.

2. Call and Put Options

When it comes to options, we have two very basic types. These are call options and put options. All other options are premised off these two major or basic types. A call option is an options contract that awards its holder rights to the underlying security but no obligations. Put options are options contracts that award the owner or buyer the rights to sell the underlying security but also with no obligation. All other options strategies emanate from these two basic types.

3. The Strike Price

The strike price is the price at which an option holder can sell the underlying stock if he or she opts to invoke their right. This price is usually fixed and cannot be changed later.

4. Expiration Date

Another useful characteristic of options is the expiration date. All options must have an expiration date. Their lives are not infinity like stocks but limited. When purchasing or selling options, the expiration date features strongly. Options whose expiration date is closer cost much less than those with a much further expiration date. Options that expire basically become worthless and of no use to anyone.

5. European vs. American

We also have American and European options. However, the difference is in the exercise of the options. American options are options that buyers can buy or sell during their lifetimes. However, European options can only be exercised upon expiry but are worthless or unusable till then. Also, you need to remember that these terms have got no regional implications whatsoever. The terms European and American simply refer to the different ways options can be exercised.

Crucial Features of Options Contracts

There are other important features we need to learn about options. One is that options are extremely flexible. Sometimes the contracts appear to be highly standardized such they can only be transacted at certain exchanges. Here are some standout features of options contracts.

1. Very Flexible

Options contracts are, on one hand, extremely standardized such that they can only be purchased and sold at exchanges. Also, such options contracts cannot be adjusted to meet the desired of each and every buyer and seller. As such, they are rather standard in nature. But there are certain option contracts that are privately arranged. In this case, a writer will sit down and discuss certain aspects of the contract with a buyer. Together they will discuss the terms of the options and arrive at a mutually agreeable contract. These terms will then constitute an options contract that is enforceable. When a writer or seller gets together with a buyer, they are able to get together and organize the terms of an options contract.

2. A Down Payment

There is an upfront payment that a buyer always has to pay. This amount is known as the premium. It is the amount that the buyer has to pay in order to have the rights to the option. Premiums are often very affordable compared to the cost of stocks or other underlying securities. For instance, the cost of premiums ranges from $1 to around $5 per 100 shares. This is much lower than the actual cost of shares or any underlying security. This amount is also consideration for the premium writer. Writers usually make their profits from the premium amount. This is how it works out. During discussions, the premium amount has to feature. Once the buyer takes procession of the options contract, he can decide to either exercise his or her rights or forfeit them. If the options are exercised then the final price should take into consideration the premium amount. However, if the holder does not exercise their rights, then they will forego the premium amount.

3. Final Settlement

During the drafting of the options contract, there is no money that changes hands. What happens is once the options contract takes effect, the buyer will take possession after payment of the premium. Settlement takes place after an options contract holder sells it or exercises their right. Remember that the options contract ceases to exist once the right is exercised or upon expiration. It is at this point that settlement of the contract takes place. In the event the option is not exercised then there is no settlement needed. The option will expire worthless.

4. Options are Non-Linear

Options contracts lack the properties of linearity which is evident in other securities such as stocks and bonds. What this means is that the profit earned after the underlying security's movement is not equivalent to the losses possible. This means that the underlying securities movement in one direction will not yield a profit that is equal to the loss possible

Trading options is considered by some to be a complex subject. However, it is only complex when it is compared to simpler investments such as sale and purchase of stocks or trade-in basic stocks and so on. Most traders get to understand this subject once they have a clearer picture of how options work.

Trading options is a strategy that is occasionally used by experienced traders to leverage securities and mitigate against certain risks inherent in the markets. If a trader holds certain stocks but expects the price to fall because of certain reasons, then the trader could use options to mitigate against the risks of loss.

Ordinarily, investors often buy low then sell high to be profitable. However, this is not always the case with options. When it comes to options trading, a trader can make money when the prices are low, when they are high, and even when the market moves sideways only.

Options trading can be extremely useful to investors in different ways. Traders can use options in order to protect their investments from losses. They can also trade directly in options and make huge and astronomical profits. However, the options trading process is an extremely risky affair. Chances of traders losing their money are high. Even the best of traders does lose some of their trades.

The risk is considered serious because traders stand to lose not just the entire investment but losses can sometimes be unlimited. This means traders can be liable for losses larger than what they bargained for. That is why it is advisable to trade cautiously and only engage in trades that are simple and less complicated. In general, the more complicated a strategy is, the riskier it is. There are other factors associated with options trade. These include time decay and implied volatility.

The options trading process is a bit more complicated compared to selling and buying of stocks. Sometimes buying or selling options is a huge gamble. It is also much more difficult to gain approval as an options trader compared to a regular trader. Also, it is highly advisable to consider the consequences and effects of trading options especially with variables such as time decay and implied volatility.

However, much as options trading process is thought to be complex and highly risky, the fundamentals are relatively easy to follow and comprehend. And that is where it all begins. A good trader needs to develop a strong foundation and a clear understanding of a concept and then building up from there. As soon as you are able to understand the basics of options trading, you will then be in a position to understand more complex features and details pertaining to options.

Reasons for Trading Options

Traders may wonder why the need to diversify into options when other securities are doing just fine. The important point that needs to be understood is that options can be extremely profitable in certain instances and offer different ways of profiting. Basically, a trader can make money in any market condition. This means money can be made when the markets are bullish, bearish, or experience no movement at all.

Experts agree that trading options offer plenty of benefits that are not offered by other types of securities. While not all traders may want to engage in options trading, there are certain aspects of it that other traders find attractive.

1. Potential for Astronomical Profits

One of the main reasons for trading options is the opportunity of making significantly large profits compared to all other forms of trade in the markets. This is possible even without large sums of money. The principle behind this approach is leverage. A trader needs not have large amounts of funds to earn huge profits. For instance, with as little as $10,000, it is possible to earn amounts such as $300,000 or even $800,000 simply by using leverage.

Take the example of a trader whose trading fund is $10,000. The trader wishes to invest this amount in Company ABC. Now the current stock price is $20 though this price is expected to rise. The trader could use the funds to directly purchase the shares and receive a total of 500 shares for his money. If the stock price was to rise to $25 within a month, the trader will have made $5 per share or a total of $2,500 in profits.

Alternatively, the trader could purchase call options of XYZ stocks with the same amount of money. The options allow the trader to purchase back the underlying stocks within a certain period of time. Now, options contracts cost between $1 and $4 depending on certain factors such as the value of the underlying security. In our example, one call options costs $2 so for the $10,000, the trader receives 5,000 options contracts.

If the trader chooses to exercise the right to sell the underlying shares in the next month, then he stands to make a profit of $5 per share. Remember that he has a right to a total of 5,000 shares for a total profit of $25,000. This clearly demonstrates the capacity and power of options as well as how profitable this kind of trade can be.

2. Great Risk vs. Reward Consideration

Like all good traders, it is essential to weight the risk posed by a certain trade compared to the possible rewards. When trading using options, then the style adapted will indicate the type of risk inherent in the trade. The above example clearly shows how profitable options trading process is. If a loss was to be incurred in the above instance, then the total loss would have been the cost of the options.

In this instance, the risk is well worth the reward because the amount set to be lost is insignificant compared to the amount of profit to be made. In general, the higher the risk than the higher the potential return. Any time that a trader considers a trade, then the risk versus reward ratio should be taken into consideration.

As an options trader, you should learn how to benefit from volatility. Volatility needs to be your friend and partner as you can benefit from sharp and sudden movements in the markets. Options are mostly affected by implied volatility which is essentially the most crucial factor affecting options prices. You need to learn to be on the lookout for implied volatility and determine whether it is low or high. This way, you will easily be able to get a sense of direction regarding the type of options to engage with.

3. Versatility and Flexibility

Another extremely appealing benefit of trading in options is the inherent flexibility. Options offer lots of flexibility with dozens of different strategies to pursue. This compares really well with numerous other trade and investment options out there. Most of these do not offer as much flexibility as options do. Also, most other securities have limited strategies and this tends to limit the flexibility that a trader has on that security.

Take stocks for instance. Even stock traders encounter certain limitations that are not inherent in options trading. There are plenty of strategies ranging from simple to compound to complex strategies. Stock traders generally buy, hold, or sell stocks. There isn't much else that they can do. This contrasts greatly with options because of the tens of strategies available to them. The versatility and flexibility inherent in options trading far surpasses that of most other securities.

Firstly, options' flexibility allows them to be traded based on a wide variety of underlying securities. The variety and range of options strategies are massive. Also, the spreads provide real flexibility in the manner in which they can be traded. Traders have flexibility and versatility when it comes to limiting risks of assuming market positions when it comes to hedging, and even simply trying to benefit from stock movements, there are numerous opportunities available.

			Calls				Strike				Puts			
Symbol	Last	Chg	Bid	Ask	Vol	Open Int	Action		Symbol	Last	Chg	Bid	Ask	Vol	Open Int	Action
☐	Jan 10 Calls			(226 days to expiration)				MAC @ 7.8							Jan 10 Puts
KGZAG	0.21	-0.06	0.22	0.30	150	8,537	Trade	2.50	KGZMQ	1.41	0	1.26	1.29	60	22,515	Trade
WBAAZ	5.50	+1.25	5.60	5.80	401	4,817	Trade	2.50	WBAMZ	0.56	-0.14	0.53	0.57	1,322	40,539	Trade
KGZAA	0.05	0	0.03	0.05	263	15,500	Trade	5.00	KGZKA	3.60	-0.10	3.55	3.65	75	7,411	Trade
WBAAF	4.20	+1.20	4.15	4.30	1,616	26,895	Trade	5.00	WBAMF	1.64	-0.31	1.57	1.63	1,500	31,061	Trade
KGZAR	0.02	-0.01	0.01	0.02	41	36,850	Trade	7.50	KGZMR	6.25	0	6.00	6.20	00	2,891	Trade
WBAAO	3.04	+0.94	3.05	3.15	2,149	75,590	Trade	7.50	WBAMQ	3.05	-0.40	2.92	3.00	531	18,620	Trade
KGZAB	0.01	-0.01	0	0.01	05	20,865	Trade	10.00	KGZMB	8.00	0	8.20	9.85	00	2,369	Trade
WBAAB	2.20	-0.72	2.21	2.25	2,179	57,337	Trade	10.00	WBAMB	4.60	-0.64	4.50	4.65	340	25,187	Trade
KPVAV	0.07	0	0.06	1.63	00	1,367	Trade	12.50	KPVMV	7.36	0	6.75	7.16	47	1,430	Trade
WBAAR	1.53	+0.50	1.54	1.60	648	47,231	Trade	12.50	WBAMR	6.75	-0.65	6.35	6.50	118	11,804	Trade
KGZAC	0.02	0	0	0.02	05	3,312	Trade	15.00	KGZMC	14.25	0	12.85	14.80	00	174	Trade
WBAAC	1.12	+0.41	1.10	1.12	1,097	36,741	Trade	15.00	WBAMC	8.66	-1.64	8.35	8.60	90	26,520	Trade
KPVAY	0.43	+0.09	0.42	0.48	57	1,305	Trade	17.50	KPVMY	11.90	0	11.15	11.65	00	3,374	Trade
WBAAS	0.74	-0.01	0.74	0.80	904	19,009	Trade	17.50	WBAMS	10.70	-1.29	10.50	10.70	312	13,426	Trade

How to Read Options Quotes

Options chains are usually found listed in two different sections. These are the call section and the put section. Put options are always listed after call options which are commonly listed first.

There is a good reason for this. First, call options happen to be more common than put options. Customers generally purchase more call options whether investing or hedging. Put options are not as common and hence second-place listing. Also, it has been the practice over the years to list call options first and put options last.

There are varying options expiration dates on the tables. Some expire in months such as June and July while others expire in October, January, and so on. Options start losing value once they have less than a month to expiration. As such, time is a major factor when it comes to options contracts. Buyers can wait for options to lose value but then they may not be of much use after purchase.

We have what is known as the strike price. This is the cost of buying a call option or selling a put option. The call options with higher strike prices happen to be cheaper compared to those with a lower strike price. The same applies to put options inversely. This means put options with higher strike prices are more expensive compared to those with a lower price.

There are plenty of different prices posted on the options tables. Of these prices, the last one indicates the most recent trade posted. There is also a change column that shows the variation in prices from current and previous days. Sometimes options operate just like stocks because traders can bargain prices and arrive at amicable solutions. This is why prices vary most of the time. Prices are also dependent on a number of factors such as demand and time left.

Options, both put and call, can be designated as being in the money or out of the money. When making a decision about the options to buy or not, you will need this information. Options that are in the money are those that have gained in value and can be redeemed for a profit. For instance, a trader may purchase a call option at $35 yet the current market rate is $39. The option will be said to have an intrinsic value of $4 which is pretty good.

An option that is out of the money is simply one that is not yet profitable. Such an option still has some time before it becomes profitable. As such, it will not fetch as good a price as options that are in the money. This is another crucial point to note.

Setbacks of Trading Options

1. Sellers are exposed to large and sometimes unlimited losses

Option buyers and holders are only exposed to small losses. However, the option writer's risk is almost unlimited. The losses that they stand to incur are so much greater than the cost of the options contract. The reason is that they have obligations of purchasing or selling stocks or the underlying stocks if a buyer or seller chooses to exercise their right.

2. Time is always limited for the investor to make profit

Options are short term in nature. Investors who use options often seek short-term or near-term price movements that they can capitalize on. These price movements need to take place within a matter of a couple of days, weeks, or months for the payoff to happen.

As such, it is crucial to make a number of assumptions. These are deciding when to buy an option and when to exercise it or walk away from the contract before expiration. This contrasts long term stock buyers who have really no time limit. They are able to invest and wait for years and even decades.

3. Traders have to qualify to trade

As an options trader, there are certain essential criteria that you must meet if you are to start trading. For instance, you must be approved by a broker. You do this by answering a couple of questions or going through a similar screening process. The broker will need to find out about your personal financial situation and your knowledge and experience with risk and understanding of how to trade options.

After the screening, then you will most likely be assigned a trading level based on your skill and experience. The broker will also take into consideration your understanding of risk posed by options trading. This level will dictate the kind of options trades that you will be allowed to place.

As a trader, you will generally be expected to maintain a minimum balance of roughly $2,000 in the brokerage account. This is the general requirement within the industry and this is a cost that you need to seriously consider.

4. Options traders can incur added costs that affect returns

There are certain strategies that need you to set up a margin account. For instance, when selling a call option contract on securities that you do not own. This margin account provides a line of credit that is held as collateral in the event the trade moves against you.

There are different minimum requirements across the various brokerage firms for account opening and so on. The interest rate and amount will depend on factors such as how many securities and cash are present in an account. You can get access to margin loans with interest rates ranging from the low single digits to the low double digits.

In the event that you are unable to repay the margin loan advanced to you by your brokerage firm, then the broker will issue a margin call then liquidate your account should you not add some funds or securities to it. This can also happen if your account falls below a certain percentage which is very possible in the course of a trading day.

You can learn detailed information about the risks and characteristics of standardized options contracts at the Options Clearing Corporation of the USA. There are also income tax regulations that you need to familiarize yourself with if you are going to trade in options and other securities.

Chapter 4: Swing Trading and Options Contracts

There are different approaches when it comes to trading options. One of the favorite strategies is swing trading. This trading style is considered ideal because it promotes a passive lifestyle where investors and traders can trade for brief periods of time and their strategies generating profits as they focus on other matters.

Swing trading is a pretty simple and straightforward process. The process consists of analyzing securities and assets in order to predict their future movements. The information used is based on the security's history. As such, technical analysis will come in handy. Therefore, learning the principles of technical analysis and how to read charts is crucial.

A lot of successful investors and traders use this strategy on a regular basis. Swing trading probably demands only fifteen minutes of your time each week. If you learn the technique and apply it to options trading, you will be setting yourself up for a very profitable passive income opportunity. However, it is advisable to learn as much as possible about swing trading.

Unlimited Profits with Limited Liability

The best part of options trading, especially with these simple strategies is that your profitability is unlimited while losses are limited. As a result, you can make money regardless of the market's trend. Once you get past the indicated breakeven point, profits will begin to exceed the amount paid as premium.

Identifying a Suitable Strike Price

Another important consideration before you begin trading is identifying a strike price. The strike price is useful as it enables traders to determine how to price options. Basically, the better the strike price in terms of affordability, the costlier the option will be. The reverse is true because options that cost more will be less expensive. Also, options that have a lot of time to expiration are more expensive compared to those with a shorter time to expiration.

Again, when the strike price is higher than the prevailing market price, the options are said to be in the money. An option contract that is in the money is also said to possess intrinsic value. On the other hand, when the prevailing market prices for the underlying security are lower than the strike price, then the options are said to be out of the money.

Sometimes the strike price and the prevailing market price are equal. In this situation, we can say that the options are at the money. Options only possess intrinsic value when they are in the money. In all other situations, they have zero intrinsic value.

Brief Introduction to Swing Trading

Swing trading is a trading strategy used by trader who seeks to hold a position in the markets for a period of time longer than one day. The most common period is between 3 to 10 days. However, sometimes the typical plan can last between 1 and 5 days. In rare cases, a position can be held for an entire month.

In swing trading, traders focus on benefiting from a short-term price movement with a large range. This is why, in reality, the definition of swing trading is actually a continuum between day trading and trend trading. A day trader ordinarily holds a position for a brief period of time ranging from a couple of seconds to a couple of hours but never more than an entire day.

On the other hand, a trend trader can hold the stock for a couple of weeks and sometimes even an entire month. Therefore, a swing trader is simply a trader who holds stocks for a period of time ranging between a few days to a couple of weeks.

Swing trading capitalizes on taking smaller profits within short trends then cutting losses fast. While the gains may be small, they tend to grow very fast over time and can deliver excellent returns at the end of the year.

Details of Swing Trading

As a trader, it is crucial to learn as much as possible about the essentials of swing trading. For instance, you should learn how to determine the best securities such as options and add these to your portfolio. You also need to learn how to trade in valuable securities such as large-cap stocks. Large-cap is a shortened term that means large market capitalization. It refers to stocks of companies with a market capitalization worth at least $10 billion. Stocks are generally labeled as small-cap, mid-cap, or large-cap.

You also need to determine the right market conditions that provide the best chances for success. The market can have two extremes. You can have a Bull market or a bear market. In such market situations, momentum carries stocks in one direction for lengthy periods of time. So, for swing trading, the best approach is to trade along the long-term trend. It is also crucial to determine the kind of market you will be operating in.

Swing traders thrive when markets are headed nowhere. This is when indices rise for a few days then descend for a couple of days only for the pattern to recur over and over. Swing traders will get plenty of chances to benefit from the short-term up and down movements.

Swing Trading Strategy

One of the basic aims of swing trading is to take modest profits of about 10% rather than 20 - 25%. As a swing trader, your focus is not really on making gains over weeks and months. Most trades last between 5 and 10 days. You will be better off making 5% to 10% gains each week than 20% over a month.

Entry Strategy

As it is, your swing trading entry strategy is probably the most significant part of your trade. This is because all your capital will be exposed to risk. However, should the stock finally move in your favor, then you should relax and plan how to collect your profits.

1. Price Pattern

One of the most important aspects of technical analysis used to determine entry points is the price pattern. The price pattern refers to the configuration of price movement. This configuration is identified by using trend lines and curves. There are a couple of price pattern signals that come into play.

A price pattern can point to a change in trend direction. When this happens then it is referred to as a reversal pattern. Alternatively, you can have what is known as a continuation pattern. This happens when the current trend proceeds in its intended direction after a brief pause.

Swing Points

Identifying swing points should be one of your main intentions with the entry strategy. A swing point is simply a pattern that exhibits three distinct candle patterns. Price patterns have been used by swing traders for many decades. The patterns are as a result of technical analysis.

A trader carries out technical analysis using price patterns in order to learn more about current market movements and also to gain insights into future market movements. When it comes to the entry strategy, your first step should be to identify any swing points.

Part of the technical analysis performed by traders involves reading charts. When traders keenly observe the technical charting of a stock's price, they are able to identify the moment when a reversal is occurring. Traders usually anticipate a reversal to happen especially after a stock has been regularly hitting new lows or highs. In these instances, the candlestick movements of the stock are closely observed.

Swing Point Lows

- The initial candle on the chart makes a low
- The second candle shows a lower low
- The third candle then results in a higher low

The information derived from the third candle indicates that sellers are rather weak and the stock is very likely to see a price reversal. To be successful in getting a good entry strategy, we need to identify stocks that have both pulled back and indicate a swing point low. Therefore, our entry strategy in this instance is to identify a stock with a low, a lower low, and then a higher low. At the point of the third candle would be a perfect entry point.

Please keep in mind that swing points are most likely to result in a strong reversal. This means that if a stock is trending downwards and the swing point occurs, then the price will stop trending downwards and will develop a strong upward trend. This is a great point to enter a trade. However, please also note that reversals do not occur without a swing point developing. You can take some time and look at previous stock charts.

2. Consecutive Price Patterns

It is always a great idea to trade stocks with consecutive down days just before the swing point low developing. This is also considered as a great entry point. When you look at your chart, you will be searching for consecutive days with an upward trend prior to the appearance of the swing point high.

As you await the development of swing points, you need to watch the left-hand side of the chart to confirm whether your stock is at resistance or support area of the chart. This is intended to improve to make the strategy more reliable.

Stop Loss Points

Traders are sometimes wrong and will lose some trades. This is because trading is ideally a game of probability. Stop-loss points are used to prevent a trader from incurring huge losses and possibly losing large amounts of money.

It is crucial that you make use of stop orders. All too often, enthusiastic traders will take profits quickly but then lose focus and cling on to losing trades. This is human and is absolutely understandable. However, as a trader, you need to completely detach emotions from your trades. Instead, you need to apply your technical analysis and stick to it.

A well-placed stop order is great because it acts as an insurance against possible huge losses. The stop order works by simply stopping trades once a certain price is attained. When the stop-loss order is triggered, it will close out a trade instantly. The order will basically minimize any possible loss. While no trader enters a trade thinking they will lose, losses are part and parcel of a trader's life. However, they really have to be kept in check.

Position Size

By setting up a stop loss, you also determine what is referred to as a position size. A position size refers to the size of shares of a stock that you are willing to take. This position is often determined by a simple formula. This formula is used to help minimize your risks while maximizing profitability.

Most traders will not risk losing more than 1% of their total trading capital on one trade. This means that if you have $10,000 then you cannot risk more than $100 on one single trade. However, you will need to work out your position size and determine your stop loss then you will be able to assess how you will invest or trade with the $100.

Candlestick Charts and Oscillators

As an options trader, you need to learn how to use different technical analysis tools. These will help make your trades more successful by helping you to take advantage of short-term price movements. To determine the trend strength and direction, you will have to use fractals, oscillators, volume analysis, chart patterns, and other methods.

Some of the most crucial methods that you should master are candlestick and oscillator patterns. These patterns provide an easy and quick method that characterizes the trend in order to identify swing trends. Here is a look at how to apply this trading strategy to options.

Applying Swing Trading Strategy to Options

Swing trading relies heavily on a number of indicators such as RSI or relative strength indicators and momentum indicators. These are used to provide information regarding market conditions. The indicators let traders known when the market is ripe for a correction after a long period of overpricing and so on. A correction in the reverse direction provides excellent market conditions for traders. Swing traders last longer in trades than scalpers and day traders.

Even then, they often exit trades within two days and two weeks. Rarely do swing traders last longer than this. Other types of traders who last longer are trend traders and actual investors. Options bought at the markets basically have very little or even limited risk on the downside. As such, they are safe to trade using this strategy. As we have already determined, options are derivatives which means they derive their value from an underlying security.

Options traders make use of graphs such as payoff and payout profiles. These enable traders to obtain a visual sense of the possible payoff upon expiration. Things to note when getting ready to trade include details such as the exercise or strike price. This price determines the level that a trader will buy as well as the price at which the underlying asset will be sold.

Payout and Payoff Profiles

Swing and options traders make use of certain types of graphs known as payoff or payout profiles. These enable them to obtain a visual representation of how much the strategy will pay off. The payoff is viewed under different circumstances such as at expiration and so on. Here is one such graph.

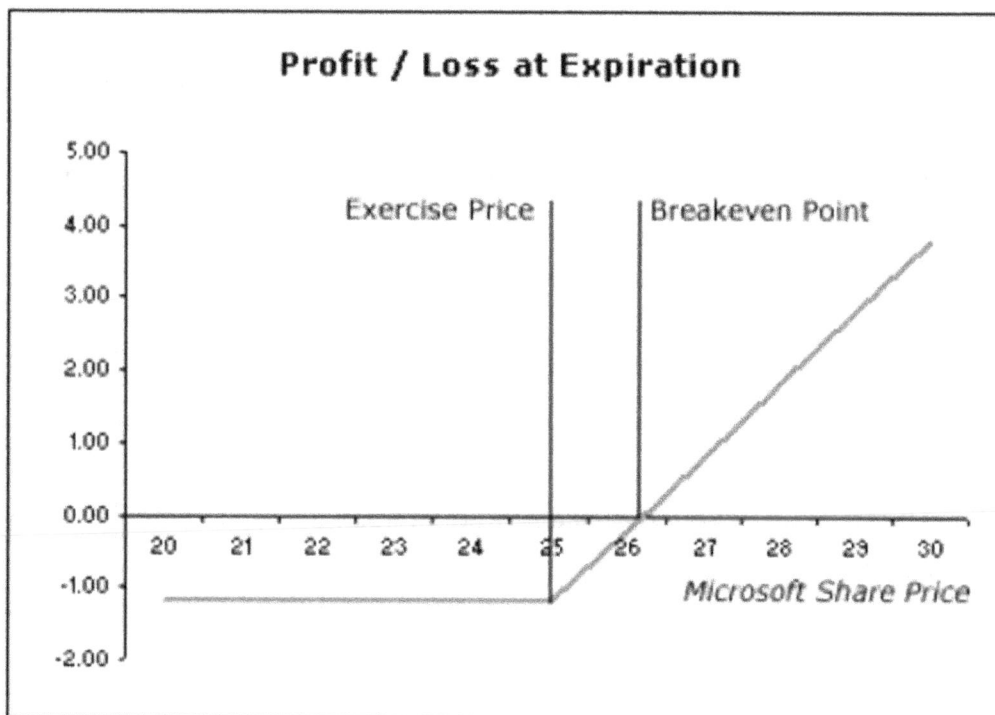

Profit / Loss at Expiration

Exercise Price | Breakeven Point

Microsoft Share Price

The graph above is an actual payoff profile for a $25 call option with Microsoft shares. If we examine the above graph closely, we note that there is a line running from the bottom left towards the top right-hand side. A close look at the graph indicates profitability at expiration when the market goes beyond breakeven mark.

However, this position also profits when you sell the underlying stock at a price higher than the initial purchase price. As such, you can benefit multiple times through options trading. This is actually the purpose of swing trading. You should aim to purchase stocks at a lower price and then sell when the price goes up, usually after a couple of days.

This is a directional strategy which is a good thing because it is great for swing trading. Fortunately, it is easy to learn some basic swing trading strategies which you can apply to options and trade successfully. Here are a couple of basic steps.

First, identify the asset you wish to trade-in. This is usually the underlying asset. The most common underlying assets are stocks especially blue-chip stocks with large trade volumes. You can use some of the indicators to help you identify stocks with large volumes for instance. Think about Bank of America stocks for instance. They make a great choice. You can also monitor a number of asset markets in order to identify excellent opportunities.

Importantly, you should identify an asset that is very close to correction. For this, you will need to use some of your tools or perhaps perform fundamental analysis. Most traders make use of momentum indicators like the RSI or relative strength indicator. The RSI is a bounded indicator and as such, it will indicate if the market is overbought or oversold. For instance, an outcome that is over 70 points indicates that the asset is overbought while any figure below 30 indicates the asset is oversold.

Any asset outside these figures is a game and can be chosen for trading purposes. If you are tech-savvy then you can use a further indicator such as the price-RSI. This will help you to attain even closer or more accurate results in your analysis which will mean better results.

The next step is to identify a market and also choose a direction. This is easily achieved through market analysis. You can use technical or fundamental analysis. In a later chapter in this book, we shall look closely at fundamental analysis. Once you learn how to conduct this type of analysis, you will easily be able to trade options and all other kinds of assets.

The best trading ratio for our purposes is anything from 2:1. Others include 3:1 or better. This means that you stand to make a larger profit against a smaller risk. As such you could easily take a directional market view based on the chosen underlying asset whether a put or call option. If your analysis shows a rising market or upward trend then a call option would be appropriate. Also, the reverse is true which means put options for a falling market. These two scenarios imply unlimited profitability with limited loss risk.

Technical Indicators

There are two indicators considered among the most important by many traders. These indicators should not be used to inform us of the best trade entry points but simply as guides that point us in the right direction. However, these two are lagging indicators and as such, not the best for our purposes. If you use them for your trades, they will result in inefficient trades that lack precision. However, they remain beneficial and useful most of the time.

There are other indicators available that you can use. These also let you know the exact points where to enter the market as well as the best exit points. You get to learn as precisely as possible where to place stop-loss orders and where to locate the profit targets.

A lot of traders have a certain aversion to day trades. They do not have the patience or time that intraday trading requires. Such traders still want to trade stocks and other financial instruments at the market and benefit from short term movements. It is here that swing trading comes in handy.

Swing trading requires you to identify a stock or other financial instrument that has the potential to make you money. Traders do not simply choose stocks to trade at random. They have to know which ones are the most favorable and which ones are not. This requires some skill so you should learn how to identify the best stocks to invest in.

Popular Technical Indicators

There are plenty of indicators that traders and investors use to enhance their trades. We shall review just a few of these and discover the best way of applying them to our trades in order to maximize profitability. It is crucial to understand that none of these indicators will make you profitable from the onset. Therefore, do not break your back trying to find the best or most profitable trade indicators. Instead, focus more on learning about a couple of extremely effective indicators as well as the strategies and methods used alongside them. Experts believe that trading strategies are more profitable when you apply the few indicators that you have mastered.

1. Moving Averages

Moving averages are among the most important trade indicators used by swing traders. They are defined as lines drawn across a chart and are determined based on previous prices. Moving averages are really simple to understand yet they are absolutely useful when it comes to trading the markets. They are extremely useful to all kinds of traders include swing traders, day, intraday, and long-term investors.

You need to ensure that you have a number of moving averages plotted across your trading charts all with different time periods. For instance, you can have the 100-day moving average, the 50-day, and the 9-day MA. This way, you will obtain a much broader overview of the market and be able to identify much stronger reversals and trends.

How to use moving averages

Once you have plotted and drawn the moving averages on your charts, you can then use them for a number of purposes. The first is to identify the strength of a trend. Basically, what you need to do is to observe the lines and gauge their distance from the current stock price.

A trend is considered weak if the trend and the current price are far from the relative MA. The farther they are then the weaker the trend is. This makes it easier for traders to note any possible reversals and also identify exit and entry points. You should moving averages together with additional indicators, for instance, the volume.

Moving averages can also be used to identify trend reversals. When you plot multiple moving averages, they are bound to cross. If they do, then this implies a couple of things. For instance, crossing MA lines indicate a trend reversal. If these cross after an uptrend, then it means that the trend is about to change direction and a bearish one is about to appear.

However, some trend reversals are never real, so you have to be careful before calling out one. Many traders are often caught off guard by these false reversals. Therefore, confirm them before trading using other tools and methods. Even then, the moving average is a very vital indicator. They enable traders get a true feel and understanding of the markets.

2. RSI – Relative Strength Index

Another crucial indicator that is commonly used by swing traders and other traders is the RSI or relative strength index. This index is also an indicator that evaluates the strength of the price of a security that you may be interested in. The figure indicated is relative and provides traders with a picture of how the stock is performing relative to the markets. You will need information regarding volatility and past performance. All traders, regardless of their trading styles, need this useful indicator. Using this relative evaluation tool gives you a figure that lies between 1 and 100.

Tips on RSI use

The relative strength index is ideally used for identifying divergence. Divergence is used by traders to note trend reversals. We can say that divergence is a disagreement or difference between two points. There are bearish and bullish divergent signals. Very large and fast movements in the markets sometimes produce false signals. This is why it advisable to always use indicators together with other tools.

You can also use the RSI to identify oversold and overbought conditions. It is crucial that you are able to identify these conditions as you trade because you will easily identify corrections and reversals. Sometimes securities are overbought at the markets when this situation occurs, it means that there is a possible trend reversal and usually the emerging trend is bearish. This is often a market correction. Basically when a security is oversold, it signals a correction or bullish trend reversal but when it's overbought, it introduces a bearish trend reversal.

The theory aspect of this condition requires a ratio of 70:30. This translates to 70% overvalued or over purchased and 30% undervalued or oversold. However, in some cases, you might be safer going with an 80 to 20 ratio just to prevent false breakouts.

3. Volume

When trading, volume is a crucial indicator and constitutes a major part of any trading strategy. As a trader, you want to always target stocks with high volumes as these are considered liquid. How many traders, especially new ones, often disregard volume and look at other indicators instead.

While volume is great for liquidity purposes, it is also desirable for trends. A good trend should be supported by volume. A large part of any stock's volume should constitute part of any trend for it to be a true and reliable trend.

Most of the time traders will observe a trend based on price action. You need to also be on the lookout for new money which means additional players and volume. If you note significant volumes contributing to a trend, then you can be confident about your analysis. Even when it comes to a downtrend, there should be sufficient volumes visible for it to be considered trustworthy. A lack of volume simply means a stock has either been undervalued or overvalued.

4. Bollinger Bands Indicator

One of the most important indicators that you will need is the Bollinger band indicator. It is a technical indicator that performs two crucial purposes. The first is to identify sections of the market that are overbought and oversold. The other purpose is to check the market's volatility.

This indicator consists of 3 distinct moving averages. There is a central one which is an SMA or simple moving average and then there two on each side of the SMA. These are also moving averages but are plotted on either side of the central SMA about 2 standard deviations away. These bands can be clearly viewed in the diagram below.

5. Accumulation and Distribution Line

Another indicator that is widely used by swing traders is the accumulation/distribution line. This indicator is generally used to track the money flow within a security. The money that flows into and out of a stock provides useful information for your analysis.

The accumulation/distribution indicator compares very well with another indicator, the OBV, or the on-balance volume indicator. The difference, in this case, is that it considers the trading range as well as the closing price of a stock. The OBV only considers the trading range for a given period.

When a security closes out close to its high, then the accumulation/distribution indicator will add weight to the stock value compared to closing out close to the mid-point. Depending on your needs and sometimes the calculations, you may want to also use the OBV indicator.

You can use this indicator to confirm an upward trend. For instance, when it is trending upwards, you will observe buying interest because the security will close at a point that is higher than the mid-range. However, when it closes at a point that is lower than the mid-range, then volume is indicated as negative and this indicates a declining trend.

While using this indicator, you will also want to be on the lookout for divergence. When the accumulation/distribution begins to decline while the price is going up, then you should be careful because this signals a possible reversal. On the other hand, if the trend starts to ascend while the price is falling, then this probably indicates a possible price rise in the near future. It is advisable to ensure that your internet and other connections are extremely fast especially when using these indicators as time is of essence.

6. The Average Directional Index, ADX

Another tool or indicator that is widely used by swing traders is the average directional index, the ADX. This indicator is basically a trend indicator and its purpose is largely to check the momentum and strength of a trend. A trend is believed to have directional strength if the ADX value is equal to or higher than 40. The directional could be upward or downward based on the general price direction. However, when the ADX value is below 20, then we can say that there is no trend or there is one but it is weak and unreliable.

You will notice the ADX line on your charts as it is the mainline and is often black in color. There are other lines that can be shown additionally. These lines are DI-

and DI+ and in most cases are green and red in color respectively. You can use all three lines to track both the momentum and the trend direction.

7. Aroon Technical Indicator

Another useful indicator that you can use is the Aroon indicator. This is a technical indicator designed to check if a certain financial security is trending. It also checks to find out whether the security's price is achieving new lows or new highs over a given period of time.

You can also use this technical indicator to discover the onset of a new trend. It features two distinct lines which are the Aroon down line and the Aroon up line. A trend is noted when the Aaron up line traverses across the Aaron down line. To confirm the trend, then the Aaron up line will get to the 100-point mark and stay there.

The reverse holds water as well. When the Aroon down line cuts below the Aaron up line, then we can presume a downward trend. To confirm this, we should note the line getting close to the 100-point mark and staying there.

This popular trading tool comes with a calculator that you can use to determine a number of things. If the trend is bullish or bearish, then the calculator will let you know. The formulas used to determine this refer to the most recent highs and lows. When the Aroon values are high, then recent values were used and when they are low, the values used were less recent. Typical Aroon values vary between o and 100. Figures that are close to 0 indicate a weak trend while those closer to 100 indicate a strong trend.

The bullish and bearish Aroon indicators can be converted into one oscillator. This is done by making the bearish one range from 0 to -100 while the bullish one ranges from 100 to 0. The combined indicator will then oscillate between 100 and

-100. The number 100 will indicate a strong trend, 0 means there is no trend while -100 implies a negative or downward trend.

This trading tool is pretty easy to use. What you need to, is first obtain the necessary figures then plot these on the relevant chart. When you then plot these figures on the chart, watch out for the two key levels. These are 30 and 70. Anything above the 70-point mark means the trend is solid while anything below 30 implies a weak trend.

Example – How to Trade Call Options

One of the easiest and stress-free ways of trading options is through buying call options. Let us look at an example just to demonstrate how it works.

Let us assume that the stock YHOO is trading at $50. According to your estimation, this stock will rise in price in the next couple of weeks. You believe that it will get to $60 within that time period. There is one way of profiting from this situation and that is to purchase about $100 the stock. If you buy it today at $50, it will cost you $5000. After a few weeks, if your assumptions were right, you could sell the same stock for $60 each and get $6000. This would result in a profit of $1000. This will amount to a 25% return on investment which is not bad at all.

However, you can do even better if you pursue call options rather than direct stock purchases. With options, you can get much better returns especially if you know for sure that a stock's price is going to rise. Let us examine the trade of a call option for 100 Yahoo! Shares. Let us say that these have a strike price of $50 but this price has a one-month timeline.

The call option is priced at $2 per share so you will buy the right to purchase 100 shares of Yahoo stock, YHOO. The strike price now is $50 but this price will expire after one month. It will cost you $2 * 100 shares = $200 to purchase this call option.

At this point, you own the rights to buy 100 shares at $50. Now in about 1 months' time, the price rises as was expected from $50 per share to $60. When this happens, then your options are said to be "In the Money".

If you are to sell this call option, you will sell it for $1000. This earns you a cool $800 profit. This is a 400% return on investment which you cannot make buying and selling shares. Now recall earlier when we spent $5000 buying shares. In this new scenario, we can spend the same amount of money buying options. $5000/$200 = 25 call options. If each option earns you $800 then 25 call options will earn you 25 * $800 = $20,000. This is an impressive return on investment and you can make huge profits this way. This is why call options are far much better choice than dealing directly in shares.

Different Scenarios

What if Stock does not get to $60 but Goes to $55

Remember that our stock, YHOO was worth $50 a share when we bought the call options. Now, what happens if after expiration of the time duration the price does not hit $60 as was desired but goes up to only $55? Then you still win because the option is "In the Money". The stocks still gain an increase of $5 which works in your favor. If you wish you can exercise your right to purchase the shares at the strike price and then sell them off at the stock market. You will then make a profit of $5 per share which adds up to, $5 * 100 = $500. A neat $500 profit for a single trade is not bad at all.

What if the Price Falls to $40 or Below?

There are two other scenarios that are possible in this case. One is that there is no price movement at all. Let us assume that the price drops to $40 or below. You will have no desire to purchase the shares because they are available at the market at a cheaper price. In this instance, your options become worthless. You will not be able to claim any money and will have suffered a loss. In this case, your options will be considered as being "out of the money". You will also lose the initial amount you used to pay for the options.

What is the Profit and Loss Implications?

One thing worth noting when it comes to options is that you stand to gain big profits but your losses are only limited to the cost of the options no matter the size of the trade. In our case above, the maximum loss that was at risk was $200 while the best possible profit was about $20,000. In future, you may want to buy LEAPs options which are long term options whose expiry dates are at least 1 year.

Chapter 5: Options Brokers and Simple Strategies

In order to trade successfully, you will need to access the markets. To do so, you will need the services of a broker. This is because the markets are not accessed directly by traders. Ideally, traders used to work with stockbrokers or brokerage firms. Traders would prepare their trades which would then be placed in the markets by the brokerage firms. This was the practice for many years and even decades.

Things are different today because of advances in the digital world. Online trading has become extremely common with thousands, and probably even millions of traders trading from different locations around the world. All these traders access the markets to place their trades or exit the markets via online brokers.

Digital Brokers

Today, you do not need to visit your broker at the office. All you need is a computer that is connected to the internet. With this, you are good to go. Simply find a suitable broker and begin trading. Brokers provide their clients with platforms that allow you to access the markets any time of day or night. This kind of easy access has changed the way things are done around the world. More and more people have been able to trade and generate wealth for themselves and their families.

Therefore, if you want to begin trading options, you start by identifying the best possible options broker in the market. You will then open a brokerage account with this brokerage which is an online platform. There are numerous types of brokers out there. They all have different requirements and provide a variety of tools and services.

Options trading can be tricky, sometimes difficult, and challenging. As such, you really need to ensure that you choose the correct broker. A lot of traders, even seasoned experts, are of the opinion that trading options carry a significant amount of risk especially when you begin dealing in more complex strategies.

The first step as it is you will have to find a broker that supports options trading. Not all brokerage firms support options trading so it is advisable to confirm this before proceeding. Ideally, you will have to look at about five or six different brokers and then decide which one serves your best interest. Virtually all brokers have pros and cons so try and identify one that has features that you like. These include helpful customer service, low costs, affordable fees, and fair charges, and so on.

Types of Brokers

We have different kinds of brokers. There are actually two main types. These are discount brokers and full-service brokers. A full-service broker also known as a traditional broker provides a wide variety of services to clients. These services include personalized advice to clients about where to invest or place their money.

These professionals serve mostly active traders who prefer to make their own financial decisions.

On the other hand, we have discount brokers who are more suited to traders who know what they are doing and wish to manage their own affairs. As such, clients pay only a minimal amount and in return get to make most, if not all their financial decisions. What they do mostly is to execute orders from clients like you. This means that when you enter a trade or a position, the broker will execute these on your behalf.

You are also likely to encounter brokerage firms that provide a combination of these services. They generally offer a bouquet of services from which clients get to choose the services they desire. A lot of options traders, including beginners and novices, prefer the discounted services. Basically, any trader that is confident enough to trade on their own and implement options strategies is very likely to be successful.

Considerations to Keep in Mind

As a trader, when searching for a broker, you should watch out for a couple of important features. The most crucial for most traders are commission charges and great customer service. However, these should not be the only considerations. There are other important ones as well. In the end, you will have to balance out your preferences and possibly sacrifice some benefits in exchange for others.

Speed of Trades Execution and Availability

Some of the most important features that you should look out for include website availability as well as its responsiveness. There are brokers who sit on trades for so long that traders lose any benefits by losing out on timing. Speed is crucial if you are to be a profitable and successful trader.

A good platform should also be responsive. There is no need for spending so much time coming up with a strategy only for the platform to fail you. Ensure that you find a good platform that is sufficiently responsive so that you do not lose any advantages based on your analysis. Also remember to ensure that you have an excellent system from your PC or laptop computer to system, applications, and connectivity. These are crucial for a successful trading experience.

Ease of Use

Another crucial aspect of any trading platform or online brokerage is its ease of use. All too often brokerage firms will present quite complex or oblique platforms that take a while to master. Some keys may be spread apart while some functions are complex and hard to master. Such platforms are not ideal for traders.

What you need is a platform that is easy to master, user-friendly and simple features. Such a platform should also contain fantastic features that save you time and support your trades. These platforms tend to make trading easier and are much better than others. Search for trading platforms offering unitary screen order forms that cover all sorts of strategies.

Fees and Commissions

Also crucial are fees and charges including commissions, penalties, and so on. It is crucial to find an affordable broker whose costs and charges are minimal. If you are not careful, fees and charges will eat into your profits. As it is, options brokerages are super careful to stand out from the competition.

Such brokerages often charge either per contract fee or a per-trade fee. These are different in many ways. Find out exactly what fees are charged, what they cover, whether they are paid upfront and soon. Other crucial considerations include market and limit orders. Different orders will cost a different amount based on certain factors. Check the fees charged and understand exactly what is being charged.

There are sometimes hidden fees. These fees could be charged on inactive accounts, not maintaining a minimum fee in your trading account, and even a general annual account maintenance fee. Watch out for commissions that are usually charged on winnings. They do add up to significant amounts with time. Avoid platforms that charge large commissions. A low-commission broker is ideal.

Two-Way Screening

You need to know that screening should be both ways. Even as you get screened by a broker, you will need to screen them as well. Your broker will be your most crucial partner from this point on so you need to ensure that you will have a positive relationship together.

An appropriate broker is one with the necessary research and trading tools and will provide the necessary customer service, guidance, and support. This is especially important for first time traders who are new to options trading. You need to also compare and contrast other traders and see who offers you the best platform, tools, and support. This is easier nowadays because most of them have been rated by traders.

Select an Online Broker

It is important to consider the tools offered by a broker and the fees he charges. These two considerations are of paramount importance. If you are a beginner or novice trader, then you will want to find a broker who offers excellent customer service because you will definitely need some assistance along the way.

At this stage, you probably won't find brokers that charge low fees. Basically, you should aim to pay no more than $4 - $10 per trade. You probably won't trade much as a beginner and novice trader. Once your skills get better and you start trading more often, then you can consider moving to a more affordable broker.

Also, take a look at your broker's software. This software should be easy to navigate and also streamlined. A good platform that is presentable, easy to navigate and user-friendly is what you should be on the lookout for. The software should provide advice on how to access all the trading tools you will need and also access to a platform that allows you to interact with other traders.

Trading Accounts

When it comes to trade and investments, a trading account is simply an account that is held by a financial institution that you open as a trader. These accounts are not normally opened directly but via a broker or investment dealer. The account is for you and is meant for your trading and investment purposes. It can hold all sorts of securities from stocks to currencies, bonds, and numerous others.

The best way to fund your account is via your bank account. This will establish and confirm your identity. It will also prove that the funds belong to you. You cannot use a check issued by a friend to fund your account.

Margin Trading Account

You can choose between opening a margin trading account or a cash account. A margin trading account comes with a credit line directly from your broker. This credit line makes it possible for you to purchase stocks, options, and other types of securities whenever you wish. You also get the chance to buy options directly.

Cash Trading Account

This type of trading account allows you to enter trades using only the cash in your account. Basically, I you have $5,000 in your account then you can only use the $5,000 for your trades. You will also be required to close one position before acquiring more purchase power.

Since this is a cash account, you are generally not permitted to borrow any cash. The good news is that any cash settlements are often processed within a day. Let us assume you transact today. Any cash settlements can be sorted out within a 24 hour period. However, this is just with some brokers and not all. There are those who take up to 3 days to process settlements.

Margin

A lot of the time brokerage firms will offer you some margin. This is additional credit that enables you to invest in more stock. A margin account is similar to receiving a loan from an institution. This means that you will pay some interest on the cash advance. This interest is charged only if you hold a position overnight. The amount of interest charged is often 2% over and above the prevailing market rates. Remember that you will be responsible for paying back this money, regardless of whether or not you earned a profit.

Margin is often handed out to qualifying accounts at a rate of 2:1. This applies to accounts whose balance is less than $25,000. For instance, if your account balance is $15,000, then you have access to a total of $30,000 which you can use to place trades and buy into positions. For account holders with more than $25,000 then you can get access to credit in the ratio of 4:1. This is a lot of money so please be careful if and when you do qualify.

Leverage and Options Trading

The reason why trading options strategy is so profitable compared to that of other securities is due to leverage. A small amount of money can leverage a larger underlying security compared to the same amount placed in stocks or bonds, for instance.

With $100, you can probably buy 20 shares valued at $5 per share. However, this same amount of money can control probably 100 shares. This is what leverage is. When it comes to profits, the options trader will make a much larger profit compared to the stock trader. Basically, if you have trading capital, then you can make a much higher profit if you choose to trade options rather than stocks or any other security. The potential is really huge and ranges in the 1000% possibility.

Options leverage is defined as the money equivalent in multiples of a single option position in relation to the true cash value of an underlying asset. When these two are compared, then the difference becomes visibly noticeable. This is why options are considered so valuable. The potential they hold is astronomical.

Example

Let us look at an example to understand how leverage works. Imagine that you have $1,000 to trade. You decide to invest this amount in Company ABC because you believe the stock will rise in a couple of weeks' time. Assume that the stock is worth $20 per share. This means that you can buy 50 shares of the stock with your $1,000. If, after a couple of weeks' time the stock rises in price as predicted to $25, you will make a profit of $250. This is not a bad deal at all.

Now instead of buying shares, let us assume you invest the $1,000 in options instead. There is a call option on Company ABC with a strike price of $20. The cost of the contract is only $2 per share. As such, you are able to control over 500 shares of the same stock. Remember in the first example you only had 50 shares.

Now with the same price movement from $20 to $25, you will make $2,500 which is far much more than the initial $250 that you would make buying shares directly. This goes to show the power and reach of leverage. If you think about it, you will realize that leverage is a powerful tool. It applies in many other situations but is at its most powerful when trading options.

Simple Options Trading Strategies

There is a wide variety of strategies used with options. You can adapt any one of these depending on certain factors. Some of these are basic and quite straightforward while others are complex and even complicated with multiple legs and so on. However, all options strategies are based on call and put options. As a novice trader, you should focus on learning some of the most basic strategies going forward. Within time, you will be able to master these and then check out some more advanced strategies later on.

1. The Long Pull

One of the most popular yet basic strategies is the Long Pull. This strategy is almost similar to the long call. The only difference here is that you will be rooting for a price fall of the underlying stock. A drop in price will put you in a better position to have the outcome that you desire.

Example

Let us assume that ABC stock is at a price of $50. Now someone puts up a $50 put option. Each costs $5 and limited in time to a 6-month period. So if you were to buy a contract of 100 shares is $5 * 100 = $500. With this trade, you stand to benefit the most if the price drops to zero. Should this happen, then you will stand to make at least $5,000. On the other hand, the downside is that you will lose the premium you paid to acquire the stocks. In our case, this is $500.

2. The Long Call

This strategy is very simple and pretty basic. It is ideal for beginners. Basically, as a trader, you find a call option and purchase it. This is known as going long. When you buy this option, you are doing so in the hope that the value of the underlying security will go up past the strike price within a given timeframe.

Example

Let us assume that a stock, ABC is trading at $50. Let us also assume that an options call is available at $5 per share for a period of 6 months. Like all others, this option contract is for 100 shares. This means that it will cost you, or any other trader $5 * 100 = $500 for the contract.

3. The Short Put

This kind of trade is the direct opposite of the long put. Traders will sell their put or go short. The thinking or reasoning here is that the price of the stock will go up or remain stagnant until expiration. The payoff of a short put is the exact opposite of a long put.

Chapter 6: Risk and Money Management

What is Risk Management?

Trading is generally not without risk and options pose a higher risk compared to other forms of securities. The risk is largely due to its speculative nature. As a trader, you need to protect yourself and trading capital from unnecessary losses and any potential losses that can be prevented.

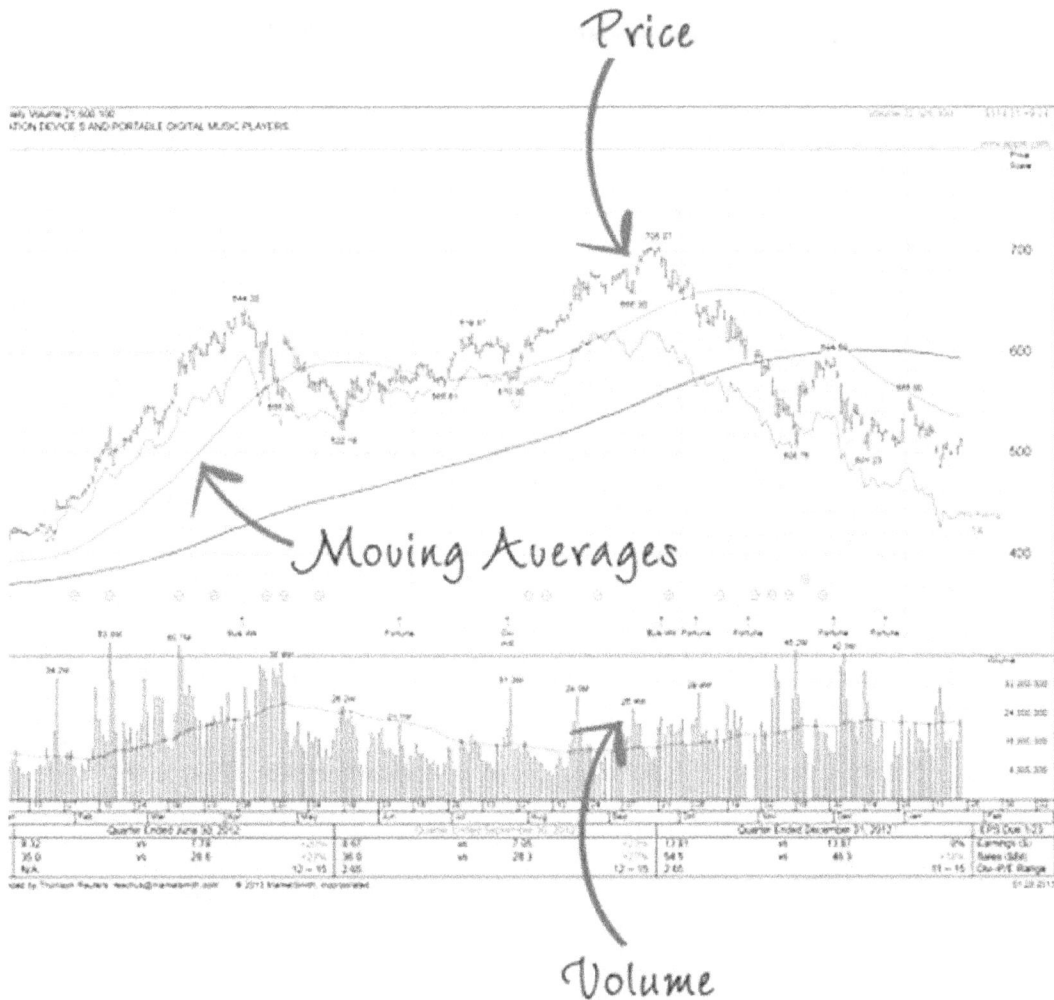

As a trader, the first thing you need to think about is not losing money. We do not engage in trade in order to lose money. A lot of beginners lose money in their early days. Some believe that this is an inevitable process. However, it does not have to be this way. With proper planning and especially proper risk management, you should not unnecessarily lose money trading the markets.

In fact, to be successful as a trader, your number one focus should be risk management rather than winning trades or strategies. A good trader is one who does not unnecessarily lose money. The most successful traders are those who manage their funds so well. To do this, you have to watch your every move and countercheck every decision that you make. For instance, if you want to enter a position in the markets, you need to ask yourself if that move is necessary and what amounts you stand to lose should it not work out.

Effective Risk Management

The options trading process does carry some risks with it. Understanding these risks and taking mitigating steps will make you not just a better trader but a more profitable one as well. A lot of traders love options trading because of the immense leverage that this kind of trading affords them. Should an investment work out as desired, then the profits are often quite high. With stocks, you can expect returns of between 10%, 15% or even 20%. However, when it comes to options, profit margins in excess of 1,000% are very possible.

We are familiar with bad investments and losses emanating from the actions of individuals or organizations that were hoping to be profitable. Numerous traders make huge errors when they trade resulting in major losses. This only happens when they know not what they are doing and when they do not take sufficient steps to protect themselves.

Remember that profits do not just show up. It takes plenty of hard work and most of all proper risk management techniques. Without risk management techniques in place, there is no need to enter the markets because you will be risking your funds. Keep in mind that trading options is a highly risky venture because it is speculative in nature. As such, you cannot trade without protecting yourself. Here are ways you can protect yourself and your trading capital.

1. Have a Trading Plan

One of the most important things is to have a trading plan. This plan details exactly all the steps that you will follow from market entry to exit. You should sit down and consider all possible scenarios. There is no need to take any risks. Once you learn as much as you can about options and trading, then you should learn how to plan your trades. Wise traders say anyone who fails to plan is planning to fail. If you want to succeed then you should come up with a trading plan which you should then abide by. Again there is no need of coming up with a trading plan if you will not implement it fully.

The main purpose of a trading plan is to ensure that you manage your money wisely and place it only well-planned and well-executed strategies. This way, you will avoid reckless moves and only put your money in strategies that are well worked out.

All too often, a trader will enter a trade without understanding exactly how it will play out. In such instances, the chances of losing money are extremely high. If you are unsure about any move, then please don't make it. A single move could imply a risk. With a good plan, all moves will be premeditated and no unnecessary risks will be taken.

2. Understand Trading Psychology

Trading options largely revolves around three major factors. These are money management, trading strategies, and psychology. You need to keep in mind that the markets can be a very emotional place so it is crucial that you remain focused and disciplined. If you do not stay disciplined, then you will lose out and others will very likely take advantage of you.

What you really need to do in order to trade successfully is to have a solid strategy, follow the strategy and stick to it. If the strategy does not follow the intended plan, then simply quit and come up with another strategy.

If you have a strong mindset, you will be able to understand when to pursue a losing trade and when to quit. If you lack discipline, then one of two emotions will take over. These are greed and fear.

Sometimes traders trade on a whim and keep posting random trades. Rather than take this approach, you really should focus on a successful strategy which you will pursue until you need to exit. You should also have good trading skills and proper money management plan. With these in place, you will be able to focus better and think in terms of probabilities and risk-reward ratios. This way, you will not leave room for emotional trading.

There are other things that you need to also keep in mind. For instance, you need to develop and stick with good trading habits. As a trader, you need to note that a winner is one who is persistent and consistent. You should develop the habit of closely studying the markets, conducting your analysis, and position sizing.

Position sizing is crucial, especially in a volatile market. As such, you need to take care of your downside risks and ensure that your position size appropriately. You should also envision the end game. Come up with a vision of where you want the trade to head then prepare to make any necessary adjustments.

You also need to accept any possible failures. Sometimes your strategies will not work out and you will lose some trades. This happens to all traders, even experienced ones. If you assume that you must succeed on each attempt, then you will be setting yourself up for failure.

3. Risks are Inherent

All types of investing opportunities carry a certain level of risk. However, trading options carries a much higher risk of loss. Therefore, ensure that you have a thorough understanding of the risks and always be on the lookout. Also, these kinds of trades are very possible due to the nature and leverage offered by options. A savvy trader realizes that he or she is able to control an almost equivalent number of shares as a traditional stock investor but at a fraction of the cost. Therefore, when you invest in options, you can spend a tiny amount of money to control a large number of shares. This kind of leverage limits your risks and exposure compared to a stock investor.

4. Time is not on your Side

All options have an expiration date and that they do expire in time. When you invest in stocks, time is on your side most of the time. However, things are different when it comes to options. Basically, the closer that an option gets to its expiration, the quicker it loses its value and earning potential.

Options deterioration is usually rather rapid and it accelerates in the last days until expiration. Basically, as an investor, ensure that you only invest dollar amounts that you can afford to lose. The good news though, is that there are a couple of actions that you can take in order to get things on your side.

Therefore, try and always or at least mostly to choose options whose expiry dates lie within your investment opportunity. Also, identify options that are at the money or very close. These increase your chances of profitability while minimizing risks and exposure. Ensure that you sell options whenever you believe that high prices are due to volatility. Instead, choose to purchase option when you believe that volatility is undervalued.

5. Naked Short Positions can Result in Substantial Losses

Anytime that you decide to short options naked presents a high likelihood of substantial and sometimes even unlimited losses. Shorting put naked means selling stock options with no hedging of your position.

When selling a naked short, it simply implies that you are actually selling a call option or even a put option but without securing it using an option position, stock or cash. It is advisable to sell a put or a call in combination with other options or with stocks. Remember that whenever you short sell a stock you are in essence selling borrowed stock. Sooner or later you will have to return the stock. Fortunately, with options, there is no borrowing of stock or any other security.

6. Prices can Move Pretty Fast

Options are highly leveraged financial instruments. Because of this, prices tend to move pretty fast. Basically, options prices can move huge amounts within minutes and sometimes even seconds. This is unlike other stock market instruments like stocks that move-in hours and days.

Small movements in the price of a stock can have huge implications on the value of the underlying stock. You need to be vigilant and monitor price movements often. However, you can generate profits without monitoring activity on the markets 24-hours a day each day.

When structuring your options, you should ensure that you use the correct strike prices as well as expiration months in order to cut out most of the risk. You should also consider closing out your trades well before the expiration of options. This way, time value will not dramatically deteriorate.

ROI or Return on Investment

The Term ROI stands for Return on Investment. ROI is a measure of performance and is used by both investors and traders to measure the effectiveness and efficiency of an investment. This includes your trading capital. ROI deliberately endeavors to measure directly the total return derived from a particular investment.

For instance, if you invest a total of **X** amount on a particular trade and then received a return of **Y** from this investment, then ROI will endeavor to indicate the performance of your investment amount and what you received for your efforts. If you want to calculate the rate of return of an investment, you will need to know the total return which is then divided by the investment amount.

One of the most important aspects of your investment portfolio is its profitability. You need to regularly monitor your investments which is best achieved using the ROI or return on investment. It is advisable to work out what each dollar invested has generated. There is a formula for working out this figure.

R.O.I = (Profits – Costs) / Costs

Even then, investors need to understand that the ROI depends on numerous other factors such as the kind of investment security preferred and so on. Also, note that a high ROI implies a higher risk while a lower figure means reduced risk. For this reason, it is important that appropriate risk management is undertaken.

A Brief Introduction to Technical Analysis

What is technical analysis? It is simply a method used by traders, investors, and other market players to examine and predict price movements in the markets. Technical analysis makes use of market statistics as well as historic chart prices.

The idea behind this type of analysis is that identifying past market performance can help to accurately predict future performance.

As a trader, you want to be able to identify the shares to trade, the best entry points, volumes, price, and the best exit points. The best way to find out information about all these is through technical analysis.

Two Different Approaches

According to finance experts, there are two basic approaches to technical analysis. These are the top-down approach and the bottom-up approach. In most cases, short-term traders will opt for the top-down approach while long-term investors prefer the bottom-up approach.

Steps to Technical Analysis

One of the first things you need to do is to come up with a technical analysis strategy. This is basically the process of developing a trading system. You will need to use some technical indicators such as moving averages. You can use the 200-day or the 50-day moving averages and follow them for a couple of days. Use them in relation to stocks or options that you have an interest in.

These will help you to identify the best securities to trade or deal in. therefore, use moving averages to identify high-quality securities that have good value, sufficient volumes, and so on. These are great candidates for trading.

Technical analysis will also enable a trader to identify the best points to enter and exit the markets. Therefore, as you plan your trades, you will need to use technical analysis in order to determine the best entry points. First, identify your preferred stock and then find its historic charts. The charts will provide you with information and indicators as to the most appropriate points to enter the markets. If your analysis is correct, then you will have no problems in the markets. However, you will also need to mark some points on the chart about where to collect profits and where to exit.

Factors Regarding Technical Analysis

Technical analysis is widely used on a regular basis all over the world. The best part is that there are programs and software that make the work a lot easier. There are also lots of experts who focus on certain specific tasks to make your work easier. For instance, there are software tools available that scan the market and list down the best stocks to trade-in. There are also tools and programs that can help identify exit and entry points on your behalf.

Finally, whenever you come up with a strategy, you should test it thoroughly before implementation. This way, you will easily be able to identify any flaws or things that need to be fixed. Once a serious trading plan is ready and tested, it should then be implemented without any due worry or concern.

Chapter 7: Speculations

In the world of finance, speculation, or speculative trading, refers to the act of conducting a financial transaction that has substantial risk of losing value but also holds the expectation of a significant gain or other major value. In the case of speculation, the risk of loss is more than offset by the possibility of a substantial profit or other compensation.

An investor who buys a speculative investment is likely to focus on price fluctuations. While the risk associated with the investment is high, investors are generally more likely to make a profit from this investment based on changes in market value than with long-term investments. If speculative investing involves the purchase of a foreign currency, one speaks of currency speculation. In this scenario, the investor buys the currency and later tries to sell the currency at a low rate, unlike the investor who buys the currency to pay for the import or to finance a foreign investment.

There would be little motivation to speculate without significant profits. It may sometimes be difficult to distinguish between speculation and simple investments, which forces market players to check whether speculation or investments depend on factors that determine the type of asset, the expected duration of the holding period and/or amount of leverage applied to the exposure.

How does speculation work

For example, real estate can blur the line between investment and speculation when buying property with the intention of renting it out. Although this would qualify as an investment, buying a large number of apartments with minimal down payments for quick resale at a profit would undoubtedly be regarded as speculation. Speculators can ensure market liquidity and narrow the range of offer prices so that manufacturers can effectively hedge price risk. Speculative short sales can also maintain a crazy bull market and prevent asset bubbles from forming by betting against successful results.

Mutual funds and hedge funds often engage in speculation in the foreign exchange markets as well as bond and stock markets.

Speculation in the Stock Market

Stocks that are considered to be risky in the stock market are known as speculative stocks. Speculative stocks offer potentially high returns to compensate for the high risk associated with them. Penny stocks with very low stock prices are an example of speculative stocks. Some stock market speculators are day traders who seeks to take advantage of price fluctuations during the trading day. As noted above, speculators are important to publicly traded companies because they are willing to invest in unproven companies, providing those companies with equity funding that enables them to grow and expand their market reach.

Speculation in the currency Market

The foreign exchange market (Forex) is popular with speculators, as the exchange rates between currencies fluctuate constantly over the long term. The forex market also offers frequent trading opportunities due to the different currency pairs available for trading. For example, the exchange rate of the US dollar can be traded relative to more than a dozen other currencies worldwide. Among the most commonly traded currency pairs include Eur/Usd (the euro vs. the dollar), Gbp/Usd (the pound sterling vs. the dollar) and Usd/Jpy (the dollar vs. the Japanese yen). Forex trading is also popular with speculators because of the high leverage that makes it easier for traders to make substantial profits with little commercial capital.

Chapter 8: Hedging

Hedging is analogous to taking out an insurance policy. If you own a home in a flood-prone area, you will want to protect that asset from the risk of flooding- to hedge it, in other words- by taking out flood insurance. In this example, you can't prevent flooding, but you can work ahead to mitigate the dangers if and when a flood occurs. There is a risk-reward tradeoff inherent in hedging; while it reduces potential risk, it also reduces the potential profit. Simply put, hedging is not free. In case of the flood insurance policy example, the monthly payments add up, and if the flood never comes, the policy holder receives no payout. Still, most people would choose to take that predictable, limited loss than suddenly lose their roof over their heads.

In the world of investment, hedging works the same way. Investors and money managers use hedging practices to limit and control their risk. To properly hedge yourself in the investment world, you need to use various instruments strategically to offset the risk of adverse price movements in the market. The best way to achieve this is to make another investment in a targeted and controlled manner. Of course, the similarities to the insurance example above are limited: in the case of flood insurance, the policyholder would be fully compensated for the loss, possibly with lower tax-deductible costs. In the area of investment, hedging is both a more complex and an incomplete science.

A perfect hedge is one that eliminates all risks associated with a position or portfolio. In other words, the hedge is 100% inversely correlated to the vulnerable asset. This is more an ideal than a reality on the ground, and even the hypothetical perfect ideal hedge is not without costs. Basis risk refers to the risk that an asset and a hedge will not move in the opposite direction as expected. "Basis" refers to discrepancy.

How does Hedging Work?

The most common way of hedging in the world is through derivatives. Derivatives are securities that move in accordance with one or more underlying assets. They include options, swaps, futures and forward contracts. The underlying assets can be stocks, bonds, commodities, currencies, indices or interest rates. Derivatives can be effective hedges against their underlying assets as the relationship between the two is more or less clearly defined. Derivatives can be used to define a trading strategy in which the loss of an investment is mitigated or compensated for by a profit in a comparable derivative.

For example, if Morty buys 100 shares of Stock plc (STOCK) at $10 a share, the company could cover its investment by closing a $5 put option with an exercise price of $8 that expires within a year. This option gives Morty the right to sell 100 STOCK shares for $8 next year. If STOCK is trading at $12 a year later, Morty will not exercise the option and will exit $5. However, he is unlikely to worry because his unrealized profit is $200 ($195 including the price of the sale). Conversely, if STOCK is trading at $0, Morty will exercise the option and sell its shares for $8 at a loss of $200 ($205 including the price of the put). Without this option, you could lose your entire investment.

The effectiveness of a derivative hedge is expressed in the form of a delta, sometimes referred to as a "hedge ratio". Delta is the amount by which the price of a derivative moves for each movement of $1 in the price of the underlying.

Fortunately, the different types of futures options and contracts offer investors the opportunity to protect themselves against most investments, including those related to stocks, interest rates, currencies, commodities and more.

The specific hedging strategy and the valuation of the hedging instruments will likely depend on the risk of an impairment of the underlying security against which the investor wishes to hedge. Basically, the higher the risk of falling, the greater the hedge. Downside risk tends to increase with higher levels of volatility and over time; an option which expires after a long period of time and which is linked to a more volatile securities will therefore be more expensive as means of hedging. In the STOCK example above, the higher the strike price, the more expensive the option will be, but the more the price protection it will offer as well. These variables can be adjusted to create a cheaper option for less protection, or a more expensive option for better protection. Still at a certain point, it becomes inadvisable to purchase additional price protection from the perspective of cost effectiveness.

Chapter 9: Spreads and Combinations

Options spreads: put & call combination strategies

An option spread is a combination of buying or selling two or more options that cover the same underlying stock or security.

These options can be put or call options (or sometimes stock options) and be of different expiries.

Each combination creates a different risk and profitability profile, which is often best represented using a profit and loss diagram.

For example, a trader can sell an AAPL Jan 540 call and buy an AAPL Jan 560 call, a type of call spread as defined below.

With all of these strategies, a trader uses the selected combinations of puts and calls to make a profit if a forecast result occurs. This is usually the case when the underlying stock moves up in a certain way - in the case of the call spread up - but for more complex trades, volatility can be expected to move, or time can be exploited.

There are three main types of basic option strategies:

1. Vertical call and put spreads

So-called because options with the same expiry date are quoted vertically in the chain of options.

Vertical spreads therefore contain a combination of put and call options if the expiry date is the same, but the strike price is different.

Examples include bull / bear call / put spreads as discussed below, and back spreads discussed separately.

Bull call strategy

Bull Call spread is a simple combination of options that can trade an expected increase in a stock's price, at minimal risk. It consists of buying options and selling a call options with a higher exercise price; Example of a direct debit spread with a net transaction cost.

It might be possible to buy a Nov 160 call for $3.50 and sell a Nov 165 call for $1.00, a net cost of $2.50 per contract:

Buy IBM Nov 160 Call 3.50
Sell IBM Nov 165 Call 1.00
Net Cost: $2.50
Should IBM rise and be above $165 at the end of November the spread would be worth $5, thus doubling the invested amount. Of course, if it is lower, the spread is worth less, with the worst case being if IBM falls below $160, whereby the spread is worthless, and all money is lost.

The trade is therefore a risk adjusted 'bet' that IBM will rise moderately over the next month.

Bear call strategy

A bear call spread is a similar trade that trades an expected drop in the price of a stock with minimal risk. It's about selling one call option and buying another with a higher strike price.

Note that this is a credit spread, meaning that we get money for a trade and, if we are right and the stock falls, we want to keep it if both options expire worthless.

So, again, with IBM $162, we might sell the $160 Nov and buy the call for $165 Nov call (i.e. the opposite of the previous one).

It may be possible to buy a Nov 160 call for $3.50 and sell a Nov 165 call for $1.00, which equates to a net balance of $2.50 per contract. i.e.:

Buy IBM Nov 165 Call 1.00
Sell IBM Nov 160 Call 3.50
Net loan: $2.50
If IBM drops below $160 as hoped, both options will expire, and we will keep the $2.50.

However, should IBM rise and exceed $160 at the end of November, the spread would have to be bought back to any value above $160. The breakeven point for trading is $162.50.
The trade expectation is therefore that IBM will fall moderately over the next month.

Bull put strategy

The put version of the bear call spread: i.e. a credit is received for 'betting' that stock will move in a particular direction (up, as compared to the bear call spread where the 'bet' was for the stock to fall). For example:

Buy IBM Nov 155 Put 0.75
Sell IBM Nov 160 Put 2.00
Net Credit: $1.25
The full credit is kept if IBM is above $160 at the end of November.

Of course, should IBM not be below $160, the spread would expire with some value (equal to the stock price less $160). Hence if this value is more than $1.25 – in the stock price is above $161.25 – the strategy has lost money.

This $161.15 is the breakeven point of this trade.

This is the put version of the bull call spread: that is, an amount is paid in advance that increases in value if the stock moves in the right direction ("down" versus "up" for the bear call spread). For example:

Buy IBM Nov 160 Put 2.00
Sell IBM Nov 155 Put 0.75
Net cost: $1.25

Should IBM fall below $155 by the end of November, the spread will be $5 (a significant increase from the original $1.25).

However, if the stock was above $158.75, the final value of the spread would be less than the $1.25 paid and the trade would have made a loss.

Butterfly

The butterfly spread can use either calls or puts and consists of two spreads that are combined into one. A butterfly widespread with calls would mean buying one call, selling two more calls, and then buying another call farther away.

A butterfly spread with puts would consist of buying one put, selling two puts farther away, and buying another put farther away.

One way to display the butterfly spread using calls is to buy a bull call spread by selling a bull call spread. The same applies to a butterfly spread with puts.

For example: Suppose a trader is bullish on BBB stock, which is currently trading at $40 per share.

The trader believes the stock could rise to $45 in the coming weeks and wants to build a position that could potentially benefit if the stock actually rises to $45.

Instead of buying a very expensive instant call, the trader decides to buy the Call Butterfly worth $40/$45/$50. The trader buys a call worth $40, sells two of the calls worth $45 and buys a call worth $50 for a total premium of $1.

The maximum profit potential of the position is calculated from the difference in the strike prices ($5) minus the premium paid ($1) for a total profit potential of $4.
The maximum profit is achieved when the stock reaches the strike price of $45 upon expiration. If the market rises above $45, the profit will be reduced until the break-even point of $49 is reached. Trading loses money if the market is above $49 or expires below $41.

When to Put it on

The butterfly spread can be useful when the trader has a directional opinion on the market or believes that the market is likely to stay within a specified range.
The call butterfly may be appropriate if the trader thinks the market may see a moderate price rise. In the case of a put fly, the spread may be used if the trader thinks the market could see a moderate decline.

The butterfly spread may also be used if IV levels are very high, making a straight call spread or put spread too expensive.

The call fly is effectively buying a call spread closer to the money while selling a call spread that is farther from the money. The put fly is buying a put spread closer to the money while selling a put spread that is farther from the money.

Pros of Strategy

The butterfly spread can have some important advantages. Butterfly spreads are limited in risk. If a trader buys a butterfly spread, their risk is limited to the net premium paid for the position.

If the trader sells a butterfly spread, their risk is limited to the difference in strike prices minus the premium collected.

The butterfly spread can potentially profit not only from price action, but also from favorable changes in IV levels.

Cons of Strategy
The butterfly spread does have some disadvantages as well. The spread can be negatively affected by unfavorable changes in IV levels.

It may also require the market to stay within a fairly tight range in order to turn a profit. Because the spread uses multiple legs, it can also cost more in commissions and fees.

Risk Management

There are numerous ways to manage risk on a butterfly spread. If a trader is long a call fly for a premium of $4, he or she could elect to cut the position if the value of the spread declines by half. Butterfly spreads can also be managed using price action.

For example, if the trader buys a $40/$45/$50 call fly on a stock and the stock reaches $45, he or she could elect to cut the trade even if the max profit has not yet been reached.

If the trader has sold a call fly or a put fly, they can set a premium level at which they will exit the trade. For example, if a trader sold a call fly for $1, he or she may decide to cut the trade if the value of the fly increases to $2.

Possible Adjustments

The butterfly spread can be adjusted any time during the trade. A trader could elect to close one or more legs of the trade at any time. This could, however, increase risk exposure or even expose the trade to unlimited risk.

Traders also have the option of rolling the fly up or down using different strike prices.

Traders can also elect to sell a fly back to the market, and to buy a new fly with more time until the options expire. Conversely, a trader that is short a fly can buy it back and sell a new fly with more time.

Traders can also use a variation of the butterfly where one portion of the spread, known as the wing, is larger. For example, a trader could buy the $40 call, sell two of the $45 calls and purchase a $52 call.

The structure of the trade can be made according to the trader's market forecast, risk tolerance and profit objectives.

The butterfly spread is extremely versatile and can be used under a variety of market scenarios. It is a fairly simple spread to grasp and may put the trader in a position to potentially profit while keeping trade risk limited.

Options Trading Part 2

Chapter 1: Introduction to Forex

As the world continues to be a globalized village, currencies as well continue to play an important role. If you have had the opportunity to travel to another country, you always have to do a currency exchange which involves exchanging the currency you have with you into a new currency of the country you are visiting. Usually, there is a currency exchange booth at the airport, having a big screen that displays different exchange rates for different countries. Suppose you are visiting Japan and you have to exchange your currency into Japanese Yen, you will have to look at the currency exchange rates. If the exchange rate for $1 is 100JYN, then for your 1000 US Dollar in your wallet, you will have 100,000 Japanese Yen. If you have ever done this, then essentially you have participated in the forex market. Today, foreign trades and businesses continue to be on the rise, and whether you like it or not, at one point in your life, you will be involved in foreign exchange, whether directly or indirectly.

Foreign Exchange (Forex)

Foreign exchange, popularly referred to as forex refers to the buying and selling of currencies with the goal of making profits off the changes in their value. Forex can also be simply described as the process of changing currencies. There are many reasons as to why you would change your currency into another. These may be due to commercial reasons, trading reasons, or tourism purposes. However, the main reason as to why currency conversion is undertaken is for the purpose of earning the profit. As different currencies get converted every day, some currencies experience price movements in an extremely volatile manner. While this volatility increases the risks of conducting forex trade, traders are highly attracted to this volatility as it brings about a greater chance of high profits.

Forex is unique because there exists no central marketplace where foreign exchange can be done. There is no one centralized exchange center, but rather, the trade is conducted in an electronic manner over-the-counter (OTC). This, therefore, means that all forex transactions are carried out in computer networks between all forex traders around the world. The forex market actively operates 24 hours a day. Currencies in foreign exchange are traded across all the time zones in the major financial centers in the world. Such a trading system means that when the trading day in the US ends, a forex market in the US begins a new day in the say Hong Kong or Tokyo. This is what makes the price quotes of the forex market to change constantly.

In the same way, we do with stocks; we can also trade currency. Trading currency is also based on a trader's thoughts. A trader will have to critically think about where the value of a given is or where its value is heading to. However, the big difference is in the fact that with forex, it very easy to trade down or up. For instance, if you think that the value of a currency will increase, you proceed to buy it. Again, if you feel that it will depreciate, you will proceed to sell it. Today's globalized market is vast, making it easy to find a buyer or a seller. A good example can be the case scenario where you get the news that an African country like Kenya is trying to attract foreign business by devaluing its currency. Therefore, you look at this issue critically, and according to your analysis/thoughts, you can see that this depreciation will extend for some period of time. You, therefore, decide to sell the Kenyan currency against another profitable currency like the Saudi Arabia Dinar. You will, in turn, gain more profits, the more the Kenyan currency devalues against Saudi Arabia Dinar. However, you will make losses if the value of Kenyan currency increases while your sell position is open.

History of Forex

As recorded by history, the oldest method of exchange is the batter system. Barter system of trade began in 6000 BC in Mesopotamia. Barter system involved the exchange of goods for goods. Later on, the system evolved with the popular medium of exchange being salt and spices. As time went by, gold coins became a medium of exchange as early as 6th BC. Gold coins were advantageous because they were portable, durable, uniform, had limited supply, could be divided easily and were widely accepted. This trend continued until the 1800s when countries decided to adopt the standard gold. This was attributed by the fact that gold was heavy, making it impractical as a medium of exchange. With gold-standard, governments were able to redeem any amount of paper money depending on their value in gold. The foreign exchange market in the early 1900s was backed by the gold standard. Countries thus were able to trade with each other in an efficient manner because it was possible to convert currencies received into gold. This went on fine until World War I when the European counties decided to suspend gold standard so as to allow them to print money that would fund the war.

The foreign exchange market experienced the first major transformation towards the last minutes of the Second World War, with the development of the Bretton Wood System. Bretton Woods System was designed by America, Britain, and France with the goal of bringing an economic order to the world. The US, with their neutrality and non-association policy, remained to be the only country that was not affected by the war. The American currency (the dollar) was seen as a failed currency, especially after the crash of the stock market in 1929. However, the dollar became one of the strongest international currencies that most international currencies compared with after WWII. The goal of establishing the Bretton Wood System was to create a stable economic environment where world economies could be able to restore their economies that were collapsing. The Bretton Wood System was pegged foreign exchange market that could be adjustable. Pegging currencies simply means that one currency can be fixed to another currency. This means that other countries could use the US Dollar to fix their exchange rates. At the time, the US was one of the top countries holding most gold reserves. This made the US dollar to be pegged with gold. Therefore, foreign countries were allowed to hold transactions in the US Dollar.

Unfortunately, due to the fact that there was insufficient gold backing the amount of US Dollars in circulation, the Bretton Woods agreement failed, and President Richard M. Nixon ended it in 1971. This resulted in a free-floating System. The European community in 1972 established the European Joint Float but also failed in 1973, resulting in an official free-floating system. The European countries, later on in 1992, held the Maastricht Treaty, which led to the creation of Euro currency. The era of the Internet: With the development and introduction of the internet, the currency market grew more sophisticated. People began to view money differently. Internet technology-enabled traders to do trade even while at home. Clearly, forex has a long history, and today, the foreign exchange market is actually the largest and biggest market in the world where each day, more than $5 trillion is traded. The future of forex presents everlasting opportunities for forex traders.

Why is Forex the Best Market to Trade?

Each and every trader has his/her own reasons as to why they prefer the Forex market. For me, I see that there are so many reasons as to why I would trade Forex online. Below are some of the reasons explaining why Forex online is the top market trade.

1. Available Technology

Today, a lot of human efforts are directed towards making our lives easier and better. This is also the same case in online trading. Today, there are many trading platforms coming up every year. Today, we also have fully established Forex trading software with regular updates. This makes Forex a very lucrative market.

2. Regulation

This trade is highly regulated and monitored. There are more than two regulatory authorities motoring Forex brokers. This is an assurance that Forex is one of the safest markets that one can trade on.

3. Working with possibilities

The basic rule of forex trade is to buy low and sell high. Forex allows for a trading method called short selling. Short selling allows you to sell assets even without owning them. For instance, your account can have 20,000 USD, and you would wish to trade it with Euro/JPY currency pair. In this way, even without purchasing Euro or Japanese Yen, you are able to do a short-selling on this pair and sell Japanese Yen for Euro despite the fact that your actual account is reading the balance in USD.

Advantages to trading forex

Here are some of the benefits of trading forex

4. There are no commissions needed

Imagine doing trade in an environment where there are no exchange fees or no government and brokerage fees? What is the feeling? Very nice, indeed! The services offered by most of the retail brokers are paid through the spread.

5. Low transaction costs

As at now, the market conditions have a transaction cost which is less than 0.1%. When conducting larger transactions, the spread is usually as low as 0.07%.

6. A 24-hour market

With forex, you can trade anytime you wish from any part of the world. There is no time limit be it in the morning, or at night you will always trade

7. High Liquidity

The forex market is extremely liquid and enormous. Under normal market conditions, a trader with just a click of a mouse is able to buy and sell currencies at his will. This means that you can never be stuck in a trade. Forex trading provides you with the capability to set up your own online trading platform that enables you to automatically close your position the moment your desired profit levels have been reached.

8. There are low barriers to entry

Most of the times when you hear about forex trade, you tend to imagine huge amounts of money. Well, the fact is that online trading stocks which require huge amounts of money, forex trading does not require a lot of money. Forex online platform offers mini and micro trading accounts whereas trader, you are allowed to deposit as low as $25 in the account.

9. It is not possible to corner the forex market

One good thing about the foreign exchange market is that it is so huge and accommodates many participants. As such, no one can control the central market price over some extended period of time.

10. Leverage

Leverage is a factor that gives traders the capability to make reasonably good profits and at the same time, keep their risks minimal. This means that a small deposit you make can control a larger total contract value. For instance, a forex broker can offer you a leverage of 50-to-1. This means that with a deposit of $50 margin, as a trader, you are able to buy or sell currencies worth $2,500.

The Challenges Involved in Trading Forex

First, when a high amount of leverage is allowed in the forex market by the banks, dealers, and brokers, traders can be able to control large positions of forex market even with their little money. As a trader, you must first begin by understanding the use of leverage as well as the risks introduced by leverage in your account. Many dealers have unexpectedly become insolvent due to extreme amounts of leverage. Secondly, in order to trade currencies productively, it is advisable that you must first be able to have a deeper understanding of the fundamentals and indicators used in economics. Particularly, in this era, as a trader, you must have the big picture in mind. You must be able to understand the economies of other countries (especially major economic powerhouses) and how these economies are interconnected. This is the only effective way that will enable you to drive currency values and be productive.

Chapter 2: What People Do Trade in the Forex Market?

The Forex market is the leading liquid financial market in the globe today. The market has various participants and commodities making it voluminous. The market is open day and night, making it control several world economies. This has made the market rise to form a good system to enable the exchange of currencies to facilitate the trade of goods and services. These products can either be traded using future or spot on markets.

In a typical manner, a contract is made between the buyer and seller about the good and mode of delivery, and the seller delivers the goods. Exchange of these goods is done by specific set standards. These standards are set in a contract, and they include:

· Quantity; it is the sum of commodities that are represented in the contract. It can be replaced in different forms which include traditional measurement of using bags or barrels, units, or imperial units.

· Quality; this is the descriptive features of the commodity that is being traded. It even includes physical characteristics.

· Price; this point in the contract which stipulates the least amount the product can be traded for. However, the agreed price does not have to be at the precise market value.

· Delivery; the contract is supposed to stipulate the delivery date, the means of delivery and time of delivery. Some of the contacts made are satisfied financially before actual delivery.

Despite these standards for the formation of a trade contract in the forex market, it is the task of buyer and seller to enforce the agreements.

There are several items people trade in the forex market includes soft commodities, precious metals, and energy.

Soft Commodities

Soft commodities' trading has risen over recent years by traders in the forex market. Traders who take an interest in soft commodities seek to diversify their portfolios on bond and stocks. Soft commodity trading is a term that is used to refer to general agriculture goods that are grown and not mined or extracted. The trade of soft products stated very many years ago. Despite being traded for a long time, it has very few participants compared to hard commodities. This section of tradable goods has a significant role in the forex market. The diversification of a person's portfolio helps him or her to have a soft cover during risky moments of trade. Some of the most traded soft commodities are:

Cocoa

A Native American discovered this plant approximately five thousand years ago. The plant was later farmed in large scale during the 15th century in Spain. The success in Spain saw the product spread across Europe than the rest of the world. This product is highly consumed across the globe at an estimation of 4.5 million tons annually. The highly traded coffee in the forex market is from the United States and the United Kingdom

Coffee

Coffee was discovered over two thousand years in Ethiopia, Africa. After several years it began being grown in the Middle East. In the current world, the coffee beverage is highly consumed by people. This has made the product to be volatile. There are two major types of coffee that are traded which are Arabica and Robusta. Robusta coffee is proven to have the highest amount of caffeine in coffee.

Cotton

Cotton has a universal influence in the current world because it has myriad uses in the world today. This character makes cotton to be among influential soft commodities. Cotton is estimated to be discovered more than five thousand years ago. The product played a crucial role during the rise and fall of different countries several years back. These qualities make the commodity be highly traded in the forex market.

Sugar

The first form of sugar is believed to be used nearly two thousand years ago. Sugar has seen its rise over the years to be a common commodity in households. This has made the volume of sugar consumption to increase steadily over the years. The United States and the United Kingdom are countries with leading consumptions of sugar.

Wheat

Cultivation of wheat began to be cultivated around 9,600 B.C. The commodity has been among the leading soft commodities because of the rising demand that is steady over the years. The market has been exploited in the United States of America and the United Kingdom because of its demand.

Orange Juice

Orange juice has been consumed fresh for years back. This was because it had a short span of time before it went bad. However, the invention of freezing made the product survive for long periods. It made various traders invest in the product. The investment caught is a rise in forex market trading. Further investment in its production and value addition has made orange juice among the traded soft products.

Precious Metals

Metals are described as elements or compounds that are hard when they are in a solid-state. Metals are mostly categorized with shining appearance, fusibility, ductility, malleability or thermal and electrical conductivity. There are different kinds of metals, and they are classified into two groups,' namely precious metals and base metals. Base metals are mostly used by people in the manufacturing industry. These metals include copper, aluminum, copper, zinc, tin, steel, and molybdenum.

Precious metals are the most focused in the forex market. These kinds of metals are naturally occurring and rare elements. These qualities make them have high value economically. These elements are unusual because they are used in industries and investments.

The group of manufacturers used these metals to make various things. These products include catalytic converters, jewelry, dental equipment, and electronic components among several things. Those who are in the investment world use these metals differently. This group of people collects bars and coins made from precious metals. Investors also have a second use of these metals after collection. They create heated speculation in the market they trade these commodities. Investors do this because these precious metals hold a better value of money than money which is printed paper.

The precious metals used in the forex market include:

Gold

Speculators use gold as the main metal in the forex market. Many investors term gold metal as a major investment vehicle. Most of gold's demand is from the traders and manufacturers in the jewelry world. Despite being dominated by the jewelry sector, gold is also used in manufacturing parts used in electronics. Many of gold consumers see the product as an investment because it appreciates value. The forex market has invested so much into this metal. There have been several meetings over the years to find a common standard of gold that can be exchanged with the world currencies.

Silver

This metal is collected by traders in two forms which are silvers or bars. People from manufacturing sector use silver to produce electronic parts or jewelry. A fraction of gold's price has been used historically to trade that of silver. This has made various traders in the forex market to tract the prices between gold and silver.

Platinum

Platinum is included in a group of six metals that are commonly referred to as platinum group metals. Platinum has two main uses by manufactures which include making catalytic convertors and marking jewelry. Investors in the forex market buy platinum metal to speculate the market. When prices of platinum escalate, they are offloaded by being sold off.

Palladium

Palladium is also included in the platinum group metals as a member. Palladium is a precious metal, and it has various uses. The main uses of palladium in manufacturing industries are making electronic parts, dental equipment, and catalytic converters. This makes the metal have a high demand by the forex traders. Another platinum group of metals includes rhodium, ruthenium, iridium, and osmium. They have less attention from the forex market because they have less economic value.

Energy

Energy trade is one of the commodities traded in the forex that influences everybody daily life. The prices of energy have the potential to affect virtually every product we consume. It cuts across the gasoline people fuel cars, groceries, clothes people wear and electronics people use. The energy sector also has a determining factor in the cost incurred of cooling and heating factories, businesses, schools, hospitals, and homes. Basically, many people would not survive without the presence of energy in the current world.

British thermal unit (Btu) is the standard form of measuring units and defining quantities in the energy sector. The British thermal unit gauges the content of heat in fuels. According to the recent survey conducted by the United States Energy Information Agency, the global consumption of energy is more than 575 quadrillion Btu, and it is projected to escalate to 736 quadrillion Btu in the year 2040. This is an increase of 28%. To put them into a finer context, the current markets such as the United States of America have a high consumption rate. The country consumes over 60 quadrillion Btu of energy which is 36% of the world market.

There are different types of energy, and they are classified into two forms. The first form is renewable energy which is easily replenished. The second form of energy is known as non-renewable energy than can't be replenished.

Renewable Energy

Renewable energy accounts for a total of about 21% of the total electricity that is produced across the globe. A further breakdown in statistic shows that it forms 12% the global energy consumption. In the current world, there are about five renewable resources that are widely known. They include
· Sola; it is a form of energy that is obtained from the sun.
· Geothermal: it is the energy which is harnessed from heat produced by the earth.
· Wind: wind energy is obtained from the air that naturally moves.
· Biomass; it a form of energy that is harnessed from the living matter such as plants and animals
· Hydropower; this is the kind of energy obtained from water that is in motion.
In the United States, renewable in the form of biomass has a consumption rate of 5% of the total energy production. The main form of biomass used is known as ethanol. Ethanol is a colorless form of alcohol that is produced from sugar or grains.

Non-Renewable Energy

Non-renewable forms of energy are highly consumed globally. Five of the main forms of non-renewable contribute to the high fraction of the total consumed energy in the world. They include:
· Petroleum products; these include crude oil and several products from refined crude oil such as lubricant oil, heating oil, jet fuel, diesel fuel, and gasoline. The most-traded type of crude oil is the Brent crude and the sweet crude.
· Hydrocarbon gas liquids; the liquid gas is produced from crude oil and natural gas. It contains alkanes and alkenes.

· Natural gas; it is a form of energy that consists of methane, and it is found deep under the earth surface.

· Coal; this is a sedimentary rock that can be burnt to produce fuel.

· Nuclear energy; it is a new form of energy production that splits atoms of uranium which produce a chain reaction of energy.

Stocks and Bonds

Shares and stocks are also very critical in the forex market. Most of the financial assets can offer opportunities in investment, and this has seen banks diversifying their portfolios. Securities are normally included in their portfolio which comprises of ownership certificates of assets that can be publicly traded. These securities are made up of stocks and bond that can be traded across the global markets. They can also be explored by local investors who are interested in them.

Stocks

A person who owns stock is paid money in the form of dividends he or she earns. These dividends are mostly paid after the company earns the profit. A person can also make more money by investing more stock when the prices are projected to go up. This means that many people will be willing to invest in the same company making these stocks be more valuable. Therefore, with time, these stocks will be worth more than an individual had bought them. The activity of buying and selling of stocks in the forex is handled by the stock market.

Bonds

A bond is an instrument of debt that indicates a person's obligation to pay. This allows companies and governments to raise money for funding different projects. In return, a person who has bonds receives interests from these institutions after a stipulated amount of time. Unlike stocks, a person having bonds is just a financer to a project and doesn't own the institution. Several foreign companies and international governments issue bonds. The three main types of international bonds are domestic bonds, foreign bond, and Eurobonds.

Chapter 3: The Principle Currencies (Most Popular Currencies, Their Personalities, and Characteristics)

You must have looked at paper money and reflect why such notes carry a lot of value. The reason is that those notes are used as a mode of exchange of commodities. The revolution of money has been a very long process. Initially, the cash used to be valued in terms of properties like cattle, agricultural materials, and other foodstuffs. Some people even could exchange such items as a form of batter trade. However, due to the lack of a good measure of a commodity, there was developed metallic money. These materials involved the use of gold or silver, which was thought to be very rare and durable. They were mostly made by the blacksmiths who acted as the bankers. To get their loan, you could borrow a certain amount of bullion, and they give you a paper receipt. Consequently, this paper receipts gained worth as the same as that of the bullion. For that case, they have developed to represent the value of the hard money.

From that time, the paper cash was viewed as the currency that ought to be used universally. The coins are very different among many countries in the world in terms of features and worth. However, due to the demand of international trade, there must be foreign exchange. This activity can develop to become the trading of currencies, which is widely known as forex trading. When specializes in forex trading, you should engage economists who can predict the behavior in the selling off those currencies.

The Monetary Unit Principle

It is an ideology that requires that all type of transactions be expressed in terms of currency. Therefore, you cannot measure your revenues or income from nonquantifiable items. Consequently, the monitoring policy is built on the following ideologies.

First, the currency supply is limited. This aspect means that money is rare; no wonder why the gold was used in early times. When something is in excess, it means you will disvalue it, but when it is limited, that is when you acknowledge it. You will always hustle and bustle to obtain items that are in limited supply. Limitations of the commodity also improve sales and earn you a significant profit.

Money is portable where one can move it across many places. That is the mobility factor that helps one to trade in many destinations. This quality is facilitated by it being light. Compare paper money and commodity money like cattle, would you be able to carry animals all the places? Their mobility is further sustained by using technology like internet transaction, e-banking, and other platforms where the cash is transacted on online forums.

Durability is a distinctive quality of money. Currency is made of unique materials that are long-lasting; this is mainly for coins and notes. This cash made to withstand harsh weather conditions like moisture and tearing easily. The further use of online funds reduces any minimal touch in money hence less wearing.

The coinage is also divisible to smaller functional units. Products and commodity come at different sizes and dimensions. That is one of the reasons that led to the failure of barter trade where different valued products were exchanged. Currency usage, therefore, accurately ascertains the measures of the commodity.

Uses of cash are also homogenous since they are uniform to every user. Therefore, it promotes standardization of product. Ensure that your money is collectively labeled and branded in a way that is well known to every citizen. Homogeneity features also help one to distinguish the original to fake notes.

The Most Popular Currencies, Their Personalities, and Characteristics

Many countries in the world desire their bills to gain value more than for others. This aspect illustrates why those countries will always upgrade their treasury to be the supreme currency in forex report.

The US Dollar

The US Dollar is the most popular currency. This bill originates from the United States, where it is the dominant force all over the world. That does not mean it is the strongest coinage, but most commodities in foreign trade are standardized using the US dollar. State officials are fond of comparing their money worth relative to the dollar.

It has some characteristics which include the prevailing exchange rate in the world where it is used interchangeably among other nations around the globe. Another thing is that it is the most consistent currency among the other currencies. Consistency means it does not fall in value in most times. Therefore, its value is always maintained.

The US dollar is the standardized global reserve unit where countries buy it as how they would buy gold as reserves. In the process where is majorly obtained, it gains its worth substantially. It is also used as the official treasury in some countries which do not have local currencies.

The USD is also an acceptable currency for precious minerals and commodities like crude oil and other treasures. Crude oil is the most consumed good across the planet because of its suitable products. In the process of buying the oil, you are enriching the dollar by a more significant portion.

The Euro

It is the world second largest currency, which is used as security for most countries in the world. It is used by many countries, mostly the European states. It is prevalent in the forex trading and very liquid when one trades it with another currency.

Euro money is very diverse because it deals with the different Eurozone. Its highest denomination is five hundred euros. A euro consists of seven denominations. Use of many such denominations enables the member states to use it efficiently and able to measure their commodity value.

It is advantageous because it has seven different sizes that make it recognizable compared to other significant notes and coinages. Its dimensions also make it easier for the visually handicapped to recognize.

It acquires various colors which usually are used for its different notes. It tones differentiation enables each denomination to be differentiated. For every penny it has is poses a different color. The most used pigment is green, yellow, and many others.

The Euro also constitutes other items like the Europe map, which is a symbol of unity. The map appears on the reverse side of the banknotes, and it also incorporates the North Africa and Asia Minor sections.

Its other essential features are security impressions. This design helps it not be faked easily. They include the watermarks which can only be viewed well when focusing it to light. There is also a security thread that is unique and jotted in tiny figures.

The Sterling Pound

It has one of the most significant values hence used as a reserve by many. Its value is higher because it usually not used by many countries except Great Britain. Due to its considerable worth, it is used as a comparing item of the currencies of other states. It is constituted by four different banknotes ranging from five, ten, twenty to fifty pounds.

It has a unique numbering which is featured in vertical and horizontal. The horizontal letters are printed in the bottom right corner where it has many colored symbols. For the vertical ones, their letters are of the same dimensions.

There are also the copyrights symbols which are included on the front and back of especially the fifty notes. The copyrights consist of the name of the developer of that pound which is featured on the left of the front of the note

Concerning the security characteristics, there are different portrays like watermarks. The image of the queen is usually hidden on the watermark where it can only be observed by lifting the note against the light.

The motion impression is another characteristic that is much concealed in the paper. Try to recheck the note in the limelight; you will be astonished to discover an image of the number like the value of that currency moving upwards and downwards.

Its texture also matters a lot where you can differentiate it with counterfeit money. The printing on its paper gives a unique feeling which other fake notes lack. Finally, it has a metallic thread embedded in every paper note than appears as a continuous dark line.

Japanese Yen

It is the third most valuable currency in the world after the Us dollar and the Euro. It is used by the Japanese to symbolize their booming industrialization. Its domitable nature is attributed to the Japanese policy of having a zero interest rate. Therefore, traders have borrowed it to exchange it with other financials at no cost. It is also famous due to its relevance in profiting from the indifference of interest rates between two currencies

Some of the characteristics include the following. First is that it has close to four denominations, which even starts at a higher rate ranging from ten thousand to one thousand yen. Its coinage also varies from one bob to five hundred yens.

It has very significant security features starting from different watermarks. This impression is hidden and can only be seen by placing it over the light. There are unusual watermarks patterns that usually shows which are hard to replicate.

It also has a delusional visual when checked keenly. Take the note and tilt it in a certain angle; you will realize that the '10000'impression changes and a word 'NIPPON 'appears. This feature is further castigated by a hologram visual. That is where the color and pattern change when tilted.

Other characteristics are micro printing, glowing of the image under a different magnification imprint like ultraviolent light, Intaglio printing, and tactile marks. All these marks are written in the Japanese language where their calligraphy is highly sophisticated.

The Major Principles of Note Issues or Monetary Policy

The economic impact determines the currency issue in any authority or government it will have in the country. It is right to say that if there is a shortage of notes, then the government should print more money. In logics, it may sound sensible, but in economic implications, this is a wrong thing to do. Having excess or insufficient cash in the economy will cause inflation and deflation, respectively. Picture yourself waking up to find a piece of bread worth thousands of dollars. You will surely be astonished. Moreover, the economic impact is that it will lose its value among other currencies in the foreign exchange rate. Below are the principles that a government conducts in the supply of coinage.

The banking principle is one of the aspects. Banks play a significant role in the economy because they regulate the currency in circulation Governments use banks in discharging or supplying the capital to the citizens. The most crucial principle related to money states that banks ought to be allowed to submit notes in relative measure to the bullion like gold, silver, and coins. Bankers would also argue that they should not be limited to issue notes because even if there is a higher demand for capital, it will lead to higher deposits. Hence nothing would change in the process as the cash would remain with them. Another thing they argued is the value of the financials is directly related to the coinage and metallic commodity hence no overflow.

The primary significant in this ideology is that the flow of cash would create an economic and elastic field. Elastic means it is expansive where it can incorporate any growth in industries that requires more treasures injections. However, when bankers are confident about supplying funds, they can over issue it leading to inflation and the consumers losing confidence. The long-term effect can even be changing of currency wholly to a new one as has been evident in some countries.

The second principle is the currency principle. The scholars involved in this ideology argue that the banking system does not care about the balance of payments (BOP). One may relate this ideology in exports and imports. Some nations may experience deficit BOP where they import more than they export. In that case, this philosophy identifies that the quantity of an issue must relate to the balance of payment. Domestic consumption of money is discouraged in this case, as countries seek the growth of their foreign exchange rate. Other governments require that there should be a reserve of financials in terms of coinage or bullion to cater for BOP deficit.

For that reason, the most significant advantage of this ideology is the security of revenues. Nonetheless, it also has some demerits of wastage and keeping high reserves of treasures and coinages. Remember that these reserves are made of expensive materials like gold, silver or copper, and even other precious minerals. Another disadvantage is that the buffer minerals stocks are less convertible to quick cash.

 The third principle is the fiduciary principle. Some other nations may practice a fixed system of distribution of treasuries. Such a policy is called the fixed fiduciary supply system. A state may deliver capital over time without even backing it with reserves. However, it must have a fiduciary ceiling level, which is the upper limit of to a quantity of the treasury; at this limit, there must be a hundred percent reserve. Therefore, contemplate on the growth of technology and demand level, which prompt capitalists to raise the fiduciary limits.

This fixation policy is fruitful because the treasurers dispatch money following the legal system, thereby having strict authority over the financials distribution. However, it is normal that when you keep treasures as a safe keep, it will earn you much cost. Another demerit is that it is inelastic and cannot readjust to steady economic growth.

There is also the maximum limit of system ideology. This philosophy is nearly close to the fiduciary system except that it has no reserve backing. There is a definite figure of currency that must be maintained, by Issuing notes beyond this limit needs one to be allowed by the authority concerned. The principle is ideal because the issuing agencies exercise freedom due to fewer reserves holdings. It also economical since not many reserves are being stored. Inelasticity and inflation can be a disadvantage because industries need to grow, and the freedom of issue leads to massive money circulation.

Talking of a proportionate money reserve is a scheme which represents another money policy control. It means that coinage issues have to be secured by a certain percentage of gold backup. The government must utilize the other remaining proportionate in the selling of shares like treasury bonds and bills. The securities sold are highly solvent and carry an attractable interest rate. This system is easy to facilitate because it is comprehensive, and it is also elastic due to its liquidity level. The demerits include the uneconomical way of using treasures as the buffer stock, which are costly. It also demonstrates a multiplier effect where incase of fewer reserves the supply contracts more, therefore, affecting the industry and trade negatively.

The last principle is the minimum reserve system. That is where the central bank needs to maintain the minimum reserves of the bullion and foreign currencies. Nonetheless, it has allowed the government to sell securities. It is elastic and flexible where the note issue is sufficient to accommodate any developmental pattern of the industries. However, it is susceptible to inflation because it induces the pressure to the government to print more cash. It also only works on areas under strong governance and free of corruption. When embezzlement of funds rises, it deteriorates, it values because it has low security of gold and other treasures.

Chapter 4: Where Do We Trade Forex?

History of Forex Trading Platforms

Forex trade started for in the ancient times of the Babylonians. During this time, the system was made up of only goods with the exchange happening between tangible goods. There was then the introduction of metal and gold and silver became popular. Therefore, it became the tool for transaction; this idea was loved by many, and therefore it became popular. After some time, political regimes started forming, and the creation of coins for trade became necessary. Gold surpassed all the coins, and it became an important trading tool, and as a result, it became restricted. The restriction created panic, as more people wanted to exchange their value for money with gold.

In 1931, the gold which was considered as a standard tool for exchange trade was removed, leading to the emergence of the Forex trade market. The market was introduced so as to have a more reliable and stable currency of exchange. However, the Forex market was not more active because only a small number of people knew how it operated. The USA introduced a new world's currency in 1944: it was the US Dollar. The use of this currency was agreed by the World Bank, GAAT and IMF at Bretton woods. There was still an issue on the use of the standard Gold, but it was solved as all the currencies for use in the Forex market were fixed at the gold standard. Bretton Woods became the most popular system of exchanging currencies, and it operated with fixed exchange rates. This system of exchange lasted for barely ten years. In the 1960s, the dollar started to devalue, and this became worse during the Vietnam War. The President of the USA then suspended the conversion of dollar to gold, which created a crisis in the Bretton Woods system, and it collapsed. The collapse of Bretton woods opened the way for a free market, where currencies were not fixed; they were allowed to fluctuate, and their behavior was determined by foreign direct investment and trade flows. Later there emerged a Smithsonian agreement that proposed the fluctuation of currencies to be confined within a given range of 2.25%. This agreement was later disputed as nations such as the USA required to value of the currency beyond the fixed point. This led to the closure of the Forex market in 1971 when it was reopened a year later, the fixed level of fluctuation was no longer functional and free-market controlled by demand and supply prevailed.

The big banks now controlled the trade by trading currencies amongst themselves, and at this time the platform was known as the inter-bank. The other banks that joined the system used the retail platform that only allowed access to currencies through the big banks. The currencies were obtained at the rates determined by the big bank trader involved; these rates were less favorable. There was a relief when the electronic platform came about in 1994. The retail traders and individuals now had access to more information about Forex trade and direct access to currency trading rates were possible. The advancement in technology made things easier as electronic now became an online trading platform, where different brokers and institution gets direct clients to buy and sell their currencies from different markets around the world. The platforms that are now in existence are the interbank, the retail, and the online trading platforms.

Market Share of Platforms

The Interbank

The interbank market is the one that has the second volume of currencies traded in a day. In the interbank, the largest bank trade with each other directly using interbank brokers. They also use electronic brokering systems such as Reuters or Electronic Brokering Services (EBS). This platform is an approved system, where banks trade with each other because of their credit relationship established over time. Apart from trades between banks, others that use interbank are institutions such as corporations, online Forex markets, and hedge funds. Small banks in emerging markets, institutional investors, and corporations do not have access to rates of the interbank platform because they do not have well-established credit lines connecting them to the big banks. Therefore, for foreign exchange needs, they deal with one bank, but at less competitive rates. The rates become even less competitive for participants that use small banks and exchange agencies to trade; remember that the banks also need to make a profit. The largest market share among the banks is JPMorgan, followed by UBS, Deutsche Bank, Bank of America Merril Lynch, Citi, Goldman Sachs, Standard Chartered, HSBC, XTX Markets, and Barclays.

Retail Traders

Retail traders include the small bank community, institutional investors, banks found in emerging markets, and corporations. As explained earlier, these platforms usual have no direct control of the rates because they are attached to big banks. The big backs, therefore, offer a rate that is lowering slightly different from what they offer when buying or selling to the other big banks. The volume of currencies traded across this platform is therefore slightly lower than that traded through the interbank platform.

The Online Trading Platform

The introduction of the electronic trading system was introduced in 1992. It then developed to online trading gave a chance for retail traders to connect with market makers, and increased the participants because of its low costs and high efficiency. This platform offers a chance for individuals to access the rates that are the same as those used by big banks. This trading platform has steadily grown due to the accessibility and continued development of technology that supports it. It has the largest market share of more than 50% with the traders, including big banks, small bank community, corporations, and individuals.

The Platform with Majority Traders

The most important part of Forex is access to the buyer or seller. Online trading has broken the barrier that used to limit how currencies were exchanged. Anyone wishing to join Forex trade can quickly get online and choose a trader. This platform is also not only used by individuals but also the big banks. Everyone in this industry constantly looks for clients and has made has easier to access them in all parts of the world. This has led to all traders to converge online to look for the best-trading partners and offers; this makes the online platform the most popular and with most traders.

The Most Popular Trading Platforms

The most popular platforms are online trading platforms with Ninja trader being the most popular in the world. The platform offers the environment for testing many trading strategies and gives historical data on the performance of currencies. It also gives daily and hourly analysis charts. It is very stable and offers high performance. In addition, it has high custom indicators and order modification. This trading platform is customized such that it allows the trader to arrange data provided and charts on the screen in a self-fitting manner to allow for analysis. The analysis is also easier because it has an inbuilt strategy analyzer that allows analysis in terms of profit factor, Sharpe Ratio, and other crucial measurable parameters. Although it is the most popular trading platform, it is not the best for use by inexperienced traders, and not supported by devices that run on IOS and Android.

How People Respond to New Platforms

People are excited about the new platforms of trading and want to maximize their trades using the new technology. There has been an increase in participation of non-financial institutions, non-dealer financial institutions, and individuals. The market trading now dominates the market today, with a share of more than 50% of customers from all segment of the market. There are no worries for individuals with little knowledge about the trade because there is available knowledge online on how to trade; some traders offer to give demos to clients using virtual money, which they later allow them to trade using real currency. Some amateur individual traders are paying for training sessions on online trading, while some learn through apprenticeship. Many people want to part of the trading system that was dominated by big banks in the world.

People are also taking advantage of the advancement in technology to access the trade all the time. The use of smartphones and tablets, among other electronic devices, has enabled many to monitor the market and place their order at their own convenient time and place. Some have resigned from their full-time job just to do Forex trading, as others do it as a part-time job. In some instances, some people have employed others to do for them online Forex trading, while others seek consulting services.

Competition among Platforms

Today, the competition among platform is very high because of the ease of access to information about currencies online and the reduction in the cost of maintenance and transactions. This is thanks to the advancement in technology. Those using different platforms always operate within a given range in terms of costs and rates because they know that any big difference would lead to a shift of clients to other platforms. The competition has made it easier for clients to get better rates at a lower cost of operation. There is competition in the improvement in the user interphase, which gives clients a better experience and flexibility in the use.

What Makes a Platform Better?

Simplicity

Nowadays, most people are going for online Forex trading platforms, and these people are either experienced or not. The platform should be simple for new users to adapt and use them correctly. There must be tools that are easy to interpret to navigate and execute important actions easily. The tools should be also visible and correctly positioned for a timely reaction. It should also be user-friendly and convenient; it should be easily accessed from many devices.

Flexibility

The level of flexibility of the trading system should also be high for maximum efficiency. The order of management of the execution of action should be clearly stated, tools for charting or engagement with the client should be provided on the same screen or page to provide timely reaction, thus avoiding time-costly procedures. Time is money, and when it comes to Forex trading, a delay can mean a loss of money.

Real-Time Information

The currency market is extremely volatile and unpredictable; this means that sometimes, it can experience shifts within a very short time. A good trading platform must, therefore, have a feature that enables the trader to view accurate real-time information and changes in the prices of the currency. In order to make wise and immediate decisions, traders need this information. The information should be provided as daily, weekly, monthly, and annual reports. New updates on the current market news updates and headlines that affect currency should also be included in the platform.

Easily Customized

Each customer has personal requirements and specific needs, and therefore, a trading platform should have options that allow for customization. For instance, a trader that wants his or her order to be made automatically should be able to do that and other important aspects of traders.

Secure

Transacting online should be secure because most of the time, it involves the supply of personal information such as names, passwords, and IDs. The logins should be safe when using the platform or switching to other platforms. This means that technology use should be high tech and up to date.

The Platforms Which Were There and Reasons for Closure

Bretton woods Forex trading system was there earlier in the history of Forex trade, but it collapsed because it was not favorable for clients who traded on it. At the time of its existence, all the currencies were given a fixed value based on the standard value of the gold. This lead to the devaluing of some currencies to an unsustainable level, such currencies include the US Dollar. The closure of this platform led to the revolution of the Forex trade in a way that the value of the currency was now controlled by the supply and demand. It has remained so until today.

Chapter 5: Choosing A Broker

A broker refers to a firm or somewhat an individual who charges a certain fee or rather a commission for executing the buying and the selling process. In other words, they play the role of connecting the customer and the seller of the product. Thus, they are generally paid for acting as a link between the two parties. For instance, a client might be willing to buy shares from a particular organization. However, he might be lacking enough information about the places that he can purchase these shares. Thus, he will be forced to seek a person who understands well the stock exchange markets. The broker will, therefore, educate the client as well as link them with the right sellers. The broker will thus earn by offering such a connection. Other brokers sell insurance policies to individuals. In most cases, the individuals earn a commission once the clients they brought in the organization buy or renews the system. Any insurance companies have utilized the aspect as a way of increasing their sales.

List of Common Brokers

IG

It is rated as one of the best forex brokers in the world. It was one of the pioneers in offering contracts for difference as well as spread beating. The organization was founded in the year 1974 and had been growing as a leader in online trading as well as the marketing industry. One of the aspects that have boosted its growth is the fact that it has linked a lot of customers hence gaining more trust. In other words, a duet to its large customer base, a lot of clients prefers selling and buying their services. The other aspect worth noting is that this organization is London based, and it is among one of the companies that are listed on the London Stock Exchange market for more than 250 times. The aspect is due to the fact that it offers more than 15,000 products across several asset classes. Such classes include CFDs on shares, forex, commodities, bonds, crypto-currencies as well as indices. Another aspect worth noting is that the 2019 May report, the firm is serving more than 120,000 active clients around the globe. Also, there are more than 350,000 clients that are served on a daily basis. The aspect has been critical in boosting its expansion as this group of individuals does more advertisements.

Some of the benefits that one gains by working in this industry are the fact that it allows comprehensive trading and the utilization of tools that enhance the real exchange of data. The other aspect worth noting is that it has a public traded license that allows a regular jurisdiction across the entire globe. In other words, one can acquire the services of this organization across the whole world with ease without the fear of acting against the laws of the nation. Also, the premises offer some of the competitive based commission that enhances pricing as spreading of forex. There is also a broad range of markets that are associated with the premises too, there several currencies and multi assets CFDs that are offered by the organization. The aspect has been critical in the sense that it allows the perfect utilization of all the services as well as the resources available across the globe. Some of the services that are offered by the organization are permitted globally, such that even after traveling from one nation to the other, one can still access their services. Since the year 1974, the organization has joined more than 195,000 traders across the entire globe. The aspect has allowed the selling its shares as well as services hence its fame.

Saxo Bank

The forex broker was established in 1992and has then been among the leading organization in offering forex services as well as the multi-asset brokerages across more than 15 nations. Some of these nations include the UK, Denmark, and Singapore, among others. One of the aspects of the organization is that it offers services to both retailers as well as institutional clients in the globe. The character has allowed the premises to provide more than one million transactions each day. Thus, it holds over $ 16 billion in asset management. The Saxo bank also offers more services to all of her clients. Such services include Spot FX, Non-deliverable Forwards (NDFs), contract difference as well as all the stock exchange options.

The aspect has been critical in increasing its customer base across the globe. Some of the services such as crypto and bond services that are offered in the premises has allowed its expansion in the sense that they are sensitive and essentials.

Some of the benefits that one gain by assessing the services of the premises are that it enhances diverse selection of quality, it increases competitive commissions and forex spread as well as an improved multiple financial jurisdiction function that is allowed across the entire globe. In other words, the premises offer services that are allowed in the whole world, and that considers the rules and policies provided in each nation. The aspect has enhanced its continued growth despite the increased competition. One is required to pay a minimum deposit of about $2000 and an automated trading solution for all the traders. There are times when the premises offer bonuses of 182 trade forex pairs to all its clients. The aspect has also been the key reason behind its increased expansion. In other words, there are various services offered at a relatively low price hence the widening of its customer base.

CMC Markets

The premises were founded in 1989 and since then, it has grown to be one of the leading retail forex as well as a CFD brokerage. The premises thus serve more than 10,000 CFD instruments that cut across all the classes such as forex, commodities as well as security markets. The aspect has allowed the premises to spread its services to more than 60,000 clients across the entire globe. The premises have more than 15 offices that are well distributed in the nation; it offers the services. Most of its actions are thus related in UK, Australia as well as Canada. The aspect is due to the fact that the premises have it is customer bases in some of these nations. In other words, its serves are well are accepted in Canada and the UK.

There are various benefits that one gains by joining the premises. One, the premise offers some of the best competitive spread to all her customers. In other words, there are a variety of services that one can choose from. Also, the premises offer some of the largest selection of currency pairs in the entire industry. There are more than one hundred and eighty currencies that one can access by joining the premises. The other aspect worth noting is that the premises offer some of the best regulated financial agents in the entire globe. In other words, there are policies as well as rules that govern the provision of services in the world. Also, it is easy to identify the premises as there are potent charts as well as patterns that are used as recognition tools.

City Index

The forex broker was founded in 1983 in the UK. Since then, the premises have gained popularity and has turned out to be one of the leading brokers in London. It is worth noting that in 2015, the premises acquired GAIN Capital Holding Company that enhanced its increased customer base. Since 2015, the premises have been providing traders with services such as CFDs and spreading-betting derivatives. The premises have been further expanding the forex services with the acquisition of markets as well as FX solutions before gaining the capital market. Nowadays, the City Index has been operating as an independent brand under GAIN Capital in Asia as well as the UK. The aspect has allowed a multi-asset solution hence offering traders access to over 12,000 products across the global markets.

Some of the benefits that one gains part of the capital holding, a large selection of CFDs as well as regulated in several jurisdictions. The organization has tight spreads as well as low margins and fast execution. In others, the premises have been time from time, offering average ranges to all the clients; hence its increased customer base.

XTB Review

The organization was founded in Poland in the year 2002. Since then the organization has been well known for its forex and CFDs brokerage. Since then, the organization has maintained its offices in several nations; it offers its services. The premise has been working as a multi-asset broker that is regulated in several centers hence increasing their competitive advantage. The premises have been trading as multiple financial centers offering a lot of services to all her traders. With a wide range of more than 2000 functions, the premises have been trading in almost all nations hence an increase in its customer base. The premises also offer excellent services that have been the reason behind its expansion. One of the aspects that have made the forex broker be thriving in such a competitive environment.

Signs of Illegitimate Brokers

Although numerous brokers have been working in the forex industry, the aspect of legitimacy has been an issue affecting the progress of some these premises. One of the elements that are considered is the vulnerability of the clients. In most cases premises illegitimate brokers tend to rob of their customers. Most of them are self-reliant and optimistic. Most of them operate above their financial knowledge hence making numerous mistakes. Most of these organization record big loses as they are relatively weak in term of management. The organization offers a lot of transactions that tend to be cumbersome in terms of management. It is worth noting that most of their operations aren't legitimate and never approved by the necessary authorities. Thus, when deciding on the kind of forex premises to seek services from, it is essential to consider some factors. Avoid assumptions that are exaggerative in terms of offering services that are above their knowledge. The aspect is harmful in the sense that they provide services that are not well planned hence recording a number of loses that befalls many clients in the long run. In other words, the drops recorded in the organization

Signs of Legitimate Brokers

Although there are numerous illegitimate brokers in the market, there are legitimate brokers who offer excellent services. Most of them provide a few unique functions. In other words, they don't give a lot of transactions. Thus, they are able to manage their operations and command profits on their premises. The other aspect worth noting is that most of the services are approved by both the clients as well as the governing bodies in the organization. The other issue worth noting is that most of these premises have employed excellent knowledge in a range the progress of the customers. In other words, all their services are focused on advancing the clients. In a nutshell, when selecting a forex broker, it is good to consider several factors. It is critical to find whether the premises are approved by both the governments as well as the clients. It is good to view the number of services as well as the transactions that are offered by the premise. The aspect is due to the fact that most of the wrong assumptions tend to provide numerous services that are poorly managed. The reviews offered by the clients of each of these premises need to be considered as they reflect whether the brokers are legitimate or not. Clients of consistent clients tend to offer reviews that are good as the services they receive manage to be excellent. The financial reports of these organization tend to be considered. The aspect is linked to the fact that they tend to reflect whether the brokers are making loses or profits. It is critical to find premises that record gains since the benefits tend to be high.

Chapter 6: Fundamental or Technical Analysis?

Forex Market Analysis

Many new traders often find it challenging to choose the vast range of methods to trade the financial markets. However, we are able to break down these methods into either fundamental analysis or technical analysis of the financial markets. In as much as some traders, today use both methods, the majority of them, however, focuses on technical analysis.

This chapter will teach you as a trader on how you can perform a technical analysis of the financial markets. We will teach you how to go about using the best technical analysis software that is found in today's marketplace. As you start trading, you will be able to learn the top technical analysis patterns that will make you become a master of Forex technical analysis.

What Is Technical Analysis?

Let's begin by understanding what technical analysis means. In financial markets, technical analysis refers to the study of the patterns of prices of particular assets. Basically, there exist many ways with which technicians use to identify patterns in the market. However, the following are the common ways;

· Technical analysis chart patterns

This analysis involves the use of technical drawing tools like Fibonacci levels, horizontal and trend lines for the identification of classical chart patterns. The patterns identified can include consolidation patterns and symmetrical triangle formations etc. These patterns are important in giving clarity on the strengths and weaknesses of buyers and sellers in the market.

· Technical analysis of candle patterns

This method involves the use of technical analysis charts like candle charts where the price levels (such as high, low, open, close) of a given timeframe with the goal of identifying the characteristics of buyers and sellers within a given time period.

· Technical analysis indicators

This analysis method involves the use of price action indicators to provide a detailed understanding of the market condition. For instance, indicators will provide signals when the market is overbought or oversold. Some indicators will provide signals when there is rising or falling momentum.

Forex Technical Analysis

The Forex market is very liquid. This means that it attracts all types of traders ranging from one-minute traders to daily traders. Forex technical analysis supports all these different types of traders involved in the market. All the different types of technical analysis, including chart patterns, candle patterns, and indicator are used in Forex technical analysis. As a beginner, we prefer that you download MetaTrader 4. MetaTrader 4 best fits the needs of a beginner because it supports multiple languages, has advanced charting capabilities, trading is automated, it can be fully customized, and you are able to change trading preferences based on your needs, for example, you can customize it to technical analysis, or provide you with trading news.

Does Technical Analysis Work?

In most cases, as humans, we tend to have limited time and focus; thus, when analyzing these factors, we are likely to make errors in the cause and effect. However, with technical analysis, a more reliable way that comes with the short-cut is provided to analysts. Therefore, analysts are able to give their full attention to just one section - price movement. Technical analysis is also referred to as chart analysis. With chart analysis, traders are able to analyze historical price movements.

The Basics of Technical Analysis

As a trader, here are some of the basics about technical analysis that you should have in hand.

· Price action discounts everything

The technical analysis derives its logical framework from Dow Theory. According to Dow Theory, the price of an asset accurately reflects all the relevant information about the asset. This means that any factor that impacts on supply and demand by default will end up on the chart. When it comes for the case of researching or the events outside price action, Dow Theory renders them useless because these are things that cannot be quantified thus may give unreliable data.

· Price moves in trends

As observed, most technicians are always seen to favor trends, including the nature of the market. This is another reflection of Dow Theory. Basically, markets can move in an uptrend (bullish market). In such a case, it means that the market will continuously create higher highs as well as higher lows and the big picture which is the price, will be seen to be jumping up and down but mostly within an upward corridor. A bearish market has similar market behaviors as it is characterized by a downtrend of lower lows as well as lower highs.

There is also a ranging market which is a horizontal trend. However, this is a trend that is not desirable to trend-based traders. This is due to the fact that traders are not able to know what will happen next, particularly when faced with ranging periods. In a ranging market, the bulls and the bears somehow have equal powers; thus, there is no side strong enough to dominate the other for a long period of time. It is also important to note that Forex statistical analysis does not give major concerns on why things happen. This means that Forex statistical analysis will not look into why certain trends occur. Therefore, as a technical reader, it is important that you be able to understand this. Most technicians do not know how to quantify answers because they often feel that trends are empirically proven facts.

Fundamental Analysis

In this era of globalization, our financial markets continue to be impacted and influenced by a large number of factors. For instance, today, the central banks of each country must administer its monetary policies, governments must also deliver their fiscal policies, and on the lowest level, companies and consumers also determine the internal economic factors. All these are factors that must be studied in order to understand how they impact on different assets and markets. Therefore, it is always very hard to know the factors with significant impacts. This can be solved using fundamental analysis.

A Comparison of Technical Analysis and Fundamental Analysis of the Financial Markets

Before proceeding into finer details, technical analysis focuses on studying price charts and price patterns while fundamental analysis, on the other hand, focuses on to study data on the economic aspects of company aspects. The economic or company data that fundamental analysis focuses on includes figures from retail sales, the reports on inflation, country's employment patterns, earnings announcements, and news from companies. Fundamental analysis uses this data to identify market trends as well as the possible changes or turning points that a particular market needs. Fundamental analysis is mostly used in stock markets and not fit for the forex market. Due to this, technical analysis has become a popular option for most traders. The reason why most traders prefer to use technical analysis is that technical analysis aids in decision making about trade. However, there are also traders who prefer to combine these two analysis methods as they present a high profitability trading opportunity.

The Pros of Technical Analysis

· Traders using forex technical analysis only need to have a few basic tools. In most cases, these tools are usually free.

· Traders using forex technical analysis are sometimes offered with high probability directional views as well as the entry and exit points from the market.

· With the advancement in technology today, traders are able to choose technical analysis tools and indicators they wish to use in helping them identify the available trading setups.

Disadvantages of Technical Analysis

· Technical analysis is widespread and widely used. Therefore, Forex technical analysis can sometimes trigger abrupt market movements, particularly when many traders come up with the same conclusions.

· There are complex markets that technical analysis fails to cover some aspects, thus calls for the combination of technical analysis and fundamental analysis.

The Pros of Fundamental Analysis

· Fundamental analysis is a perfect tool for understanding market trends (i.e., why a market is going down or up).

· Fundamental analysis, when combined with technical analysis, can enable traders to know the long term market trends.

Disadvantages of Fundamental Analysis

· It is easy to have cases of conflicts. This is because there are many fundamental analysis tools, and some of these tools may show bad data, thus giving the wrong indicators.

· Its time consuming because it involves keeping track of all the different news announcements.

· It is not a guarantee that the market will respond to the things said by fundamental analysis. For instance, if data on the Japanese economy suggests that it is weak, it is not a guarantee that the Japanese Yen will go down.

· It requires traders to master the outcomes associated with different economic data like inflation reports. To learn these outcomes takes a longer period of time.

Here are the benefits that come with both analysis methods

· Using the analysis, traders are able to make sound judgments relating to trade based on the information on the chart.

· The analysis information can enable traders to look for a potential trade setup

· Traders are also able to identify where they can find potential trade setups Through the analysis, traders are able to learn how they can manage the identified trade setups.

Chapter 7: Third Approach: Relational Analysis (Pros and Cons)

Forex highly relies on relational analysis. So, what is this relational analysis? Every decision made or taken by a trader investor or even speculator is based on money and only money. To understand this, then one must understand bonds. Bonds are the basic ingredient that allows one to borrow and even lend capital. How does someone interpret these bonds? But before we dive into the interpretation of these bonds, it is best to look at the words that are mentioned in between the bond interpretation. Yield is one of those words.

Yield is divided into three: there is the nominal yield, current yield and lastly, yield to maturity. This is one of the most basic things in trading and also applies in forex trade too. Yield maturity is where one analyzes the bond market over a long period of time. It is also known as the yield curve. The nominal yield is the interest rate that the bond issuer agrees and promises to the bond purchasers. It is also known as the nominal rate. When one determines the current price of a bond, then calculating its current yield is easy. The current yield is, therefore, the annual interest over the current price of the bond.

Equity markets are very risky and also have high returns. Forex trading is one of these equity markets. The higher the risk then, the higher the returns one gets. For one to succeed in forex trading, then he or she must be a high risker. These equity markets are, therefore, good for long term investments. The equity markets are also where the buyers and sellers aggressively transact in terms of stocks or shares. These stocks show a representation of claims in businesses. These businesses are majorly listed on the public stock exchange or maybe even private. This information thus gives one a clear vision of what relational analysis is in general.

What is Relational Analysis in relation to both Technical and Fundamental Analysis?

Fundamental analysis is considered a long term method for trading. It tries to look at the value of stocks and shares in terms of basic economic factors like the impact of its value to the economy. The things looked at include: the revenue, expenses, income, growth of the company, a competition the company may face, and the expected returns to the company. The goal of this kind of analysis is to look at the upbringing and undermining factors too. This type of analysis does not look at the nature of the market.

Technical analysis is considered a short term trading method. It helps one to evaluates the investments according to how the market is. It does not look at how the company is in terms of its economy. It looks at factors like history pricings of the shares, trading volumes over a period of time and lastly is the industry trading trends. The goal of this type of analysis is to look at the history of trading so that one can be able to tell of the future.

What does technical analysis offer?

The first is trend analysis which is one of the most influential advantages. This is by checking the forex graph over time. This helps one to learn their way into selling and buying shares. It was always good to check the past in order to deal with the present future. The checking of the graph helps a buyer or seller in the forex trade to do business and get profits is one of the best things that come out of this kind of analysis. The market is looked into keenly.

The other advantage is that one can know the point of entry or even exit. This is important for any buyer and seller. The analysis of the past and present helps one to know the curve of the market. What do I mean by saying the curve of the market? The curve may go up, meaning that the curve is good and it may go down, meaning the sales and buying of shares is down too. When the curve is up, it means that it is a good entry time, and when the curve goes down, it means that one is advised to exit.

It also fast and inexpensive. This means that one does not require a lot of money to do it. All one needs is a smartphone or a laptop and some data or WIFI to look up these past graphs. One will also just need to look at these graphs keenly. Looking at something does not cost anything, just being able to view what is needed. This was maybe done in a very short time like one day, which is unlike fundamental analysis. Thus, this then explains how fast and inexpensive this method is to all people.

One earns a lot of information. This may be through the research of the forex trade. Looking keenly at the curve can explain a lot of things and answer a lot of questions. For one to succeed in forex trading, then he or she must be a high risker. The forex markets are, therefore, good for long term investments. The forex markets are also where the buyers and sellers aggressively transact in terms of stocks or shares. It gives one an easy way to earn money depending on whether they know to work their way through the forex curves and market.

How then is the shortcoming of technical analysis in relation to relational analysis?

One may read the technical information wrong. This is possible since one is looking just at the graphs. The way of learning is observation in this case. The eyes can deceive someone in many cases. And since we are dealing with graphs, a person than one may not understand the information that is shown by these graphs. These graphs someone who knows and understands these graphs. This then limits the number of people who use this technical analysis. This is such a bad disadvantage which limits the people to learning and understanding forex life in short.

The other is bias-ness of the information. Technical analysis is based on the curve graphs and does not look into the economy. It is important to look at the economy to see if one will get to see if the forex world is doing good or not. It is important to know that booth the economy and graphs are important in forex trading. Since the technical analysis way only approaches the graphs, then it limits the information it gives. Then the combination of both the graph and economic information both important at all times. The technical analysis should thus be revised.

Why chose relational analysis?

One thing is to avoid the news. This helps many buyers to base their trades off the news. It is difficult to keep ahead of the news and events going on around the world. The news affects the markets, but before the people receive their news, the big companies usually have made their moves in terms of buying and selling of shares. It is then important to look at the curves for one to predict the future in forex trades. It is also nice to follow the news, but it is all up to you.

Another thing is that one can focus on the price of the forex shares or stock. Prices and also numbers are key to how and when one can place their trades. When one focuses on the pricing, then one can cut out the news events and gossip that circles the information centers or outlets. One feels in control of their decision, and one is able to approach a trade with confidence due to the information might have. This is one way in which technical analysis can remove the baggage of other issues. One has to learn the curves and just trade.

Also, one trades with less emotion. Fundamental analysis requires a lot of information that is from without. The news can always bring up: fear, greed, nervousness, and excitement. These emotions can make someone make you turn on decisions one might have made before. One should not let such things come between them and their trading. Technical analysis deals with a personal level of knowledge; this gives someone the confidence to take charge and risk to trade. Someone will always trust themselves; thus, this method is the best to use. It makes one be their own boss.

Lastly, one can trade any chart without knowing the market. Focusing on the prices, support, and also available resistance and lastly, a few other indicators - these are things that allow one to transact in other markets without any issues easily. The things to look at that make markets different are the volume and the earnings of the stocks or shares, which greatly does not apply in forex trade. One has to gain a lot of information, especially if one misses out on important things like the news. The decision is entirely up to you as the trader at all times.

Chapter 8: Volume Price Analysis (VPA)

In forex trading, it comes under different terms. It prompts one always to look forward to achieving lots of maximum profits in this investment. Trading in international exchange requires your intelligence to realize the points where one can generate the maximum returns. One must be skilled in knowing the price movement involved in the currencies at hand.

There are times a particular currency trade lower than the other; at this rate is when you cite the best point to make your trade. Those individuals able to identify the best point can immerse a higher profit. This field necessitates one to acquire knowledge in particular areas. That involves skilled speculations and investment practice. By risk-taking any currency, you stand a chance of benefitting more. Therefore, investors are advised never to fear to risk a profitable avenue.

Volume is a pivotal indicator in learning the general price movement of a specific stock or security. It usually increases every time a buyer or a seller trades in their shares. It is, therefore, symbolizes strength in the forex trading. Imagine when purchasing in an area where the volume falls even when the price lowers or decreases, then you will assume the market is weaker. Therefore, an active demand is demonstrated by a higher quantity of sales.

Features of Volume Trade Analysis

You must have seen how a chart of forex trading looks. First, the trading composes of a graphical diagram where there are different types of currencies are positioned either above the graph or its sides. The charts have a stoichiometric oscillator or scale that moves up and down in measuring the behavior of a stock trade.

A trend is an instrumental figure of the volume trade analysis. A pattern syndicates both aspects of a value change and the volume in confirming its strength. The direction is achieved when one simulates the behavior of the indicator over certain a period. It also averages the percentages increase and decrease of how currency stock is fairing with another in the market.

How can one precisely measure the trend and interpret?

In a good market, one can determine the trend where the percentage of the volume is multiplied with a value increase of the previous measure. The figure is then summed to the price volume trend value the previous record.

In recession time, the price-volume trend is reached when one multiplies the percentage price decrease in consideration to the previously recorded volume. The calculated figure is then added to the other trend value.

There are different interpretations concerning the trend analysis. These interpretations are based on the divergence or the dispersion of the same. Such could read that higher price influenced by higher volumes trend indicates the price trend upward. Lower price influenced by a decreasing volume trend shows a price downturn in terms of its divergence

A decreasing value followed by a neutral value or a higher figure; or a higher price accompanied by the decreasing number. This situation demonstrates that the trend movement is weaker.

The items used in measuring such a trend usually are referred to as the indicators. These indicators are of various types of which are starred in the volume price analysis chart. They, therefore, represent a scale that is moving in any level of trading on the currencies.

These scales are like waves because of their re moment at a high wavelength and low points. The higher score means the economy is trading at a booming point. The lower peak implies the market is receding. Moreover, the horizontal line of the oscillator means the market is constant, where it has minimal change. It is up to you the investor to speculate the point the trend and predict what the market will behave next.

The Different Types of Indicators in the Volume Price Chart

These indicators always follow specific movement criteria where some of them may be of trending markets and others of the range-bound market. Trend marketing looks like they are moving in one direction, whereas a range one seems like a sideways one that runs in a specific range.

The first indicator is the Relative Strength Index (RSI). This indicator compares the magnitude of stocks overbought and stocks oversold. When this scale reads a higher peak, it means the currencies are overbought, and when it leads a low level, it means the stocks were oversold. Investors using the scale should be aware that the significant drop and rise effects can create a false impression in analyzing the trend.

The Moving Average Convergence Divergence (MACD) is another indicator. It illustrates the two exponential averages that measure the distances between the moving trends. Convergence means objects are close to each their while divergence shows they are far away from each other. There is a centerline passing along the exponential averages which shows. It is plotted to show when the proportions are equal and when they are crossing on each other. Traders will always target where the MACD is farther away that shows a higher momentum. At this juncture, you are likely to immerse a good return of investments that you are trading.

Bollinger band indicator is used to measure the standard deviations of a simple moving average of the scales. This scale measures the volatility of a particular stock. During extensive volatile periods, the bands widen and stretch away from each other. At lower volatile, the groups move close to each other and contracts. Such an aspect warns speculators t of the possibility of volatility where they should be in a rush to invest before the price comes down.

The super trend indicator measures the trend direction. One can carefully study the course of the pattern of the market and realize the point to reenter the market after a pullback. Take a situation where the downtrend is marked in red, and the uptrend is in green when the indicator switches from the red to green is an alarm of an abrupt pullback.

Steps in Analyzing Stocks Trading in Volume Price Analysis

First, contemplate on the charts and its features. Recognize the scales side in the diagram and the type of indicator available. Also, meditate on the chart type and its readings. Check on the different types of currencies provide in with the graph and looks at their forex valuing. This preparation stage is essential to orient you with how you will use the present features of the given graph.

Test and examine how the oscillators behave at a particular movement. You can even adjust the scale to a higher point and lower point to notice their behavioral pattern. Try to read the given currencies and identify the trends the indicators are following. This activity is like a rehearsal schemes before you start doing the real trading of stocks. Rehearse it over and over again until you are satisfied, you can follow the patterns appropriately.

Take an example of the currency pairs you prefer to use. Always determine the ratings and use those that you feel will perform accordingly. Let takes a sample of US/EURO trading. You will realize after going up, and down the scale, there is different movement of the indicators. You may recognize that when the Euro is depreciating the USD is appreciating and the vice versa. Take other examples of that combination and deliberate on the magnitude of returns they show.

Conduct research on how the program works. Do not rush in placing your odds on particular forex movement because you may end up losing your money. Always is a risk manager when doing the tasks. Remember that this scheme is full of risks. A professional stock player will always try many attempts to read the sequence and the pattern of the trading. Always compare the risks and the rewards of various stocks involved.

By now, you will have generated the different playing techniques applicable for successful trading. Read all the symbols in the chart and identify what they mean. Such may include the symbols of the different currencies. Identify the point of highest price returns and risks. Recognize the volumes indicators. Terms like the overbought, the oversold, purchase price, sales commission, and others should be fully understood.

By this time, you ought to try to make a purchase where you can recharge your account. First, you should look at the oscillations levels of the indicators. The knowledge of observing the trend and the currency variations matters a lot because you will be in apposition to choose the profitable points. Always look at the peak where if the indicators correlate it means you will have a break-even point. That is the end which there is neither a gain nor the loss. From this point, you can easily predict a profitable area.

The game is as impressive when you keep on earning lots of money. Even if you lose do not despair since this is a risk-taking operation. Always remember that the volume price analysis shows good returns when the overall price moves correlatively with the volume. If you are underscoring a particular pairing currency, try another one frequently. You will realize you can speculate their profit margin. The exercise will give you a host of portfolios to practice where the returns will be fruitful at intelligent speculation.

Chapter 9: Mechanics of Trading (Underlying Math of the Trading Account in Terms of Leverage, Margin and Risks Management)

Before you get started, here is a recap to keep in mind. In any business, there is a level of risk involved.

Forex trading is a high-risk business too, that requires proper skills to venture in it. To mitigate risk and enable low-income earners to engage in this business margin and leverage are instruments that traders can use to be accommodated by the market. But before we embark on understanding what margin and leverage are, we have to equip ourselves with knowledge about pips, spread, and lots.

Define a pip

A pip is the smallest increment or decrement or the last decimal place of a currency quotation.

For all currency pairs, a pip is 0.0001 except currency pairs involving the Japanese Yen whose pip value is 0.01.

For instance, in the event that there is a movement of the EUR/USD from 1.3220 to 1.3221, then that is defined as the pair having moved a single pip upwards. For the USD/JPY, if a currency moves from 98.00 to 98.01, it will have moved one pip. It is worth noting the difference in the number of decimal places for currency pairs involving JPY.

How can one define a spread?

Spread is the difference between the bid price and ask price.

The higher the spread, the higher the cost of trading. Therefore, always find brokers that offer the best spread to maximize profits and minimize losses in a given trade. Usually, spreads range between 3 and 10 points on particular currencies and between 5 and 15 on cross-currencies. You will note that cross-currency is a pair that do not have USD as one of the currencies in the pair, for example, EUR/JPY.

When buying a currency pair, you will use the asking price. The ask or offer price is usually higher, and you pay the spread on entering a position.

When you sell a currency pair, you apply the bid price. Here you pay the spread on exiting your position.

What is a lot?

The standard lot is $100000, and a mini-lot size is $10000. A trader would require very large amounts of cash to trade. For traders with little capital to take advantage of participating in forex trading, they use margin and leverage.

What is Margin?

Margin is where a trader is only required to deposit a smaller affordable percentage of the minimum lot. For example, you may only be required to deposit $1000, which enables you to trade $100000. $100000 is the minimum acceptable mini-lot by most brokers.

There exist two types of margin, namely a **margin of interest and a fixed margin.** In the case of using the fixed margin, the trader has to invest a fixed amount of capital as per the policies of the brokers to ensure they maintain financial security as per the leverage preempted in that specific trade.

For example, in leverage of 1:100, the expected standard mini-lot is 10000 of the trading currency units. This implies that one has to ensure a deal by the margin of 100 units of the deposit currency if they need to open a position with one lot. 10000/100=100, this is regardless of the currency you are executing a deal.

There is a difference in the margin of interest. In this strategy, we ensure the deal is within a certain margin of the traded percentage. The sum counted has to be based on the current rates. The other factors that have to be considered in this type of margin are the traded currency and the trading asset currency.

For instance, if the currency used to deposit the trade commodity is in USD. And the interest margin is marked at 1% as of the volume of the deal. When a trader makes the decision to conduct a trade deal with EUR/USD, the lot volume is 10000 EUR hence the rate of the execution of the deal will be:

PAIR	BID	ASK
EUR/USD	1.3580	1.3586

To find the needed margin, we conduct the following arithmetic:

1% of the total of a single (1) lot = 10 000 *1/100 = 100 EURO.

This will be later converted into USD as shown below:

100 = 100*1.3586 = 135.86 USD = 135.9 USD approximately.

Which is equivalent to $135.9

What is a Margin call?

When you deposit money in your trading account, we call that initial deposit initial margin or just account margin. The minimum security varies from broker to broker. This margin is usually about 1% to 2% of the respective lot.

For example, if you have a lot of $10000, with a 1% margin, you will need to deposit $100 in your trading account. Therefore, if you had $1000, you can control up to $100000.

Note that **usable margin** is the money available in your account for trading and sustaining trading losses. In the event that a trader's money goes lesser than their margin requirements, the broker automatically closes some of their positions to avoid further losses which may attract negative balance.

For instance, when one opens a regular Forex account with $4,252. They are said to open a single lot of EUR/USD, which has a margin requirement of $2000. Since the person started at $4252, the margin that they can use remains to be $4252. However, in the event that they opened one lot, which had a margin requirement of $3565, their remaining usable margin will be $3565. Now, the margin call comes when one exceeds the usable margin.

For one to avoid margin calls, they can implement an effective account balance monitoring strategy, or they can implement the stop-loss orders strategy hence minimizing risks.

Generally, you need to understand your broker's policy on margin, and always remember that too much margin is not desirable as it only amplifies the risk.

The lower the margin requirement (meaning, the higher the leverage), the greater the potential for higher profits *and* losses. Low margin requirements are desirable when your trades are good, but not so enjoyable when you are wrong. It is advisable not to overlook the margins. They are very real, and they are the determinant of your trading success. Be on the lookout.

What is Leverage?

Leverage is where a trader uses various financial instruments or borrowed capital, such as margin, to increase the potential return of an investment. Leverage will help an investor to get the opportunity to execute deals with a volume that exceeds their initial investment by over 100 times.

Leverage magnifies your expected profits to a large extent.

One thing you need to remember, leverage is a two-way sword. The same way it magnifies your profits, your losses will also be magnified in a similar measure.

A successful trader needs to choose a margin with leverage that they can afford the profit/loss results.

Leveraging can be defined in terms of either a ratio or a margin percentage — the ratio displays as what constitutes an investment in relation to the profit. While the percentage defines the amount of profit, a person is able to make when they trade a certain amount of money.

The relationship between leverage and a margin can be shown as:

The leverage = 100 / Margin Percent

Margin Percent = 100 / Leverage

Leverages are always displayed in the form of a ratio such as 400:1.

When trading, we are supposed to consider various aspects of the market, including, spread and the type of orders we will apply in a given situation.

Types of Orders

There are three types of orders
- Instant orders
- Pending type of orders or Limit orders
- The stop-loss type of orders

Instant Order

A market order is a type of order where you execute at the current market price. We know that going long on a currency pair (buying) means purchasing the base currency and selling the quote currency and when going short on a currency pair (selling), the opposite applies.

Therefore, before you go long on a currency pair, you expect the price of the base currency to rise in future so that you can go short (sell) when the price is higher, hence earning a profit.

When executing a market order, a proper analysis should be done to avoid unnecessary losses.

Pending Order

A pending order is where you set a target price, such that when your set price is attained, your order is executed.

For example, if you want to go long on a given currency pair, you will let the price of the pair to drop to a low level where you will purchase the currency pair and hold it as the prices rise. Once your sell limit is reached, your sell order is automatically triggered and executed.

Employ the stop order technique

A stop-loss order is a special type of pending order which limits the magnitude of loss a trader can incur, just in case, the market works against their predictions. For instance, you can set your stop loss to be 20 pips from your entry price in the opposite direction to your prediction.

Take Profit Order

In your trading, you can set a price that once your currency pair attains, you scoop the accrued profit, and that point of taking profit becomes your new entry point for the trade, and next profit will only be calculated from this point. You should choose this position carefully to avoid early exits from trades as this reduces your profits. At all times, you should consider slippage.

Slippage is the difference between the price at which an order should be executed and the price of actual execution. This slippage can be attributed to the slow internet or servers' response.

Managing Your Trading Risks

To manage risks in a successful way, one does not only need to monitor their trades closely but also, they need to have a tested and proven strategy which they can use to minimize the chances of incurring losses. Everyone, from the trading experts to the newcomers, they need to understand the basics of loss minimization to ensure they remain on the profit-making side and not lose more than they make. This book has come up with some strategies which will help you understand the losses and how to minimize them regardless of your trading status effectively.

· Come up with a plan and stick by it and do not get swayed

In the trading field, you have to formulate your trading methodology. You can base the methodology or trading model on your analysis. You should test the methodology process for effectiveness. After you have formulated your plan, evaluate the plan to check for profitability. Some of the major parts of the plan should include the highest stake you can afford to lose and the highest amount you intend to invest at one specific time and at a specific interval or in a day. Exit the trade after achieving those limits to avoid losses.

· Avoid investing every cent you got

It is true that the highest risks also earn the highest. However, do not literally apply that strategy with forex. It may or may not work for you. You have to portion your money in bits and ensure in every investment you earn a profit or sell before you lose everything. Keep some money to get the trade going even when you lose what you've invested currently?

· Implement the stop orders strategy

With a stop-order strategy, one is able to reduce the risk and loses in this agile market. Develop and implement a very one-of-a-kind stop-loss strategy that helps you exit the market whenever you lose a certain percentage of money in one sitting.

· Embrace diversification

When one diversifies, their portfolio is minimized. Avoid investing everything in a single trade. Keep the amount diversified. Ensure that you do not trade in one position for more than 10% of the time spent of your trading capital. You should involve the use of tools to help with the interrelation of the facts to avoid loses. For instance, having a long position in a EUR/USD trade and a short on in USD/CHF trade, you only have one position. This increases the risk of incurring losses. Check all the relationship between the positions before settling for any of them.

Chapter 10: Discipline in Trading (Why It Is So Important? Psychological and Money Discipline)

Just like any activity that generates revenue, discipline is highly recommended as it helps shape growth and encourages good decision making. Decision making for any trading need insights and proper management to avoid premature conclusions. Forex trading for beginners' outlines reasons why discipline is important in trading. A lot of beginners have been reported to have made bad decisions and ended up quitting before they make a living out of their investment and it is advisable always to follow instructions and have self-discipline because it is what drives the business. Forex trading is not a governing fortune, and just like any other venture, it needs sacrifices and discipline at its core.

The first thing to be discussed is the psychological discipline with regards to forex trading.

Psychology is all to do with the mind and how it functions about making important decisions in life or career. Making the right decisions at a mature season is important for trading as it is not an average work as it seems.

The brain does many things, and concerning trading, it tends to give the body many signals which are mostly triggered by emotions. It is advisable not to make decisions when emotionally challenged i.e., rapid changes when one makes a loss or too much celebration that can end up in unplanned investment. To reach a clear decision, one ought to have a discipline measure that helps when one has a psychological problem or torture.

Forex Plan

For beginners, it is important to have a forex plan in which it helps in executing laid programs. Forex, as discussed above, needs an open mind and dealing with the exchange in currencies need a proper plan where all the possibilities are exhausted. Do you think you can control yourself and make wise decisions even when you are down? You might be in for a rude shock as things do not always turn out as anticipated.

A forex plan is perfect for it will limit you from making undocumented decisions which can result in loses or major mistake in trading. It means that one will be guided by the plan, and it is advisable to stick to the plan. This will see a beginner escalate in trading business with time and with the right way of implementation of business ideas and expansions.

Checklist

As the name suggests, a checklist is a list that keeps a forex trader in check and balance. This also acts as a book for rules to follow during the implementation process. A beginner should have a checklist for they are new in the venture, and some trading disciplinary element is sticking to the plan. This is almost similar to a trading plan, but it deeply outlines the pros and cons during the beginning of the forex venture. One will be revisiting the list to make sure everything is in place and shy away from impulse reaction towards a loss or a win.

Outlining Risks

Every business has a risk, and it is the risk that makes many businesses successful. For a beginner in forex trading and with no experience in business, having a risk measure is Paramount

Profit Outcome

This is the opposite of risk outlining. As you look at the loses that you may incur at forex trading as a beginner, having hopes for business is also an important item as it is the reason one is getting into the business in the first place. Some forex traders always rush to implementing and using up their profits by putting back into the business and it not advisable. Everything should be simultaneous, and forex trading cannot be operated with greed and hope to get immediate results. Excitement should be tamed using a profit outcome to protect earnings and initial capital

Working Journal

A journal in forex trading for beginners is important as it keeps one on toes on different forex ideas and implementation. The journal outlines a journey one has come in forex trading and help in making future decisions. This, in summary, looks like a reflection of the past, and one should constantly check so as not to repeat the same mistakes and make better future choices. This also helps in learning how to run the forex business and effects of each decision made.

When all these are set and ready to go, trading your money with discipline may save you from hurting through unfavorable markets. To trade with conscious, here are some insights on how to walk the talk and stick to disciplined measures

Stop Chasing Markets

Greed is an enemy of many in forex trading, and a beginner should be careful. Be content with small winnings and stop chasing different markets as it may work against your method of trading and one can incur more loses than profits

Stick to One Method

This is mainly a challenge to many beginners who get their first profit and want to explore more methods in a single day. Markets can be different, and some identified methods might not be that suitable for other markets on forex trading. Therefore, it is advisable to identify only to get one proven way to get some profit and stick to it so long as there is subsequent revenue coming in. This is a discipline also that makes a beginner Know how to handle markets in forex trading and not to get too excited with-profits.

So why is it important to have discipline on forex trading?

Discipline in all aspects of life requires one to have self-regulation where no matter what comes in between, you can control yourself. This also applies in forex trading as a beginner is required to follow the set rules to the latter without beating themselves up for impulsive trading. The importance discussed below can be taken down among the principles one should have to become a good forex trader and to make profits at the end of it all because that is the core reason for starting up a business. Remember, it is not about regulating your life, but regulating your business circles to avoid risking loses.

To avoid loses

Risks are an essential part of forex trading as it is a game that one challenge themselves in coming out of it alive, however, they should not dictate the order of the day as it is the reason one is in the business, to make profits. Money discipline in handling forex trading is one trait that will help you in getting more profits and avoid unnecessary loses.

Forex trading done with emotions will not see the light of the day as you will focus on bringing back the already lost money and end up losing everything. This is impulse buying which also is seen when one gets more profit, and they think the various markets will favor them and in turn, get all the profits lost or even worse part of the capital. This means that if you are looking forward to successful forex trading, then be psychologically and monetary discipline to avoid such loses and have just enough profits. This is arguably the main reason why one should be disciplined for no one embraces in any business whatsoever the case and is advisable to keep it in mind more so for beginners in forex trading.

Enables money control

Nothing beats training the mind to be disciplined for it helps control the money flow in forex trading. Some impulse traders apply the phrase 'if I die, I die' which should not be the slogan at any given point. Discipline trains the mind to control emotional trading and right decision making that impacts the outcome of the end of day returns in forex trading. If you can control the money, that means when you make loses, you will not take all the profits and put back into business immediately, which is something that can cause even loses. A discipline forex trader would control the mind and even stop trading the same day until the next day when they lose or as one would use the phrase 'we live to fight another day' which is a good gesture of discipline.

Helps avoid cunning insiders

Insiders are common in businesses where someone can tip you or give you top-level secured information so you can pay them. This is not something new in forex trading, and sometimes the so-called insiders might be internet conmen. When people see your fingers moving high or even when you are desperate, some people might want to 'spice' up your profits by duping you to believing that they are aware of some information on different markets in forex trading. Without discipline, you might end up giving up all the money, and your business could collapse any minute.

Duping is common in trading with insiders luring beginners with lucrative opportunities and probably huge profits that only exists in an ideal world. But when you have discipline, such cases do not occur as everything you are doing is placed on paper and plan implemented accordingly.

Chapter 11: Trading Psychology

Trading psychology in the forex market is a large thing. It is not inadequate for skill or enough academic knowledge to apply in the forex market because psychology is often used to gain profits. People who only used available skills and academic knowledge without including psychology aspects are prone to make mistakes while trading in the forex market. This phenomenon is the origin of primary mistakes committed in the market. These mistakes are regularly repeated over time by different types of forex traders. These forex traders are of different nationalities, cultures, social backgrounds. This is a familiar character that is displayed by among people. The trait of making mistakes is what makes people referred to as humans.

Another common trait observed among forex traders is fear. This trait creates either flight or fight response in an individual's life. Poor handling of flight or fight response has made several forex traders decline in what they do in the market. It is very difficult to reverse how we human beings have felt for a period of over millions of years. However, it is very easy to change how we respond to these feelings by observing how successful traders in the forex market have handled themselves. The process goes ahead to task human beings to implement successful findings in real-life situations while marketing in the foreign exchange market. This chapter will help beginners in the forex market know how to respond and behave in forex trading. It will be guided by the trading psychology angle of view.

Fear has the potential of creating a limiting effect on a person's behavior while trading in the forex market. A person's mind is has a natural tuning that it will want a perceived safe place. The safe place provision in mind is very crucial in mind success and its success. This phenomenon can also be experienced during trading in the forex market. It occurs when a person is making or is going loses in the forex market. The natural instinct that pops in an individual's mind is to pull out his or her from the trade. This is a contingency plan in a person's mind to avoid loses or further losses in the market.

Nevertheless, the problem at hand has the potential of leading a person away from a trading strategy that is carefully thought of and planned. The situation can make an individual commit more a common mistake of making hasty decisions. Many people make a mistake of making hasty choices and decision with the aim of salvaging the breakdown situation. This circumstance can make a person to lose more money than what he or she could lose or create if the investment was left to play out with the market forces. The mind of a person in very many instances loves to focus on the short term survival conditions. However, traders in the foreign exchange market are advised to think and plan for the future critically. This will enable a clear plan of the long term position despite losing the gains in the short term position.

When an individual participating in the forex market understands trading psychology, he or she has an added advantage in the market. Psychology understanding in the forex market helps an individual to eliminate fear while making critical decisions about his or her investments. When an individual is aware of fear in front of him or her, he can get the courage to face the obstacle with correct psychology. The same drill is used in the forex market by successful traders in the realm. The successful traders understand the psychology of the market and are not afraid to take risks which have high chances of failure. However, these risks with low success rates have the highest earnings when the market storm is over. Understanding market psychology will help beginners in the forex market have the ability to establish control of reasoning and logic. These are one of the utmost aims of nearly every single forex trader.

Different Types of Trading Bias

Forex market traders have the ability to easily feel confident in their potential to remain collected and calm. This feeling is a common phenomenon before the forex market trading sessions begin to open. However, the narrative switches to the opposite side when the trading sessions are opened. It is very easy for emotions to pop in when a person is faced with a real-life crisis. The same case happens when a stock trader is faced with real financial decisions face him or her over his or her investments. Despite these feelings cropping up in the realities of life, people have the ability to learn and work through or around.

Those who trade in the forex market are not supposed to give in to these feelings. Feelings that are prone to face forex traders include greed, excitement, or fear while trading their investments in the foreign exchange market. If these feeling overcome and cloud their judgments, these traders are prone to make mistakes that are very costly and can't be reversed. The beginners in the forex market are supposed to evaluate themselves before undertaking the challenge of forex trading. They are likely to fall under this category of psychological biases;

· Overconfidence bias; the market will head here
· Anchoring bias; this means that probably
· Confirmation bias; this proves I'm right also
· Loss bias; I hope there will be a comeback of commodity prices

A keen individual who is observant will notice how these bias overlap. Therefore, no matter which angle a person takes these biases will boil down to creating fear in a traders mind. These biases will be discussed in lengthy to help an individual be aware of his or her emotions.

Before expanding these biases, a trader is supposed to know on which way to use so as to avoid risks. To avoid the presented unnecessary risks while trading, he or she is advised to use a demo account that is free of risks. These demo accounts have the ability to give person leverage in trading in live markets. While trading in the live markets using demo accounts do not put a trader's capital at risks. This will help a forex trader to practice how to control emotions when the mark is declining. This will help him or her while trading the live markets.

Overconfidence Bias

The first lesson a beginner in the forex market is supposed to learn is how to train his or her euphoria. It is the first lesson in the trading psychology of forex market. Humans are, most of the time, self-focused creatures. Our ego plays an important role since we always want to validate what we know. These egos tend to go a notch higher to make people prove a point that they are not ordinary people and are better than the average people. Available hints that corroborate with these thoughts do a job of reinforcing our images. It is made possible through a very discrete feeling of self-love.

This feeling makes a cropping problem to forex traders while trading. The traders are prone to being very overconfident, thus succumbing to overconfidence bias. It a very common occurrence for a trader to have a good streak in the forex market and consistently make gains. The trader is predicted to have thought if he or she can't make mistakes or the market will still favor him or her in the future. A trader is discouraged from having these thoughts because it can end up being his or her greatest fall in the trade of forex. An individual in the forex market is supposed to be keen on looking at details of the gains he or she makes. The forex trader is supposed to also go into details in the sessions he or she also makes losses in the market.

Having this strategy in hand makes a person in the forex market will make a person stay on top of his or her game. A person is supposed to make mistakes in this life. The same thought is applied in the forex market as traders also are also allowed to make mistakes in the markets. Being able to make mistakes and prove one wrong is advised for because it will help the individual during the long term run. A person is supposed to be able to accept that making mistakes can't be avoided in life. This is a common occurrence to the beginners because everything in life is a learning curve.

Anchoring Bias

Anchoring bias is also a common occurrence in the forex market. The situation is created when a trader creates a comfort zone in the mind while undertaking an analysis of the market. These forex traders tend to make a mistake of thinking that the market will remain the same as the present. This mistake is made from the thought of the presents having a very similar depiction of the past occurrences for a while. This bias is derived from the studies of social life just like the other biases. Anchoring is a habit created by forex traders that solely rely on what the trader already knows. This forms the basis of decision making in the forex market. A trader with this kind of mentality has a closed edge of thinking. He or she does not put into thought the changes forex market can bring to his or her investment in the market. This has seen several traders have a decline in their investment because this mentality anchors the trader to rely on irrelevant and obsolete information simply. This phenomenon will make the forex trader have difficulties in the market. The anchoring bias elucidates itself when a trader holds a single position for a very long time. This is because he or she fails in considering other option the forex market can provide. A person is afraid to get out of the comfort zones and explore other options and alternatives. A beginner is supposed to be prepared to try several of the market offers. However, anchoring on one position can make a person rely on outdated information leading to loses.

Confirmation Bias

This form of bias is common among professional forex traders in the market. A person's decision will be anchored by the kind of information he or she looks for. These decisions do not have to be the best decisions made by a person. However, they always justify a person's actions and strategies by the information available in the market. There is always a problem when a trader does this continuously. Because a person will not improve his or her way of solving a situation, this will only make a person make other mistakes. A person makes a loop of uncountable mistakes in the forex market trading psychology.

This phenomenon appears when a trader keeps on researching on things he or she already knows. This action leads too much wastage of precious time. This action can be detrimental because a trader can go beyond losing time to losing capital and motive to trade. A trader in the forex market is encouraged to trust his instincts and intelligence. This will enable him or her to create new market strategies improving his or her profits margins.

Loss Aversion Bias

This form of bias is drawn from the prospect theory. Humans tend to have a very distinct way of assessing loss and gains. This is done along contrasting the perception of the standard belief they have set. The situation is clearly depicted in the forex markets. Various traders tend to focus on the risks available before investment rather than the possible reward after investment. The situation makes fear a powerful motive compared to greed. Therefore, while trading, forex trader with this mentality tend to make low amounts of profits. However, those traders who are ready to overcome loss aversion bias have ha different tale. They have the ability to make huge amounts of profits when their trades are successful.

Chapter 12: Money Management and Trading Plan

What is money management?

Money management is the regulation that will assist you in gaining maximum profit, reduce your losses rates, and help your trading business to thrive. Do you know what separates veterans from a novice in this industry?

Well, they know how to navigate this sector. Veterans learn the ropes of this simple yet complicated task until they conquer. Money management can either make or break your hustle. And, that's why it's essential.

Here, survival comes first; forget about the profit. And money management is one of the survival tips. Additionally, preventing extreme loses should be your number one aim. For you to be a success, you need to be knowledgeable. But how can you achieve this? Proper education is a must. Study the trends of the two currencies you are investing in. Also, you need to be ready to embrace change, as this industry is always unpredictable. You also need to be disciplined to be a successful trader.

Money Management Tips You Should Know

The following are some money management tips:

Risk per trade

You need to understand what are the risks involved during an entry. Check if the profit you will be low in comparison to the loss. You should invest 2-3% of your trading size. The money you invest shouldn't affect your livelihood. Besides, having a side hustle isn't such a bad idea. To save yourself the trouble, use a risk calculator to determine the risk involved.

Go with the market flow

In this market, you should be aggressive, but just to the right extent. Just like in cooking, you need salt for a savory stew. But, too much of it can spoil the broth. You shouldn't risk too much. Stop chasing the market. Meaning, you shouldn't jump into every opportunity that comes your way. Instead, carefully check your options.

Opening up numerous trades, to get enormous profit is a terrible idea. Investing per hour or per day could turn disastrous and, your account can blow up.

You know professionals in this industry do, they sit back, analyze the market, and when the right opportunity presents itself, they strike.

Patience is a virtue you here and trusts me; you need it.

Have a realistic goal

Your goals should be well defined. You want to make profits. But that wouldn't happen every damn time. Don't set your expectations too high. Expectations hurt. Study the market well, especially on the pairs of currency you want to trade.

After doing this, place your bet, and wait on the congratulations method. There is no quick money without working for it. Lastly you can't win without a strategic plan. A plan guides you towards the right direction on the forex trading journey. Strive to adhere and stick to it.

Manage your emotion

Fear. Greed. These are two emotions that can mess you up. Fear can limit you from taking risks. And greed can lead to huge loses. This could be a huge setback to your career. Nonetheless, take a break when experiencing hefty loses. After all, you need to recover. If you fear to try to take small trade stacks. You will get there. Keep your emotions at bay. Whether during entry or exit level, learning to manage your motions gives you confidence. Try to be neutral and go with the flow.

Learn how to manage a financial crisis

With every opportunity, you get, try to maximize your profits. Often, it's difficult to predict a market. And in forex trading, things can turn quickly in few minutes or even seconds. When bad comes to worse, you should be ready to overcome it. Bad trade exists. And at times you can experience extreme loses. Don't lose hope. Your powers are limited here, and the market is uncontrollable. When it's too much for you, leave some trades. Open them when you experience profits.

Utilize stop losses

The good thing about stop losses is that you can't lose all your money in a single trade. They provide a tempo to any business. When you're unable to keep track of the market, stop losses help maximize your profits and reduce your losses rate. You can consider stopping losses like; chart stop, percentage stop, volatility stop, time stop, and margin stop.

Understand leverage

Unfortunately, leverage is not good a good option, if you are venturing into this industry. It offers the opportunity to accelerate your profits and also, stimulates your chances of getting a loss. The higher the leverage, the higher your level of risk exposure. Take leverage with caution to avoid inconveniences later. Usually, you can get one according to your status. In this case, a retailer trader or a professional trader.

A Trading Plan

Do you know why most traders don't succeed? They don't have a trading plan. Most people view it as of less importance. Instead, others keep procrastinating to write it later. And claim they don't have time. The result is they encounter frequent losses. A trading plan acts as a root of a tree; it's the foundation. Once the uprooted the tree is not more.

What is a trading plan?

A trading plan is a theoretical framework of what your plans, including your end goals when trading. Also, it's an organized to-do list. To succeed, you need it. Actually, it's a guideline that shows you what to do something and when to do it. A trading plan may consist of: money management, rules, financials goals, methods, and when to open and close positions.

You need to be disciplined to follow your trading plan. You should not only strive to follow it but also implement it. You can record a trading plan on paper, your phone, your tablet, or your Pc.

With a good trading plan, you enjoy the following benefits;

· The trading plan assists you in becoming objective, as the market does not influence your decisions

· Improve your trading strategy.

· Rate your performance.

· Ensure you reach your target

What to consider before making a trading plan?

You should consider the following tips:

Asses your skills

Are you ready to enter this market? You should ask yourself this question first. The industry is not for the faint-hearted. You can ask yourself numerous questions like;

· Why should you venture into forex trading? To what extent can you risk your money? Your goals and also the time frame to achieve a particular aspect.

· Include your goals, strengths, and also weaknesses.

· Lastly, you can decide on what approach you want to use in drawing your trading plan. Is it fundamental or technical approach? A technical approach focuses on math and the probabilities in the trading. On the other hand, the fundamentals approach depends on the news. Often, it's objective and is influenced by economic or political factors.

Limit your scope market scope

There are numerous markets involved here. Focusing on a particular aspect on a time frame in a single market is advantageous to you. You can research and become well versed with it. Also, you get to learn the characteristics of that market.

Have goals

A goal pushes you in the right direction. Goals drive you to wake up and start trading. With goals, you can include the amount of money you are willing to lose before exiting or the rewards you are eager to accept. Your goals should be realistic.

Do your research

Check on what is going across the globe. Check if the overseas market is up or down. The research will ensure you gauge the market before it opens. Check the frequency of how much profits or losses you can get in a day, an hour or per week. Also, look at how many times you can trade at these periods. After doing all this, you can draw a plan. Lastly, you can decide to test your plan to ensure you aren't doing anything wrong.

What's your risk tolerance?

Trading has its ups and s downs. Every day will not be a bed of roses. Include the levels of risk you are willing to undertake.

Also, risk tolerance will help you control your emotions. Meaning, in case of huge success or a loss, you will know the direction to take.

Have a checklist.

Just like the name suggests, a checklist keeps you own your toss. With it, you can monitor your progress. You can review the trading plan any time you want. Hence you monitor your expectations and aspiration.

Include your entry and exit of each trade, the support, and resistance you encountered. Also, try journaling and record your progress each day. Lastly, you can record lessons learned and how to improve later.

Patience

Even with a trading plan, you should be patient. Include patience motto in your trading plan, and ensure to read it daily. Patience enables you to make excellent trading decisions. Waiting for the ideal opportunity will not be a nut-cracking task. But, a rewarding task.

A trading plan is just as important as money management. For your trading career to blossom ensure you create a trading plan. At least with it, all your visions can be met.

Chapter 13: Examples of Simple Operations with a Step by Step Guide to Do the First Operation

Before we look at the examples of simple operations, I prefer that you should first have Forex market concepts basics. Don't worry; the concepts in trading currencies are quite simple, despite the overwhelming size of the market. Here are some of the concepts that you must first understand as a forex investor:

· Have a good understanding of the major currencies

As a trader in the forex market, you must have a good understanding of the eight major economies. This is the only way you will be able to determine the opportunities presented by overvalued or undervalued currencies. This is totally different from stock market where you are presented with the opportunity to choose from a thousand stocks. These are the eight countries that dominate the forex trade in the market:

· New Zealand
· United States of America
· Eurozone
· Switzerland
· United Kingdom
· Japan
· Canada
· Australia

The financial markets of these eight countries are considered to be the world's largest and most complicated. Giving your focus on the listed countries will help you to know when to take advantage of earning interest income in different financial markets. Every day, economic data from these eight countries is released. Always try to look at these data so as to stay on the right track while assessing the economy of each country.

· Have a good understanding of the Yield and Return concepts

As a forex trader, always have it in your mind that yield drives return. Therefore, when trading in the forex sports market, you get the opportunity to buy or sell two underlying currencies. Currencies can only be valued in relation to another, thus quoting of currencies is done in pairs.

A case example is the pairing of the Euro and the US Dollar. If we have Euro/US dollar pair quoted as 1.3240, it simply means that 1 euro can be purchased by $ 1.3240.

In every transaction you carry out at the forex, you are involved in buying or selling the currency of your choice. In the real sense, you are purchasing a new currency from the currency you have sold. It is also good to note the central bank of every country sets the interest rates for its currency. This is the factor that makes every currency in the world to have its own interest rate. With this, it means that it is in as much as you are getting an interest in the currency you are buying, you also have an obligation to pay this interest in the sold currency.

Case Example 1

Assuming that you want to trade with NZD/JPY pair and in the currency market, New Zealand sets its interest rate at say 9% while Japan sets its interest rate at 0.5%, how will you analyze this?

In this case, you have to begin by looking at the basis points. Basis points are used to calculate interest rates in the currency market. In simple terms, a basis point is 1/100th of 1%. This means that rates set by New Zealand can be seen as 900 basis points while the rates set by Japanese rates as 50 basis points. Therefore, if your decision is to trade on NZD/JPY pair, you'll definitely get earnings of 9% interest. However, you will be required to make a payment of 0.5% in order to get a net return if 8.5%, which is just equivalent to 850 basis points.

You also need to be aware of the leverage offered by the foreign exchange market. The foreign exchange is also one of the markets that offer tremendous leverage; in most cases, leverage as high as 100:1. This means that with as little capital as $100, you can control assets worth $10,000. However, when the deal is too good, you have to think twice. Leverage is a double-edged sword; while when you are correct, you can make massive profits, you can also in a similar manner make huge losses when you are wrong.

It is therefore clear that you should be careful with leverage offered. Suppose we have a 10:1 leverage, then the 7.5% yield we obtained in the NZD/JPY pair will have an annual return of 75%. In such a case, suppose you are holding a 200,000 unit position, using equity worth $5,000 of NZD/JPY pair, you will be able to earn an interest of $9.40 each day. This translates to $94 after ten days and an annual earnings of $3,760.

· Carry Trades

One aspect of currency values is that they never remain stationary. This dynamic nature of currency values is the factor that resulted in the carry trade. As a trader, you also have to understand carry trade. To be a carry trader, you have to look at both the interest rate that comes with the differential between 2 currencies, but you also have to the possibilities of currency value appreciation.

Case Example 2

Carry Trade has had wonderful opportunities for profits in the past. For instance, between 2003 and 2004, the pair of Australian Dollar and the US Dollar offered a positive yield spread of up to 2.5%. I know you may see this as very small; however, its return was 25% with a 10:1 leverage. This period also saw the Australian dollar appreciating by 42% from 56 cents to 80 cents when compared to the U.S.D. As a trader, this means that if you traded, you would have by default got positive earnings as well as has a tremendous capital gain in the investments made.

Another Carry trade opportunity happened in 2005 between the US dollar and Japanese Yen pair. The currency appreciated from 102 to 121.40 and then settled on 117.80 towards December. In the same year, the return was 2.9% thus the carry trade with an appreciation of 19%, was more attractive. Furthermore, during this time, an interest rate of 3.25% was spread between USD and JPY. Without leveraging, as a trader, you would get earnings of 22.25%, and if leverage of 10:1 would be introduced, you would have a 220% gain.

Forex Trading Examples

The CDF examples below will give you an insight into how forex trading works. We will look at how buying and selling is done;
· Case Example: Buying of EUR/GBP pair
EUR/GBP currency pair currently trades at 0.8698/0.8923.
You have done your analysis, and you think that the EUR/GBP price will go up. So, you decide to buy a €30,000. The margin rate in the EUR/GBP pair is 3.34%, meaning that when depositing, you have to do so with a position margin of 3.34%. As such, your position margin will be;

= (3.34% x [€30,000 x 0.88105])
= £882.81

First trade outcome: Positive trade

Suppose you made the right predictions and then the next hour witnessed an increase in prices to 0.8799/0.8956. Seeing this, you make a decision of closing your long trade. You now sell at 0.8798.
This means that the price has moved 101 points favoring you (0.8799-0.8698)
Therefore, you will get a profit of
([€30,000 x 0.87990] – [€30,000 x 0.86980])
= 26397 - 26094
= £303

Second outcome: Losing trade

In this second case, your prediction went wrong, and there is a drop in the EUR/GBP prices over the following hour. Suppose it drops to 0.8490/0.8625. You have a feeling that the price will continue dropping and therefore, the only way to reduce losses, you now make a decision to sell at 0.8490 in order to close the trade.

Your price basically has moved against you by 433 points (0.8923 - 0.8490).

The loss that you will incur therefore is

= ([€30,000 x 0.89230] – [€30,000 x 0.84900])

= 26769 - 25470

= -£1299

Case Example: selling of EUR/USD pair

Currently, EUR/USD trades at 1.12150/1.12160. Assuming that in your analysis, you come across some data indicating that in the coming days, the euro is likely to fall against USD. Therefore, because you are convinced that the EUR/USD price will go down, you decide to take a risk and sell the €30,000.

The margin rate for EUR/USD is 3.34%. This tells you that you are required to deposit 3.34% of €30,000 as the position margin.

Position margin for this case will be;

= (3.34% x [€30,000 x 1.12155]).

= $1123.79

Again, you have to put in your mind that id the price moves against you, there can be possibilities that you can lose more than this initial position margin.

First Outcome: A winning trade

Suppose you predicted correctly and over the next hour, EUR/USD drops to 1.11150/1.11160. Seeing this, you make a decision of closing the short trade. You then buy, and the current price is now 1.11160

The price, therefore, has shifted in your favor by 99 points (1.12150 - 1.11160).

As a trader, your profit will be;

= ([€30,000 x 1.12150] – [€30,000 x 1.11160])

= 33, 645- 33, 348

= $297

Second Outcome: Losing trade

Suppose you made predictions, but unfortunately, these predictions were incorrect and actually the EUR/USD prices increases in the following one hour into 1.12452/1.12361. Again, you think that this price will continue to rise. Therefore, you want to play safe by minimizing your loss limits. So, you close the trade. You proceed to make purchases by a buying price of 1.12361.

The price will move against you by 211 points (1.12361 -1.12150).

The loss you will incur will be;

= ([€30,000 x 1.12361] – [€30,000 x 1.12150])

= 33, 708.03 - 33, 645

= $ 63.03

How Liquid Are Different Forex Pairs?

You have already learned that traders make profits by taking advantage of the differences between currency pairs. I know that you have been wondering about how someone can expect a given currency to move. You should understand that this depends on how liquid a currency is. In other words, by saying liquid, we mean how much of this currency is being sold or bought at any given time. For a currency pair to be considered as the most liquid currency pair, it must be the most have the most supply and demand in the Forex market. Basically, financial institutions, importers and exporters, international businesses, and forex traders are the people generating this demand and supply.

Foreign Exchange Speed

In foreign exchange, speed refers to the difference found between the bid and ask price of a given currency pair. For instance, suppose EUR/USD has a Bid price of 1.14468, and then the selling price is 1.14469, by default; the spread of this pair will be 0.0001 which is equivalent to 1 pip. Therefore, a trader who entered a long EUR/USD trade when the Bid price was 1.14468, his trade will only be profitable when the pair gets sells over 1.14469.

Currency pairs like EURCZK have a wider spread and thus for traders to realize considerable profits after a larger movement. The bid price as at now for this pair is 24.4475, and the asking price is 24.4275. This means that the spread between this currency pair is 0.0200, which is equivalent to 20 pips. This means that this currency pair usually has movements of 20 pips a day, and in order for traders to make a profit, they will have to carry out a multi-day trade.

Forex CFDs

Many times, you have heard or come across Forex CFDs and wondered what they might be? Well, here is an explanation for you. Basically, we can make Forex trade in two ways; first, using the CFDs and secondly, we can trade forex through spot Forex (or margin). With spot forex as we have already discussed, we will buy and sell the actual currency. For instance, you may be involved indirectly purchasing dollars for Japanese Yen, and when the value of the dollars increases, you may again exchange the Japanese for dollars thus getting more money back unlike what you initially spent. Contract For Difference (CFDs) as the name suggests, is a contract representing the price movement of financial instruments. In relation to Forex, CFDs simply means that rather than you as a trader to make large amounts of currency purchases and sales, you can take advantage of the profit on price movements even without owning the actual asset.

Glossary

· **Forex exchange.** It is popularly known as forex. It refers to the buying and selling of currencies with the goal of making profits off the changes in their value. Forex can also be the process of changing currencies.

· **Bonds.** It is an instrument of debt that indicates a person's obligation to pay. It allows companies and governments to fund their projects. It is a means of borrowing done by companies and governments, and it also applies to lend too.

· **The monetary unit.** It refers to all transactions that involve currencies. It is also the value of or measure of revenues, income, or non-quantifiable items. It provides an estimate for them.

· **The interbank.** It is one of the commodities that have the second volume of currencies traded in a day. It trades directly with interbank brokers; thus, change in currency is fast. It also uses electronic brokering systems example is Reuters. The bid interbank Fx spread is the amount the traders are willing to buy a currency at while the offer marks the point at which the traders can sell their products.

· **A broker.** It refers to a firm or somewhat an individual who charges a certain fee or rather a commission for executing the buying and the selling process. They play the role of connecting the customer and seller of the product.

· **Fundamental analysis**. Is the analysis of diverse factors that affect the market at ago and not only the chart.

· **Technical analysis**. Is the analysis that involves the use of technical drawing tools like Fibonacci levels, horizontal and trend lines for the identification of classical chart patterns.

· **Relational technical analysis.** It involves a short-term strategy to trade in the forex market. It looks at the former graphs or past trading graphs to help a buyer or seller in the trade. It does not look into economic issues.

· **Volume price analysis.** This is the indicator in learning the general price movement of a specific stock or security. It usually increases every time a buyer or a seller trades in their shares. It shows the strength and weakness of currencies.

· **A pip.** It is the smallest increment or decrement or the last decimal place of a currency quotation. For all currency pairs, a pip is 0.0001 except currency pairs involving the Japanese yen whose pip value is 0.01.

· **Checklist.** It is a list that keeps a forex trader in check and balance. It also acts as a book for rules to follow during the implementation process. It helps to discipline the new trader into the forex trade appropriately.

· **Loss aversion bias.** This is a form of business that is based on prospect theory. It is a distinct way of knowledge loss and gains. This kind of business is done along with contrast the perception of the standard belief they have set.

· **Money management.** It is the regulation that assists you to gain maximum profit, reduce your losses rate, and help your trading businesses to thrive. It may help your business be done or to be broken. It makes discipline which makes a successful trader or entrepreneur. It helps one to learn the ropes of any kind of trade.

Conclusion Part 2

Thank you for making it through to the end of *Options Trading*, let's hope it was informative and able to provide you with all of the tools you need to achieve your goals whatever they may be.

The next step is to begin to implement these tips, ideas, and strategies slowly but with certainty. It will only be a matter of time before you then begin implementing credible strategies for huge rewards. Options trading can be vastly profitable. However, it is sometimes viewed as a double-edged sword because it can sometimes be risky.

The risks only occur when traders do not apply their knowledge or strategies as required. If you come up with a surefire strategy, then you should stick with it to the end. This gives you a much better chance for success so always back-test your strategies and then implement them with confidence.

Finally, if you found this book useful in any way, a review on Amazon is always appreciated!

Day Trading for a living

How to buy the first stocks and earn money with tools and discipline.
Swing trading strategy and how to invest in the stock market by reducing losses through diversification.

Martha Guertin

Day Trading for a living Part 1

Introduction Part 1

Achieving financial freedom is possible than ever! Today, there are millions of opportunities to make, multiple and manage your money. You can literally break out of any financial bondage that you are going through and begin to live the life of your dreams.

Instead of allowing your life to be run by a 9-to-5 lifestyle, you can create a life that supports your dreams. You can literally carve a new way of living that will empower and energize your life. And you can start doing that by learning and understanding the financial market.

There are trillions of dollars being traded through the financial market every day. Money changes hands quickly and people make profits, which are accumulated to transform their lives. Trading experts like George Soros, Paul Tudor Jones, Richard Dennis, and all others have amazed great wealthy by understanding the financial market and you can do so.

Today, there are a lot of tools, resources and tremendous information to enable you to be successful in trading the financial market. It all starts with a burning desire to succeed and commitment to do what it takes to become a champion in trading the financial world. And these things don't require money!

Once you have the desire, commitment and determination to succeed, you can then specialized in trading a market: forex, stocks, exchange-traded funds (EFTs), options, bonds, and much more. You will need to become an expert in trading one market and then move onto the next. Each market requires an understanding of specific strategies, techniques, and tips for success.

You can decide to use any of the following trading styles: scalping, day trading, swing trading, and position trading to master the game. All that you have to do is to understand your craft and choose the suitable trading style that meets your personality, trading plans, and trading goals. You must be in sync with your trading style and trading plan in order to be successful over the long term.

Just like every game, there are rules for success. To be successful in any market, there are rules to follow. And you'll be learning many of these rules that highly successful and seasoned traders use to make consistent profits in the market. Instead of playing to lose, you will be playing to win consistently and building your portfolio.

Mindset is critical for success. If you are going to do well in trading, you will have to develop the mindset for successful traders. In the next few pages, you will get to know what kind of mindset it takes to succeed in any kind of market you choose. You will also know the kind of market you have to choose to become the best of yourself.

Trading is a business. And if you think like a business owner and investor, you're going to do well in the long term. By adopting and practicing the appropriate risk management policies and practices to your trade, you will be making money consistently in a bull and bear market, when you gain an in-depth understanding of the field. This will enable you to reach your financial and profit goals faster than you ever dreamed possible. Enjoy your ready!

Chapter 1: The Basics of Trading & Investing

"Calling someone who trades actively in the market an investor is like calling someone who repeatedly engages in one-night stands a romantic."

> *Warren Buffet*

If you've been thinking about making money in the financial market, the very first question you need to ask yourself is which approach you're going to use. How do intend to make money in the world of the financial market?

Well, there are two main ways to play in the game: trading and investing.

Each has advantages and disadvantages. Each has the ability to enable you to achieve the goal of making more money in the financial market. The key is not to be critical and judgmental but to choose your approach and then focus on being the best at it.

Knowing the difference between trading and investing also helps you to know what you are doing. You have to be familiar when to trade and when to invest. And you must understand the principles, strategies, mindset, and philosophies required to be successful at each end of the game.

What is Investing?

Looking at the high levels of financial problems over the world, many people have developed a strong thirst and hunger for investing. Today, many people have become investors without even knowing what investing means and how to succeed as an investor. To do well at investing, you have to commit to learning regular via books, courses, seminars, videos, blogs, and podcasts.

Investing is simply the process of building wealth systematically by buying financial securities and holding them for a long period of time to accumulate profits. The financial instruments used for investing might include stocks, bonds, mutual funds, and others. The combined value of these financial instruments makes up the investment portfolio of the investor.

An investor is generally, a long term thinker. He is not looking to get in and out of the financial market over a short period of time. He is looking for the best financial instrument that is safe, sound and has the ability to compound his money over a long period of time. Therefore, most investors like reinvesting their profits in order to compound the value of their portfolio over time.

When it comes to investing, one of the most successful investors, include Warren Buffet, Charlie Munger, Benjamin Graham, John Templeton, John C. Bogle, Carl Icahn, Carlos Slim and many more. All these people have become successful investors because they have committed themselves to be the best at playing the game of investing.

What's Trading?

Trading has been the age-old way of making money. Our ancestors make money by buying low and then selling them high in order to realize a profit. They time the market and look at the needs of people to buy the right goods in order to realize a profit from trading activities. By consistently trading wisely over a period of time, they accumulate profit huge amount of profits.

Trading in the financial market is no different. A trader is not thinking about buying financial security and holding it for a long time in order to realize a profit. The trader is thinking about how to make a huge amount of profit by analyzing the market, picking the right financial instruments and trading them wisely to do well in over a period of time. This approach to making a profit in the financial market is known as trading.

Even though trading and investing have a certain amount of speculating in them, traders tend to speculate in the market much more than investors. They have to trade more to make more profits. Therefore, they are constantly on the go, trading more and more to make a profit. The key is to know what your odds before trading. Traders have a belief that the market is always moving, and if they know the direction of the movement, they can make money. The rising and falling of prices in the market are where the trader makes money. The trader analyzes the market and finds the best opportunity to make money by trading with at the right market timing. The trader leverages volatility to make money in the financial market.

The most successful traders in the world include the following: George Soros, Paul Tudor Jones, Richard Dennis, John Paulson, Steven A. Cohen, John key, Jimmy Wales, Ed Seykota and many others. All these people have become financially successful by learning the basics of trading and then mastered the game of trading in the financial markets.

Difference Between Trading & Investing

Once you know what trading and investing means, the second thing you have to look at is how both games are being played. Understanding the difference between the ways each game is played will help you to develop the right mindset to succeed in anyone you have selected for yourself.

1. **Goal:** The goal of investing is to build wealth by buying and holding financial instruments over a long period of time. Traders focus on understanding and the timing of the market to make short term gains through trading activities.

2. **Profit:** An investor makes money by buying, holding and reinvesting profits in order to increase the value of an investment portfolio. A trader makes a profit by buying and selling financial instruments over a short period of time.

3. **Risk:** Both investing and trading involve risk, even though the latter involves a high amount of risk. Investors focus on reducing risks by investing in companies whose stock will do well in the future. Traders reduce risk by trading with money they can afford and also setting up stop-loss orders.

4. **Return:** Investors generally make a return between 10% to 15% annually through dividends from stocks or any financial instrument they own. Traders make between 10% to 15% return monthly by trading financial instruments.

5. **Cost:** Investors have low study when it comes to their selecting and managing their investment portfolio. Traders, however, are always actively trading so have ongoing costs related to brokerage commissions and taxable gains.

6. **Equity Research:** Both trading and investing involves a form of due diligence and research. Investors take a long period of time to study financial statements, financial ratios, industry reports, and all others before making investment decisions. Traders make quick decisions by looking at charts and reading the financial news about the market.

7. **Time:** Generally, investing is suitable for people who want to be passive. They just have to invest in the right place and forget about it for ten or twenty years. Traders, on the other hand, make money in seconds, minutes, days and or months.

After analyzing trading and investing, you want to know which best suits your style and personality. If you're the type that likes a hands-off approach to making a profit from the financial market, you might want to consider investing. If you are the type that likes the hands-on approach to make a profit from the financial market, then you might want to go for trading.

The most important thing is to decide your approach to playing the game of money and then decide on becoming the best at. Fred Trump said, "Know everything you can about what you're doing." After you select your way of playing the game of money, you have to learn everything possible to excel and become successful. The key is always a commitment to learning, growing and developing.

Speculating Vs. Gambling

When it comes to trading, there are two main types of operations. You can either speculate when trading or gamble. The latter is considered unethical, unsocial and diabolic, but many people gamble in the financial market all the time. If you are thinking about being a successful trader, you need to understand the glaring difference between the two.

Investopedia explains the two operations in the following:
"Gambling refers to wagering money in an event that has an uncertain outcome in hopes of winning more money, whereas speculation involves taking a calculated risk in an uncertain outcome. The speculation involves some sort of positive expected return on investment—even though the end result may very well be a loss. While the expected return for gambling is negative for the player—even though some people may get lucky and win."

When you are trading, you can decide to speculate or gamble: but you have to understand the consequences of your actions on your trading capital. When you study the explanation by Investopedia, you would realize that speculation involves some form of research, analysis, and homework, which enables the trader to have a "some sort of positive expected return on the investment."

This does not mean the trading activity cannot lead to a loss. It might! But through the act of research, the trader will be able to reduce the risk of loss regarding the trade.

Measuring Odds

Even though there a certain amount of uncertainty regarding the trader, the speculator is trading with the knowledge of the odds. After doing a thorough analysis and knowing what the odds are, the speculator proceeds into the game. Even though there is a possibility of loss, you know what the odds are and still move forward with the trade.

Risk Assessment

The problem with trading is that most people trade with no idea of the market and whether the odds are against them when they are trading. Because the gambler has no clue what the odds are, he trades with a high amount of risk and usually gets beaten in the market. The gambler takes an uncalculated risk and bears a higher risk while the speculator takes a calculated risk and bears a low risk.

Trading Objective

Ideally, the main aim of speculation is to make short term profits on the price difference arising from the volatility of the market. When you speculative, you're anticipating the implied volatility of financial security and hoping to make profits out of it. On the other hand, gambling focuses on making money by betting on price movements in the marketplace.

Decision Making

In a speculative activity, the trader makes decisions based on insights obtained from the marketplace. Information is gathered, reviewed and analyzed carefully in order to provide light for better trading activities in the financial market. Gambling is a game of chance: building on chance, luck, and blindness. Since people do not study hard, they trade blindly and ignorantly on chance.

Utility

A healthy level of speculation is helpful for the market. It is considered socially acceptable. But gambling seems to involve aggressively looking to make a profit based on the price movement of financial instruments in the market. Gambling destroys, kills and wears down investor confidence while speculation helps to build it. Knowing these frames of thinking is crucial to excelling at trading financial securities.

Once you know the difference between gambling and speculating when trading in the financial market, the next step is to look at which securities are available and how they can be traded. By adopting the right market analysis and strategies, you can become highly successful in your trading activities.

Chapter 2: Different Types of Market

"If investing is entertaining, if you're having fun, you're probably not making any money. Good investing is boring."
George Soros

After you decide that you want to make profits by trading or investing, the next thing you have to become good at is understanding the financial market and learning how it operates. If you are going to do well, you have to decide to become a professional trader or investor.

Most people save their hard-earned money and then they stick it in their bank account. Then, they look for companies and individuals to trade or invest it for them. While there is nothing wrong with that way of thinking, you are entrusting your money into the hands of someone based on his or her knowledge of the market.

Wouldn't be very good if you start learning about the financial market and gaining understanding about how many are made in the market? Even if you still get professional money managers to still manage your money, you'll be in a better position to track and manage your portfolio wisely to avoid any kind of financial surprises that may happen.

Therefore, your secret to success will first deal with understanding the financial market, the securities that are being traded and how to get ahead in the market.

What's the Financial Market?

The financial market is the marketplace where financial securities such as stocks, bonds, derivatives, and all others are traded. In each financial market, there are various parties: the selling parties, the buying parties, brokers, money managers, regulators (the stock exchange commission).

There is a small financial market and there are big ones. The New York Stock Exchange (NYSE), American Stock Exchange and NASDAQ are among the largest financial market in the world. Typically, every country has its own financial market where citizens and foreign investors can invest in organizations in the country.

In the financial market, people are buying money and others are selling money. Typically, investors are looking to generate returns by buying securities in the financial market. Organizations, in turn, uses those payments as a form of leverage to promote business growth. Therefore, the financial market serves a link between traders, investors, and entities.

Types of Financial Market
The following are the various segments that make up the financial market.

- The Stock Market
- The Bond market
- The Money Market
- The Forex Market
- The Options market

The Stock Market

A share of stock is, first of all, a claim on the part ownership of an underlying company. It gives the shareholders to the right to lay a claim on the earnings, dividends and the gains of a company. Both individuals and institutions can buy shares in all publicly traded companies listed on the stock exchange commission.

Types of Shares

Basically, there are two types of shares: common shares and preference shares. Common shares enable shareholders to have voting rights and exercise their opinion about the election of directors, auditors or any other thing during the annual general meeting (AGM). Shareholders with preference shares do not usually exercise voting rights, but they have the right to receive dividends and asset locations when the underlying company has been sold.

Shares are a form of equity financing, used to raise money from the general public into a publicly-traded company. When investors buy shares, they own a percentage stake of the underlying company.

The Pricing of Shares

The pricing of shares in the stock market is regulated by the supply and demand forces of the market (buying/selling). For instances, when the buyer of sellers of an underlying stock outnumber those buying, the price of shares is likely to go high.

On the other hand, when the number of sellers outnumbers the number of those buying, the price of shares is likely to go down. Nonetheless, there are regulatory bodies, which ensure fairness in the pricing of various stocks. Apart from the supply and demand forces of the market, financial reports and company growths also contribute to the price of shares in the stock market.

Unlike investors who like to buy and hold stocks for a long period of time, traders prefer to make short term profits in the stock market by trading on the difference in the market. In the market, there is a bid price and an offer price. The bid price is what the buyers are proposing to sell the shares of stocks, while the offer price is what sellers are willing to sell the shares. The distinction between the bid price and the offer price creates a spread. For a trade to take place, either the bid price or offer price will be accepted by the parties.

Types of Stock Market

There are two main types of stock markets: the primary stock market and the secondary market. The variation between these two financial markets is actually determined by the size of the underlying companies doing their listing on them. The main role of In addition to this, the regulation and fees involved in the listing also determine which companies use in their listing.

The Primary Stock Market: The primary stock market is where many companies get listed when they release their initial public offering (IPO). The primary stock market is preferred by small and medium-sized companies looking to leverage equity financing to raise capital to expand and grow their company.

By listing and selling shares of the company to the general public, the initial shareholders cash in on their initial stake in the company. There are various stock exchange markets in countries providing a listing of various stocks.

The Secondary Stock Market: This is the large the stock market where trillions of shares are sold on a daily basis. Most often, the companies that are listed on the stock market do not trade their own shares in the market. The shares of stock that are being traded on the secondary stock exchange is simply common shares of other shareholders in the underlying company.

The secondary stock market has a high amount of exposure and access to large institutional investors and this is why many companies aspire to have their companies listed there. Some of the secondary stock markets include the following the NASDAQ, the New York Stock Exchange, and the American Stock Exchange.

The Bond Market

The bond market is where long term debt securities or financial instruments are traded by the general public. The bond market involves the bond issuer, the entity engaged in the buying of the debt security and the bondholder, the entity engaged in the selling of debt security. Bonds are basically are a type of loans.

The Dynamics of Bonds

When you buy a bond, you're agreeing to loan your money to the issuer with the promise of receiving a fixed income interest rate at regular intervals prior to or at maturity. A bond has a coupon, which is known as the interest rate required to be by paid to the issuer for the underlying debt security.

The interest rate is paid either annually, or biannually. The maturity is the expiration date for which the associated bond is expected to yield the stated returns for the bondholder.

Difference between Bonds & Stocks

Stocks are a type of equity financing vehicles where investors share in the profit and loss of the project or company in which the funds are being invested. On the other hand, bonds are credit financing vehicles where the creditors do not share in the profit and loss of the project or the company in which the funds are being invested. They are simply entitled to their principal and the associated interest at maturity.

Difference between Bonds & Money Markets

While the money market is also built on credit financing, it is different from the bond market since debt securities are held for a short term period. Typically, money market trade debt securities for at least one calendar year. However, bonds can be held for even up to fifty years. Based on the time of the bonds, there are short-term bonds (it takes one to five years), middle-term bonds (it takes five years to twelve years) and long-term bonds (it takes twelve years to even fifty years).

Types of Bonds

According to the SIFMA, the total global bond market is estimated to be over $100 trillion. While stocks and bonds are securities, the main difference is the type of claim that the investors have. There are various types of bonds that are traded in the bond market: government bonds, municipal bonds, corporate bonds.

Government bonds are the type of bonds issued by the federal or central government of a country in order to raise money from individuals, investors, banks, and institutions to finance projects. Due to the state backing associated with government bonds, they are considered to be risk-free. Yet, there is no risk in trading any kind of security. You still have to look at the tide before buying bonds.

Municipal Bonds: These are debt instruments that are issued by states, municipalities or cities in order to raise funds to finance community projects. These bonds are issued in anticipation of tax revenue with the aim of facilitating projects before funds have been mobilized for the associated projects. Municipal bonds are always empowered by the govt so they also carry less risk.

Corporate Bonds: These are bonds issued by banks, finance companies and organizations with the goal of raising funds to finance corporate projects. Normally, corporate bonds carry higher interest rates than the usual government and municipal bonds, but they also come with some amount of risk as compared to the latter.

All the various types of bonds are usually traded on a wide decentralized market, facilitated by brokers. However, many corporate bonds are still sold via the exchange market. In the US, about 90% of the bond market is heled by pension funds, mutual funds, and other institutions while only 10% are held by individual investors.

The Money Market

The money market is where short term debt securities such as loans are traded. The period of time for this type of loan is at least one year. Investors who are looking to make short term interest on their funds trade assets in the money market. The main participants of the money market are government bodies, merchant banks, financial institutions, money market funds, and others.

The money market has become very popular and a significant of most economies because of its ability to boost liquidity for individuals, corporations, and governments. All borrowing and lending of debt instruments in the money market are done over the counter, with a few done on a wholesale.

The following are some of the money market instruments traded:

- Treasury Bills
- Repurchase Agreements
- Certificate of Deposit
- Commercial Paper
- Municipal Notes
- Eurodollar Deposits
- Federal Funds
- Asset-Backed Securities
- Mortgage-Backed Securities

The Forex Market

The Forex Market, also known as the foreign exchange is the most liquid and largest financial market in the world. On a daily basis, there is an average volume of over $ 5 trillion transactions traded globally through the forex market. While the market is wide and huge, it is largely decentralized and operated over the counter with banks/financial institutions being the main players.

The forex market generally involves the trading of currency pairs between parties: an exchange of foreign currencies using global exchange rates for the transaction. That is, paying for one current with another one. The main reason for the foreign exchange is due to international trade, investment, and transmission of debt instruments between countries.

The foreign exchange market is traded 24 hours during business working days (except weekends) and it is not geographically bound. While profit margins in the exchange are little as compared to another financial instrument, the high volume of trade generates an enormous amount of profit over time. Mostly, currency conversion and trading are carried out by banks and financial institutions.

The Options Market

A derivative is a financial instrument whose value is derived from an underlying financial security. For example, the juice is a derivative of an orange. That means the value of the orange affects the juice obtained from the orange. In the derivative market, traders and investors get the chance to trade the derivatives of other financial securities, rather than doing so directly.

In a general sense, the derive market is where options trading takes place. Options are generally derivatives of all groups and classes of financial securities. The options market is divided into two main classes: exchange-traded options and over the counter options.

Exchange-Traded Options: This is why standard option contracts are traded. They are regulated and monitored through a well-structured exchange commission with enforcement and regulations of the underlying contracts assured by the Options Clearing Corporation. The following are examples of standard traded options: stock options, index options, bond options, and futures options.

Over the Counter (OTC) Options: These refer to the type of option traded between individuals with no regulation from any external bodies. The private entities or individuals involved in this type of contract can decide to customize their contract to meet the demands of what they have both agreed upon. The following are examples of OTC options: currency rate options, interest rate options, and swaps.

Chapter 3: Which Market is Best for You?

The efficiency, credibility, and liquidity of the financial markets have been foundational to the largest economy in the world.
Dan Gilbert

To be successful as a trader in the financial market, you have to focus on an asset class that you're competent in. This will enable you to make more intelligent trades and become better in your quest to build more profits. But then, how do you know which market is suitable for you?

You know, many people ask, "Should I invest in the small-cap market or the big-cap stock market." Some dear folks will also say, "I have some amount of money in my trading account, what do you recommend me to invest/trade? The stock market or the money market which do you want me to enter first?"

While these questions are all reasonable and make sense, one thing you have to know is that trading and investment is more about the person rather than the market. Just because someone is making a lot of money trading in options does not mean you should also jump into the options market. There are a lot of factors that influence success.

There are traders who even copy the style and trading routine of the successful ones, but they still fall short of the profit levels that they wanted. It is very important that you understand that being successful as an investors/trader requires you to have "a circle of competence," as Warren Buffet would say and also a trading mindset that causes you to excel in that regard.

Analyzing Yourself

It all starts with analyzing yourself. That's where you get to choose the right market that is essential for your success. The key to trading success is not to waver from one place to another looking for one single trade that you can place your trade and hit the jackpot. You have to; first of all, conduct a thorough personal analysis and assessment of yourself.

"Know thyself," as they say is the first thing you have to do when you are looking to determine the kind of market you want to trade and make your money from. When you have a clear understanding of your trading goals, plans, objectives, personality, and approach, you will be able to choose the market and trades that will help you get there.

To put it in another way, we will say that you need to, first of all, have a trading plan. Based on your trading plan, you will know what kind of trade you can place that will enable you to achieve the profitability goals that you have set for yourself. This requires you to conduct a thorough analysis of yourself and then ensure that your goals are in line with the assessment.

Developing Your Trading Plan

If you want to build a tower, you'll need to have a building plan. If the pilot wants to fly a plane, he/she needs a plan. The plan serves as the roadmap to be able to get to the right destination. That also means that without the right trading plan, it will be challenging and difficult to get to the right destination. You will find yourself falling back and not reaching your desired profits.

There are a lot of traders who do not think that it's important to have a trading plan. They say things like this: "I don't have a trading plan, but I seem to do well in the market. I think I'm kind of just lucky." While luck is important to be successful in the market, just having mere luck will not make you super successful. If you are already doing well without a written down trading plan, know that you still have a trading plan.

There is a subconscious trading process that you follow to trade. What you need to is sit down with yourself, analyze everything, evaluate all your wins and losses and then find the process you followed before the majority of the wins were made. Also, find the process you followed before the losses were made. You can then filter them out and develop a system of trading that will make you generate a consistent profit.

Having a trading plan is very important. It does not only help you engage in disciplined trading, but it also enables you to produce consistent results over time. When you follow your trading plan, you will make fewer mistakes and make better choices, which will lead to higher profits in your trading account. It also prevents you from just playing by chance and hope.

A trading plan is your personal blueprint to make all trading decisions and a guide to achieve all your goals and ambitions. Your goals might be different from another trader. Your personality and traits might also be different from another trader. And this is the very reason why you have to make sure you create a unique trading plan that will suit your goal and personality.

The following entails what should make up your trading plan:

1. Your trading motivation
2. Your trading goals
3. Your trading skill assessment
4. Your trading time
5. Your trading risk tolerance
6. Your trading capital
7. Your trading routine

8. Your trading strategies
9. Your trading market
10. Your trading record-keeping system

Your Trading Motivation

Success coach, Brain Tracy said, "Motivation requires motive." If you don't have a strong reason for trading, you'll give up after the first few losses. If your reason for trading is not strong enough to make you keep going even in the ought to times, you will be more likely to fall off when things are not going on your favor. This is why you need to figure out the purpose of trading in the market.

Why do you want to be a trader? And why do you aspire to make a certain amount of profit that you're craving? You have to analyze and find your true motivations for trading. Ideally, your motivation should be to "excel in trading the financial market (or a type of market)." When your motive for trading is to become excellent or best at trading, you will keep moving forward even when people are falling off.

Your Trading Goals

Your trading goal is the roadmap for your success. To be successful at trading, you must have clear, written and specific goals. Your trading goals must be clear-cut, determinable, feasible, practical and time-bound (SMART). If you are fuzzy about your trading goals, you'll not achieve them.

You have to be clear about them and write them down. For example, your goals can be: "I grow my trading portfolio by 20% in the next 12 months." Set your trading goals based on what you hope to achieve in the future. You should develop your trading goals after you have done a deep analysis and assessment of your personality and trading style.

Your Skill Assessment

What is the level of your skill in trading: beginner, middle player or seasoned? To achieve your trading goals, one of the areas you have to work on is your trading skills. Rich dad said, "Skills make you rich, not theories." When you do not have the right skill set to enter the game and win, you are not going to make it.

Constant working and developing your trading skill is what will make you confident and be successful in trading in the market. The pros know the level of their skill and what amount of risk they can bear with every trade they make; this enables them to be confident and focused on their trading.

Your Trading Time

How much time do you have to commit to your trading? In order words, what is your time commitment for success? What part of your day do you want to dedicate to trading in the market? If you are already employed then, you might want to consider using early morning and evening for your trading activities.

Decide on how many hours or minutes you would like to commit to your trading in order to be successful. Also, how do you plan to use your time so that you will be productive over time? Your time commitment will also determine which type of trader you will become: day trading, swing trading, position trading, and scalping.

Your Trading Risk Tolerance

What is the level of your risk tolerance? In an individual trade, how much risk would you like to take? What amount of your trading capital do you want to engage or apportioned for trading and investments? Knowing your trading risk limit will help you to avoid losing all your money in the trade.

Many people have forgotten to set their risk limit and mistakenly lost their entire money in the trade. Use stop-loss orders to manage and cut your losses. Develop a risk/reward ratio that meets the needs of your trading. For example, let us say that your risk/reward ratio is 1: 4. Well, that means that for every $200.00 invested in a trade, you are looking to potentially gain $ 800.00. For beginners, it is better to set a lower risk level.

Your Trading Capital

In the game of trading, there is a high level of risk. You need to understand the risks of trading before apportioning your money to it. To ensure that you mitigate the risk and maximize your money, analyze your risk level first. Then, proceed to fund your trading account with the amount of money you can afford to risk in the game.

If you are not sure of your trading skills and analysis, you can start trading with a demo account. This will help you build your confidence and risk tolerance level before starting to trade. You should only exchange with money that you can allow losing in the market. Do not use leverage for trading if you are ill skilled about the market.

Your Trading Routine

Your trading routine involves the step by step process you will be following to prepare, place a trade and evaluate your position. This trading routine needs to be based on your personality, time commitment, and trading goals. This will enable you to do well in trading. To be a successful trader, you have to be organized physically, emotionally and psychologically.

You might want to start every trade through some form of mental preparation or imagination. And then, you proceed with doing your homework through fundamental and technical analysis of the market. The next step will be placing the individual trade and finally evaluating your outcome.

Your Trading Strategy

What are your entry and exit strategies? Trading is a game of timing. To be successful, you have to know which time to enter the market and which time to get out of the market. If you don't know this, you'll find yourself making a lot of mistakes in your trading activities. The buy signals indicated the time to enter the market and spread your net for a profit.

Your exit strategy is even much more important. When it comes to your exit strategy, two things come into play: loss target and profit target. What level of loss would like to entertain when the market goes against you? At what level do you want to place a stop-loss order? You need to also avoid being greedy: what profit target will you want to achieve so that you can get out of one market and move on to the next?

Your Trading Market

Which market are you likely to be very successful and profitable at? What is your area of competence? Instead of juggling various financial market, it is best to focus on one or two markets and become the best at it. What is your level of expertise regarding the various financial markets? Where would you be most likely to be very successful?

Knowing which market to trade also boils down to understanding the volatility of the market, the dynamics of the supply/demand, trading time of the market, the price movement of the market, possible profit margin per unit trade and many others. Remember that a stock trading plan will obviously be different from a forex trading plan. Your market determines your trading plan.

Your Trading Record Keeping System

There are a lot of traders who ask whether it is important to record your trading activities or not. Well, you have to look at your trading as a business. Just like any business, you need to keep your financial, operation and marketing records to be successful. Just like Peter Drucker said, "If you don't measure it, you can't manage it."

To manage your trading business effectively, you have to keep clear and clean records of your trading activities. This will enable you to make regular review and analysis so that you can make corrections about your trading system. By keeping records, you can see trends and correct them before they become something big and huge.

The Right Mindset for Successful Trading

Once you have your trading plan in place, the next area of focus must be your trading mindset. When you look at trading from the surface level, what you might want to see are the strategies, the smartness, and the market analysis. While these things are very important for a successful trade, you need to understand the underlying factor for successful trading is a winning trading mindset.

If you do not think, behave and act like a winner, you will never become one. If you do not think, behave and act like a successful trader, you will never become one. Success in trading starts from within, the mind. Reports have shown that only 10% of traders become very profitable and successful in their trading activities. What is the most underlying factor of their success?

In an article published by Corporate Finance Institute, it says, "*Being a trader is not just about formulating better strategies and performing more extensive analysis, but is also about developing a winning mindset. According to many studies of traders, what separates a winning trader from a losing one: It is not that winning traders formulate better trading strategies; it is not that winning traders are smarter; it is not that winning traders do a better market analysis? What separates a winning trader from a losing trader is their psychological mindset.*"

Your mindset is thus, the foundation for your trading activities. If you have the right mindset, success will gravitate towards you much more quickly than you ever thought. But, if you have the wrong mindset, then the right strategies and analysis might not help that much. You'll still be making the wrong trading decisions due to wrong subconscious programming.

Successful trader, trainer, and investor, Nail Fuller said, "You do not first become a successful trader and then become a successful or happy person. In fact, you must first be a successful person, even if you're mostly faking it, in order to become a successful trader. You must first be able to follow-through with mindset shifts, proper belief systems about trading, different and better habits, goals and plans on how to achieve them before you will be able to attain consistent trading success."

The 7 Mindset of Successful Traders

The following entails the seven mindsets that all successful traders have. To be successful, you need to make sure you work on yourself and think in the same manner. When you have the right mindset in place, you will be very successful when you start leveraging your trading plan, strategies, and routine for trading.

1. Self Confidence

This is the first key that unlocks the door of trading success. If you don't believe in yourself that you can become a highly successful trader, nobody will. If you doubt your ability to make it in the market, that will become your own self-fulfilling prophecy.

First of all, you need to believe that you can make it, only then can you be successful in the long term. Always see yourself as a successful trader and regard yourself in that way, even if you seem to be failing. Your belief in yourself and trading ability is the catalyst for your success.

2. Emotionally Disciplined

This is crucial for success. You need to get a handle on your emotions. If you can't get your emotions under check, you're not going to go far with your trading. When it comes to trading, many people simply over trade or they are afraid to trade. You have to learn to manage your emotions of greed and fear.

If you do not you will end up making costly mistakes. You have to learn to control your emotions and not allow your emotions to control you. A key characteristic of highly successful traders is their ability to ability to discipline their emotions when it comes to trading. They stick to their trading plan and focus on doing the right things that will enable them to be successful in the long term.

3. Optimistic Mindset

Entrepreneur and investor, Gary Vee said, "The biggest obstacle to success is lack of optimism." Most people see problems, obstacles, mistakes, and losses as a problem. And that is the problem. Instead of seeing their loss or mistakes as a learning experience, they get bitter and beat themselves. You need to rewire your thinking.

See problems as a learning experience. We make mistakes my learning. When you make mistakes in trading, do not develop negative self-pity, learn from that mistake and be determined not to repeat it again. Look out for the best in every negative occurrence. When if the market is falling and prices are coming low, find ways to make money, even in a down market.

4. Get Comfortable with Risks

If you're the type that is afraid of making mistakes, then the best thing you have to do is stick your money in your bank account. Trading involves uncertainty and risk. Even after you have done a thorough analysis and evaluation of your market, you still cannot predict the market with 100% assurance.

The key is to trade, knowing that the odds are working in your favor. So, what are the odds? Do an objective analysis of the market. Be comfortable with taking risks. Know that trading is a little different from investing. Investing your money is a certificate of deposit and collecting your interest is different from trading. You have to analyze and take a well-calculated risk.

5. Commitment to winning

If you're not committed to becoming a successful trader, then you're not going to make it. You have to commit to winning before you can do what it takes to make you win. Commitment requires hard work, focus, and patience over a long period of time. You have to decide what you are going to do whatever successful do to become a success in trading.

That means taking time to do the right analysis before trading. Successful traders do not gamble at the game. They are not reckless, careless gamblers who are just betting against the odds. They prepare for each trade and evaluate the trade. They take courses, read books, attend seminars, consult with experts and pay the price to get to where they aspire to be.

6. Discipline

Discipline is closely related to commitment. Becoming a successful trader requires hard to things well. It means doing those things you don't feel like doing. And what are some of those things? Reading stock markets, analyzing markets, reading the financial news, reviewing deals, performing mathematical calculations about the market.

You see, it is easier to spend time going through your Facebook newsfeed than to take a book about day trading and just read. It is easier to open your computer and then just start trading, rather than spending hours to study the market, develop a trading plan and follow a trading routine to place a trade. Doing hard things require discipline. And that is what separates those who do well from who fail.

7. Consistent Good Behavior

You need to have good behavior towards the market and your trading. Consistent good behavior will lead to a consistent profit over a period of time. When you consistently make a good trade, you'll be profitable in the long run. You cannot just stop doing the right things just because you have the profit target you have set for the year. You need to ensure you stick your plan, strategy and trading plan even though you have become successful.

And there is no need to change the game plan, once it's working. Develop the addiction to doing the things will make you successful. When you have positive addictions, they will combine together as a force that will enable you to become successful in life. You have to avoid the temptation of going to your old lifestyle just because you have done well.

Market Volatility

All the financial market have a certain amount of volatility. The amount of volatility in the market helps to fathom the approximate amount of profit that can be made over a period of time. To be a successful trader, you need to understand the importance of volatility.

The Economic Times defines market volatility: "It is a rate at which the price of a security increases or decreases for a given set of returns. Volatility is measured by calculating the standard deviation of the annualized returns over a given period of time. It shows the range to which the price of a security may increase or decrease". To trade in a financial market, you need to analyze the amount of volatility in the market.

Financial security with a highly volatile market means that there is a rapid change in its related prices over a period of time. When the price of security takes a long time to change, it will indicate that the market is sedated or has low volatility. When it comes to stocks, there are highly volatile stocks and stable stocks. Those with highly volatile stocks poses the right condition to trade and make a profit.

Profits are made based on the volatility of the market. For example, when the price of a stock was at $ 30 per share. Then it moves to about $ 45 per share in a two-month period, and you hopefully bought the stock, you will make a profit of $ 10. You made this profit because of the market volatility. If the market were to be stable or neutral to volatility, you will probably make no profit. This is why volatility is essential for trading.

Types of Volatility

Before you place a trade, you have to analyze the volatile. In a market like options, volatility is very important to make profits and cash in on options. You have to understand the two types of volatility and then learn how to recognize them regularly while placing trades: historical volatility and implied volatility.

Dan Passarelli admonished, "Failing to analyze components like implied volatility and historical volatility before placing an options trade is a mistake that commonly results in losses that could have been easily avoided." The fastest way to make losing trades is to avoid looking at these two volatilities.

Historical stock is straightforward. It measures the past prices of financial security by itself or another security over a period of time. You can be able to analyze the historic volatility of an asset by looking at the price chart. The more price changes the financial security experiences, the more volatile it is. For example, a stock with 20 price fluctuations will be considered highly volatile than a stock with 15 price fluctuations.

Then comes the implied volatility which is the "*volatility experienced by the underlying stock, stated in terms of annualized standard deviation as a percentage of the stock price'"* (Money Shaw). While historical volatility is based on the past, the implied volatility is based on the future. The historical volatility is highly objective while the implied volatility is highly subjective.

The first is based on the facts while the other is based on opinions of how the market will look like in the future. Traders and investors look at the historical volatility and then base on careful analysis of the underlying financial instrument, they make future market predictions on the volatility of the market. Before you place your trade, ask yourself what your implied volatility of the market is.

Bearish & Bullish Market

In the world of trading, some of the terms that you will hear over and over again are "bull" and bear market. If you do not understand what these two terms mean, you will simply not be effective in any kind of market that you might be participating in. No matter the amount of money you have in your brokerage account, you will have to constantly understand the status of the market.

Bull and bear market is the technical language used to refer to two main things: how the market is doing at the moment and how investors feel the market will most likely do in the near future. Generally, markets are either moving upward, downward or stable. The prices of financial instruments in the market are either appreciating, deprecating or neutral.

A bull market is experienced when the prices of financial instruments are rising up in value steadily for a period of time. For example, the prices of stocks in the market seem to be going onward and upward in value; the earnings of companies grow and there is a high level of employment with a high standard of living of people.

When these things are happening, investors believe that the market and the economy will keep moving upward for a long time. Due to this belief, investors begin to spend money in buying financial securities, hoping that an upward trend in price will lead to profits in the short term. Demand exceeds supply, which causes the value of financial securities to increase again.

Conversely, a bear market is experienced when the prices of financial instruments are going down in value steadily for a period of time. For instance, the price of stocks begins to see a sustained decrease in value, reduction in the earnings of companies and high level of unemployment. These seem to slow down the economy and investors begin to feel that this trend will remain for some time.

When these indicators begin to show, investors feel "bear" about the market and they begin to get fearful. When they are fearful, they sit on cash and withdraw their money from the market because the value of financial instrument reduces begin to lose their value rapidly.

During these times, many people hardly trade or invest at all. They tend to watch and wait for the market to return to the normal trend. In the bear market, supply exceeds the demand and the price of financial securities becomes relatively cheap. Buying activity slows down and this causes many financial assets to drop to the low levels. To have a clearer view of a bear and bull market, you need to understand and conduct market analysis through fundamental and technical analysis. This will guide you to make better trading decisions.

Chapter 4: Market Analysis & Evaluation

"Without data, you're just another person with an opinion."
W. Edwards Deming

The keys to consistent profit in trading is making good trades. When you make good trades over a period of time, you'll achieve consistent profits and your trading portfolio will skyrocket. But when you keep making bad trades, you'll just keep making loses. The key then is to develop a trading plan that enables you to make good trades consistently.

As part of your system to ensure that you make good trades, one of the essential things is preparation. Just as someone, ones said, "Success is when preparation meets opportunity," when you prepare yourself and do your homework, you will be positioned to make good trades. That means doing your homework is a prerequisite for making good trades.

If you do not do your homework, your chances for making bad trades will be very high. Typically, a bad trade is when you based your trading decisions on luck and gambling. But you see, you can't experience consistent success in the marketplace when you're operating by luck. In fact, luck can enable you to make a win at once, but you will not be able to sustain it.

Instead of glorying on your luck, the best thing to do is to evaluate how those "lucky wins and gains" were made, and then develop a trading routine and system that will be designed to enable you to make good trades on a consistent basis. And you see, not all good trades might generate profit at once, but you'll realize that you'll be getting better results and returns via your trading.

Overview of Technical & Fundamental Analysis

While there are a lot of things that constituent the homework t required to be done for attaining consistent success, one of the essential things that need to precede every trade is market analysis and evaluation. When it comes to analyzing and evaluating security before making a trade, there are two ways of doing that: technical and fundamental analysis.

The goal of the trader is to make good prediction and forecasting about the market, based on an objective analysis of the market. Based on those forecasts and prediction, trading decisions will be made for which profits will be attained, depending on how right the predictions. Technical and fundamental analysis help traders to invest wisely by getting a good overview of the market and making good trades.

Therefore, to be a successful trader, it is very important that you learn and master these two methods of analyzing the market. While the two methods have conflicting approaches, you will be better off having a fair knowledge about how to use both of them to make better forecasts, make good trades and good profits on a consistent basis. Your commitment to analyzing and evaluating the market before trading will be the key to your trading success.

Understanding Fundamental Analysis

Investopedia defines fundamental analysis as the "method of measuring a security's intrinsic value by examining related economic and financial factors. Fundamental analysts study anything that can affect the security's value, from macroeconomic factors such as the state of the economy and industry conditions to microeconomic factors like the effectiveness of the company's management."

For example, the intrinsic value of a stock helps to know whether the stock is worth investing in the first place. A stock with a good intrinsic value means that the underlying company is well run and the economic conditions are moving in its favor. However, when the stock does not have a good intrinsic value, investors do not even want to proceed further.

After measuring the intrinsic value of the stock, investors want to know whether it is undervalued or overvalued by the stock market. To do that analysis, compare the intrinsic value against the current share price of the stock. Usually, when the fundamental analysis proves that the intrinsic value is less than the current share price, then the investors will buy it.

This analysis ensures that financial securities are bought at fair market prices. For investors who are looking to hold the stock for a long period of time, their long-term success will largely be determined by their ability of the underlying company to do very well financially in the future. Therefore, investors also want to look at the future growth prospects of the company before investing.

A good intrinsic value, an undervalued share price and a good prospect for future growth indicates that the company is strong. Investors also want to look at price per earnings and dividend ratio and dividend payment history of the company. When all these factors are good, a buy signal and entry signal is indicated, prompting investors to buy the underlying stock and hold it until they realized their projected earnings from the stock.

However, when the company is weak: falling intrinsic value, falling share price and no good prospect for future growth, investors will go short on the stock. They will sell the underlying stock because either value will reduce drastically over a period of time. Some investors might use put options to hedge their stock to avoid being plunged by the downward movement in the price of the stock.

If an investor is buying a bond or any money market financial instrument, fundamental analysis can be performed by looking at key indicators such as interest rates, GDP growth of the economy as well as other related financial instruments. This will help the investor to know whether the bond has been fairly valued or overvalued.

Types of Fundamental Analysis

When you want to perform fundamental analysis of a company, there are two main approaches to use: qualitative approach and the quantitative approach. The assumption here is that you can't just value a company based on its inherent intrinsic value or figures on its financial statement. There are other factors to consider as well.

The Quantitive Approach to Fundamental Analysis

The quantitative approach to fundamental analysis is the main way of valuing a stock. What you want to do is to examine the financial performance of the underlying company by looking at the audited financial statements of the company.

The financial statements, which are made up of the income statement, balance sheet and statement of cash flows will be used in addition with financial ratios to evaluate the underlying company. Thus, to analyze and evaluate the stock, it is incumbent on the investor to develop the ability to read and understand financial statements.

Balance Sheet: This indicates the assets, liabilities and shareholder's equity of the underlying company at a particular point in time. The assets are the resources controlled or owned by the company. The liabilities are debts incurred by the company to run its daily operations while equity reveals money contributed by the shareholders. There is also retained earnings, making up the accumulated profit over the years.

Income Statement: This reveals the revenue, expenses, and profit made by the company within a specified period. It tells the company's performance during a particular point in time. The income statement is produced on a quarterly and annual basis.

Statement of Cash Flows: This is a helps to know the liquidity of a company. It enables investors to know how cash is flowing or being used by the company to achieve their stated objectives and to produce a return on investor's equity. It unveils the cash flow from investing, financing and operating activities. Finally, it shows the current cash of the company at the bank.

Qualitative Approach to Fundamental Analysis

When you're talking about the qualitative approach to fundamental analysis, you're looking at a way of measuring the performance of the company without looking at the numerical values. The concept of the qualitative approach is based on the fact that there are some intrinsic features of a company, which cannot be seen on paper, but greatly impacts the company's growth.

These factors are said to be what gives rise to the financial statements of the company. That is to say, that the qualitative fundamentals are what enables the company to produce wonderful results in the financial results over a period of time. Some of those qualitative measures include the following:

1. *The business model*: This is how the business generates money from operating activities.
2. *The brand*: This is the competitive advantage of the company that drives sales and revenue.
3. *The management*: This entails the team of leaders (managers and directors) responsible for executing strategic objectives and making it profitable.

4. *The corporate governance*: The policies, standards, and structures that govern the day-to-day running of the company by the management.

5. *The industry*: the market value, market share, competition, business seasons, statutory regulation and industry growth prospects over a period of time.

In fact, the future prospects of a stock can be predicated on the strength of the company's business model, brand, management and corporate governance structures. This is the reason investors still want to make sure that the company they are investing have strong qualitative features as well as strong quantitative figures.

Example of Fundamental Analysis

Let's assume that ABC Company is currently trading at a stock price of $ 150/per share. Instead of gambling and running ahead to buy the stock before a friend said so, you decided to perform intensive fundamental analysis on the company. Upon your analysis, you realized that the intrinsic value of the stock is actually four times lower than the stock price, $ 600.

You were really fascinated about the company and then decided to buy 500 shares of stock. That will be $ 75,000 ($ 150 per share multiplied by 500 shares). Well, you have bought this stock at a discount price with an expectation that the company will do well, in the long run, to ensure that the stock price goes up to $ 600.00.

This is the assumption that fundamental investors usually use when they are looking for stocks to buy. They believe that at the of the day, stock prices will move up to match up with their inherent intrinsic value because their qualitative and economic factors will drive that growth. Even though they do not know how long this will happen, they believe that this will happen in the near future and they will get the future value of their money.

If after five years on the line, the stock price jumps to $600 per share, what will be the value of your holding? It will be $ 300,000.00. In this way, the value of your invested capital has multiplied about over four times the amount invested. Please, take note that this example has been oversimplified for the purpose of explanation.

It is because of this that Warren Buffet, the God Father of Fundamental Investing said, "You don't want to worry about when. If you're right about what, you don't have to worry about when." Warren Buffet believes that the stock price will go up in value to match up with the company's intrinsic value. It was based on this philosophy that billions of Berkshire Investment Portfolio have been built over the decades.

Technical Analysis

Technical analysis is the method of making a profit in the financial market by forecasting the prices and volumes of securities. It's not based on looking at the underlying company and measuring its intrinsic value. Instead of going to look at the fundamental values of a company, a technical analyst will rather leverage the market trading volume and the historic trading prices to forecast the future. Based on the forecast made, the relevant trading decisions will be made in order to yield a profit.

Technical analysis focuses on evaluating the future prices of security by looking at external statistics such as price trends, price movements, trading volume, and many others. By using technical tools along with those technical reports, the future prices of the underlying security can be made to reap a profit in the long term.

Technical analysis can be used for trading all kinds of securities: stocks, bonds, EFTs, options, currencies, and commodities. It can virtually be used in trading any type of financial market or financial instrument. But it requires that practitioners become very effective in the use of it. If you can use technical analysis to make the right forecasts on a consistent basis, you will be on your way to profit.

Due to the complexities surrounding technical analysis, many fund managers are using computer programs that have been designed to indicate buying and selling signals. A buy signal tells you when you should get into the market while a sell signal tells when you should get out of the market so that you can avoid making losses or cutting your losses.

While it is okay to use computer programs, if you do understand them, there are other factors that might impact the computer software that will not be revealed to you. And this the reason why studying and understanding technical analysis is very crucial to your success.

The Assumptions of Technical Analysis

Just like fundamental analysis, there are assumptions that are used when practicing it. These assumptions form the theories and concepts for which technical analysis is being used in forecasting the price of various securities in the financial market. Before you start using technical analysis to make trading decisions, you have to understand the assumptions surrounding it.

The following are the assumptions of technical analysis that you must take note of before practicing it.

1. Market prices are a reflection of fundamental factors

Technical analysts make on their assumption on the fact that the prices of securities on the stock exchange are the reflection of their internal, fundamental factors. The basics for this assumption arrived as a result of a series of writings and theories founded by Charles Dow.

Charles Dow indicated, "Markets are efficient with values representing factors that influence a security's price, but market price movements are not purely random but move in identifiable patterns and trends that tend to repeat over time." Due to this research, analysts believe that stock prices are simply a print of all fundamental factors that affect the underlying security growth.

2. Prices of securities move in trends

Charles Down revealed that the movement of prices of securities are not haphazard and random as most people think, but rather they move in trends. He revealed that there are short term, medium and long term price trends that all financial securities follow.

By analyzing and studying these price trends, traders/investors can be able to make better buying and selling decisions. This is the reason many traders base their trading decisions on the historic trading statistics of an underlying asset.

3. History will often repeat itself in another way

While history repeats itself, it is very important that history will not repeat itself in the same way. This is the reason many technical analysts use a lot of tools to make new trading decisions based on the historic data of underlying securities. By using market moods and emotions and chart patterns, the technical analyst is able to tell how history will repeat itself in the current circumstances.

How to Use Technical Analysis

Usually, technical analysis is practiced by traders who are looking to make short-term gains in the market. Traders make a profit through various or difference between two price points. They want to buy low and sell high so that they can make a profit. When they continue doing the same thing over a period of time, the cumulative result leads to a trading profit in the brokerage account. This is how profits are made through technical analysis.

To make the right trading decision, there is a need to understand when to buy and sell because timing is everything. Technical indicators help to know when to buy and sell in the market. By making the right analysis and indications, you will be mostly to make a consistent profit over a period of time. The following are technical indicators that you have to learn to use:

1. *Trading Volume*

The price movement of a security is influenced by the supply and demand forces of the market. The more people need and want the stock of a particular company, the more the selling shareholders increase the price in order to make a profit from the opportunity risk they will bear when they sell the stock.

On the flip side, when the sellers outweigh sellers, there is a likelihood of prices coming down in order for selling shareholders to make a profit from the sales of stock. The more liquid the market, the better because it indicated the prospect of buyers and sellers in that market.

2. *Price Trend*

Price trend lines are based on past chart patterns of the underlying security. Studying the chart patterns and the historical trend lines will give you insight into the movement of the security: whether it is moving upward or downward. Trend lines show the direction and speed at which price changes with time.

3. *Support & Resistance*

Support and resistance focus on leveraging the price history of securities to tell buy and sell signals. Support levels indicate buying while resistance levels indicate selling the underlying asset to move on with the next trade. The criteria used here is that support is where traders in the past have already trodden or gained profits before.

Resistance levels are the price history levels where the price of the underlying security simply prevented further price advancement in the past. Since history repeats itself, buyers look to sell at resistance when the same determiners show up.

4. Simple Moving Averages

Simple moving averages are used by technical indicators to determine the future price trend of security by calculating the average daily selling price over a period of time. This helps the analyst to know the rate at the price of a particular financial instrument will move. When the figures are plotted on the graph, and short moving average crosses the longer moving average, buy/sell signal is indicated based on the current status of the market.

5. Momentum-Based Indicators

What happens when there are no clear trends in the market? What happens when the market is stable and you can't possibly know what's going to happen next? Momentum based indicators are used in these situations to help identify the price movements of the associated asset. Some of these indicators include Chicken Money Flow, moving average convergence/divergence and Bollinger Bands®.

Difference Between Fundamental and Technical Analysis

Before you start using the contrasting schools of thought for analyzing the financial instruments, you might want to look at the difference between them. This will help you to understand the risks, limitations, advantages, and disadvantages of a particular type of asset.

1. Fundamental analysis focuses on measuring the intrinsic value of an asset while technical analysis focuses on using price trends and volumes to forecast and predict the next big thing that will happen in the market.

2. Fundamental analysis uses income statements, balance sheet and cash flow statements to determine the financial performance of the stock of an underlying company while technical analysis looks toward the charts and patter reports of the financial market.

3. Fundamental analysis focuses on the internal and surrounding operations of the underlying company to make evaluations while technical analysis focuses on the external reports of the security to make an evaluation.

4. Fundamental analysis is founded on the inferring that the value of a stock can be determined by looking at the critical and integral basics of the company while technical analysis is based on the assumption that the price of a stock is simply a print out of all company/industry/economic fundamentals.

5. Fundamental analysis focuses on making long term profits by looking at fundamentals of the underlying asset while technical analysis focuses on short term and medium terms profits by looking at the price and trading volumes.

While it is good to gain skills in either of the market analytical methods, you have to focus on combining the two to make a good trading decision. In this way, each analytical method will serve as a way of complementing the other.

For example, when a company announced new acquisitions, an increase in sales revenue with profit and all other positive growth prospects, it causes a spike in stock prices. This causes prices of stock to go high. In this regard, it is very imported to take into account this fundamental industry new to make better trading decisions.

Similarly, when a subsidiary of a company goes through bankruptcy, lawsuits and terrible negative news, it creates panic in the market and causes the price of the underlying stock to go down. You have to use both technical and fundamental news to make good trading decisions during this time.

The key to successful trading is to do your homework. If you do not do your homework, you will be exposing yourself to many deadly and reckless mistakes that will simply wipe out your trading capital. When you work on yourself and develop your analytics skills, you can be able to make better trading decisions that will enable you to do well in the market.

Chapter 5: Guide to Day Trading

"Professional day traders—those who trade for a living rather than as a hobby— are typically well-established in the field. They usually have in-depth knowledge of the marketplace, too."
Justin Kuepper

The internet is replete with stories of many people who became rich through day trading. There are several fantastic stories of how many traders have bought their dream cars and dream houses through day trading. As a result, a lot of beginner traders associate day trading with profits, riches, and affluence. While it might be true that some people have made it through day trading, you need to understand that becoming successful in day trading is not automatic.

Just like any game, you need to be prepared to learn the skills and the rules of the game before you can be successful. If you don't understand and practice the rules of the game, you'll not be able to achieve your desired result. And that is exactly what happens with day trading. Being a day trader does not guarantee automatic success, you have to learn the art of day trading and master the tricks and hacks of the game.

One of the exciting things happening in recent times is the fact that many people have quit their day time jobs to become a full-time day trader. In fact, many corporate professionals working with top-notch trading houses and financial institutions have just become day traders. This has made day trading almost popular, serving as a job for many people.

Therefore, there are many day trading professionals today, trading for a living as opposed to trading to make some extra money or just as a hobby. You see, when approach day trading with such a serious mindset where you see day trading as a something that requires much attention, dedication, and commitment to win, you will be on your way to winning.

Just imagine a man with a family of three. He has to generate enough money through day trading to fee his family and also have savings set aside. To be able to surmount all this risk through the art of day trading, he must be dedicated to mastering his craft and excelling at the game of day trading. This is when winning becomes a necessity.

Justin Kuepper rightly pointed out that: "Professional day traders—those who trade for a living rather than as a hobby—are typically well-established in the field. They usually have in-depth knowledge of the marketplace, too." when you view day trading as a profession, you focus on gaining all the inside secrets, tips, and strategies required to be successful. That is why many professional traders succeed in the game as compared to hobby traders.

But that doesn't mean you should quit your job. What you need to do first and foremost is to use day trading as a profession with its own rules and games for success. Strive towards becoming excellent and not just making money. Do not focus on the results, focus on the process and you will always get the results? This is essential to surviving and thriving as a day trader.

The Basics of Day Trading

What's day trading anyway? Well, day trading is the act of buying and selling financial security for only one trading day. That means that the holdings of the day trader do no exceed one trading day. For swing traders who like to hold their positions for weeks, day traders buy and sell for within one trading day. By the time the market closes, they evaluate their gains and losses.

While day trading is okay for all the financial market, it requires a high amount of market volatility for it to be worthwhile and fruitful. If you invest in a market that is stable or sedate, you will not be able to realize a profit from the trade because the low volatility of the market will not cause it to make a profit.

For this reason, day trading usually happens with the forex and the stock market. Even with the stock market, some stocks are not being traded because of their historically neutral volatility. Day traders focus on making a profit on short-term moves of a financial instrument. They time the market and use technical analysis to trade. There is also a popular notion of trading based on financial news and market behavior.

Day trading is considered to be high risk because of the relatively short term that is required for the underlying financial instrument to move before profits are made. As a result of this idea, many new traders shy away from day trading. But with a good understanding of how the day trading market works, you'll be able to mitigate the risks and position yourself for a big catch of profit just like many seasoned and professional day traders do.

Since the trading day is limited to only a day, you might not achieve huge profits per single trade unless you trade in a high volume. That means you will be most likely making small profits per trade, but the cumulative amount of these profits for a month or quarter will yield a bigger return if you trade wisely. It is good to be realistic in your goal setting as a day trader so that you do not get disappointed with small margins.

While profits are good, you will have to remember that out of every gain, you make as a day trader, taxes and brokerage fees will be paid. This is one of the reasons you have to choose a broker with a good trading platform that meets your needs and helps to cut down the costs associated with your trading. Consider reviewing several brokers before selecting a broker that can help.

Lastly, you need to make sure you stay away from scam brokers who create deceptive websites and promising you of astronomical gains within a short period of time. You have to understand that day trading success does not happen without putting in the hard work. Avoid chasing the get rich scheme of scam brokers.

Choose the right broker with the tools for you to excel in the game. Above that, you must know that you have to put in the time and the work to be successful. Do not fall for those scam testimonials. Look for experts in day trading and follow them, as opposed to those scam broker firms. It takes time, patient, practice, and dedication to be successful in day trading. Learn from the experts.

Traits of Successful Day Traders

If you're going to be successful as a day trader, you'll have to think like a successful day trader. Always remember that success in day trading starts with the mind and continues with action. At the end of the day, it is what you do that really counts. If you follow and do what successful day traders do, chances are that you will also be successful.

With that said, here are the traits of successful day traders that you must emulate over a period of time to be successful.

1. *Education and Experience*

You need knowledge if you're going to be a successful day trader. Just think about it: How can you see an expert who knows nothing about his field? It's not possible, right? To do well in day trading, you have to become hungry to learn and gain experience. You must study an put what you study into practice so that you can be successful in the game over the long term.

When you are just getting started with day trading, practice due diligence. Learn how to use technical analysis to know how the market is moving before placing the trade. Always focus on how to gain an in-depth knowledge of the market, your trading style, and strategy.

2. Adequate Risk Capital

Risk capital is simply money that you can afford to lose in a game. When you lose your risk capital, you can still put food on your table and shelter over your head. In day trading, there are a lot of things which might happen to make a trade go bad. Therefore, it is always advisable to enter a day trading with money that you can afford to lose, that is your risk capital.

Do not be too overconfident and then use a high amount of leverage to trade. When you do this, you will be exposed to tremendous financial loss. Ensure you are well-capitalized before you commence your day trading because you will need money for everyday trading activities. Also, make room for losses that you might incur in the game.

3. Self Discipline

If you're the type that can't control your emotions, then day trading might not be good for you. To be a successful day trader, you have to learn control and manage your emotions. This is crucial and essential for success because day trading focuses on little price movements to make profits, which might sometimes end up in losses.

Even if you have a winning trading strategy or plan, you still have to discipline yourself to follow it so that you do not allow your emotions to mislead you. A day trader needs to be emotionally balanced and stable before, during and after trading in order to be successful in the long term.

4. Unique Day Trading Plan

You need to have a day trading plan if you're hoping to do well. Luck and planning are keys to success in day trading. But, you need to have the right trading plan and trading mindset that will create that luck. Your trading plan should be focused on how to trade when to trade and what to trade in the market.

Many successful day traders focus on the highly volatile and liquid market because there is a high potential for price movement and changes before the trading day closes. This is crucial for success. If the market is not moving, you will not be able to make a profit in the market.

The general trading plan of many people is to short sell in a down market and then long a financial instrument in an upmarket. To make the right trading decision, you have to create your due diligence strategy. You might want to look for key features such as company news earnings report and market moods prior to trading and know what is going on.

Day Trading Strategies for Success

Arbitrage Trading

This kind of trading strategy focuses on capitalizing on pricing errors in two different markets that are trading the same or similar financial instrument. In this case, a day trader will quickly buy the financial instrument and sell it on another market to make a profit off the price difference in the two financial markets. This profit is made by a quick observation of the market and looking for where pricing inaccuracies exit.

While arbitrage trading is a simple way of making a profit as a day trader, you need to take note these things do not happen all the time. But it is very important to look at the price of a financial instrument from the various trading market in order to find where the pricing error exit and the make a profit from.

Institutional day traders make use of analytical software in their trading activities. This enables them to quickly track and monitor any price imbalance in the market and leverage arbitrage to make a huge amount of profit from the price differences. As an individual trader, you will to stay up to date about the market and use more than market for your trading activities.

Take an example of arbitrage trading: The stock of ABC Company is selling at $11 per share on the London Stock Exchange, but selling at $ 10 on the New York Stock Exchange. You quickly realize a profit from the price imbalance between two stock market.

To profit from the price difference, you decided to buy 100 shares (total cost: ($ 1100) of ABC company on the New York Stock Exchange and then simultaneously sell them on the London York Stock Exchange (total revenue: ($ 1100). In this case, you made $ 100 from the transaction, risk-free in just a few minutes of analyzing and placing the trade.

Range Trading

A range of trading is focused on leveraging price ranges to determine entry and exit points for day trading activities. A price range is formed when an asset fluctuates high and low consistently for a period of time. Instead of grumbling about the consistent movement of prices, seasoned traders try to make a profit by finding support and resistance levels.

When you plot the movement of the underlying security, you will observe two main things: A resistance is created at the top of the range and support is created at the bottom. Seasoned traders look at other technical factors that might impact the volatility and the price of the underlying stock. Factors include trading volume, liquidity and the relative strength index of the support and resistance levels.

The more the underlying security has support and resistance points in the chart, the stronger the trend. On the other way round, the less the price reacts to the support and resistance levels, the weaker the range trading will be. Seasoned day traders make a buying decision at support and then sell at resistance range levels.

For example, a stock is at a lower support level of $ 20 and the upper resistance line, $ 35.00. The trader will like to buy the stock at around $ 15.00 and the reap profits from the range trading. Once the stock rebounds, a stop loss will be placed at $ 14.00 in order to avoid the loss that might occur when the stock breaks from the support level. It is important to combine other technical factors before making a move. Analyze your risk/reward ratio for the trading before you proceed.

News Based Trading

Every day, things happen. Some of these things can affect market psychology. Therefore, seasoned traders tend to study and examine the impact of the things that happen on the market and make trading decisions that will capitalize on those events. This type of trading strategy, which is based on using news related to the stock market to trade, is known as news-based trading.

Supply and demand in the financial market are affected and influenced by the moods/emotions of investors. When bad things (for example, poor earnings and corporate governance) happen, investors become fearful and then begin to sell rather than buy. This reduces the price of financial securities. As a day trader, you can profit from this buy trading with the news reports by initiating selling decisions.

When good things (for example, better earnings and good corporate governance) happen, investors tend to be greedy and then they begin to buy the underlying security. This creases traffic in the market and causes the price to go high. It is very important to buy at the point of good news and the wait to make a profit and then get out of the market.

Insurance stocks tend to go high when certain bad things happen. This should prompt you of a bullish market. For example, when a flood takes place and people are very affected, many people use this medium to buy and use insurance products. This causes the market to experience better economics as compared to other industries.

High-Frequency Trading

Many institutional traders use sophisticated trading software and programs to analyze trade and make a higher profit in the market. Most of these software tools are relatively very expensive and out of reach of the average day trader. So, you might not benefit from using these sophisticated systems for trading.

The tools and programs are used to exploit entry and exit points to make short term profits in the day. The following are some of the trading patterns recognized by the system for day trading decisions are Elliotte wave patterns, flags, and channels.

Should You Day Trade for a Living?

Day trading for a living is very different from just playing in the market because you just want to earn some extra money. If you are thinking and considering building a career as a day trader, you have to look at certain things before making your decision.

1. *Set your living expenses aside*

The beginning of everything is hard and rugged. If you want to become a day trader, you need to avoid the fallacy that you will make a lot of money over a short period of time. Stay objective. As Donald Trump said, "It gets worse before it will get better."
Plan for the hard days by setting aside your living expenses for least six months to a year. Also, you might consider having another stream of income to support the

ups and downs of the day trading. This will avoid having your trading account dried up because of lack of capital.

2. Start Small

If you're getting started with day trading, you have to start small. You can't just put all your trading capital in a few trades because someone told you so. Avoid being egotistical and start very small. Look for stocks or financial instrument that you can easily get started making a profit at before jumping int the big areas. This will help avoid making huge losses at the beginning.

3. Commit Time

Success in day trading can be time-consuming, but you have to commit the time required to be successful in the field. Sometimes, things can be very challenging and boring, but you still have to devote the time required to study the market, analyze and place your trade. By staying focus and trading wisely, you will be successful in your day trading.

Chapter 6: Guide to Swing Trading

"I have two basic rules about winning in trading as well as in life: (1) If you don't bet, you can't win. (2) If you lose all your chips, you can't bet"
Larry Hite

As the market grows and expand, many traders have come to realize diverse ways of trading that meet their needs and enables them to achieve their goals and dreams. Many individual traders in the market have come to like and enjoy swing trading, due to the flexibility it offers. Instead of having to worry about holding security within a few minutes or hours, you can hold it overnight and wait for a swing to fly.

Recently, swing trading has become very popular. It has been embraced by professional and beginner traders who are looking to bet on price changes to generate profit from the market. For many professionals, the joy of not having to be looking at their computer screens every minute of the day makes them enjoy swing trading.

When you are using swing trading, you will be trading in the market for just a short or medium term, from a day to several weeks. Most traders spend quality time studying the market and analyze trends when they are not trading. They keep on evaluating and analyzing the direction and price movement, place a trade and then wait for the price swing to catch the profit.

While swing trading might sound logical and easy on paper, you must know and understand that your success in swing trading will be determined by a myriad of factors that I had talked about here. While it is true that swing trading is less active than day trading, you need to follow the rules of the game if you are going to be successful in the long term.

What is Swing Trading?

Basically, swing trading involves the trading style of capturing profits in the financial market over a period of days or weeks. A swing trader is not looking to hold the stock or financial instrument for a long period of time. The trader's goal is to capture profits in a relatively short period of time and then move on to the next swing trade.

To be successful in swing trading, you need to have a trading plan and routine that outlines what you will be doing in the morning, afternoon, evening and over the days to keep track of the market. Your trading routine has to make room for preparation, the time that you set aside to analyze and look at a number of stocks, which are very promising to yield swing-trading profits over time.

It's key to understand that many institutional traders do not usually deal with swing traders. Their portfolio is large enough that they do not waste too much holding the financial security for a couple of days. So, the majority of people you in the swing trading market selling or buying financial instruments are simply individuals who are either managing their portfolio.

Doing well with your swing trading will involve the knowledge of technical and fundamental analysis. The key is that you have to understand how to use the macro and macroeconomic indicators to set new prices and trump in the game. Fundamental analysis is used in alliance with technical analysis to validate trading decisions, which have been made by looking at the current market condition.

The Psychology of Swing Trading

Swing trading is quite different from day trading. Therefore, you need to have a mental program designed to enable you to succeed therein. If you don't have the mindset of successful swing traders, all the rules, strategies and formulas may not help you. Thus, what you need to do before entering swing trading is to mentally prepare your mind for the game.

To achieve success in swing trading, the following are the mindset shifts you need to make:

1. Long term perspective

Instead of just focusing on a couple of wins or losses in a day, you need to focus on the overall trade that you intend to place in a week and what percentage of profit you hope to gain out of it. Put in another way, focus on the average percentage of profit that you would like to accrue from your swing trading at the end of the month or quarter. That is how to measure progress.

2. Don't personalize your losses

There're many people who just get hooked up and fed up of trading just because the market has gone against them. You need to be emotionally neutral to losing and winning. Bruce Kovner rightly noted, "If you personalize losses, you can't trade." To be successful in the long term in swing trading, you have to learn from your losses and develop a trading plan that will yield a consistent success over time.

3. Develop a swing trading plan and stick to it

This is the key to success. You need to develop a tailored plan for your swing trading, or else, you continue being emotionally swung from one trade to another. This is very important if you want to remain emotionally stable. When your plan is working, just follow and stock to it. Success will be quite predictable. Make changes to your plan only when the market changes.

The Benefits & Risks of Swing Trading

What are the pros and cons of swing trading? You've got to know about it. You're gambling in swing trading if you don't know the risks and rewards associated with your trade. What differentiates between losers and winner is that winners know the risks revolving their trade and then develops an approach to mitigating their risk so that they win consistently.

Losers simply trade, failing to make the right adjustments required to make their trading success. The following entails the risks/reward associated with swing trading:

Benefits of Swing Trading

1. Less Trading Time

As compared to day trading, where you are placing trades more often, swing trading usually involves less time to trade. You can simply place a trade per week or just one trade per month. And you do not have to worry about the market fluctuations.

2. Generating Short Term Profit

The whole essence of swing trading is focused on how you can be able to generate short term profits by analyzing the market carefully and making the most of price movements. You might not huge profit from this little price swings, but when you calculated your wins over time, it will be worth it.

3. Using Technical Analysis

Instead of worrying too much many fundamental indicators for trading, you can just use technical indicators to make your buying and selling decisions. This will ensure that you capture any upsurge movement related to price and profit in the marketplace.

Risks of Swing Trading

1. Short Term Risk

The challenge of swing trading is that you'll be making short term profits, but also assuming short term risks of price changes in the marketplace. Prices of financial instruments may fluctuate in and out within days and weekends before settling. When you swing trade, you might bear this short term risk. Again, that is where technical and fundamental analysis comes in.

2. Unprecedented Market Changes

You can't control the market. You can only control yourself. Sometimes, you can do all your homework and still miss it when the market somehow moves against your trade. Just hope this doesn't become your normal trend. Make room for losses as a result of unprecedented market changes.

3. Missing on Long Term Trends

When you engage in swing trading, your goal is to make short term profits over a long period of time. As compared to position traders who focus on long term trends to make a significant amount of profit, you will be missing on those long-term trend and profit margins.

Picking the Right Securities for Swing Trading

Regardless of your plan and desire for swing trading, you have to first of all select a market and then choose financial security to trade. If you don't know which market to trade: either stocks, bonds, money market, options or currencies, you'll not be making any progress. Therefore, before you consider trading, decide on the kind of market you want to focus on.

1. The Size of the Market

If you are looking towards practicing swing trading, you have a wide area to cast your net: small-cap, middle cap, and large-cap stocks. You have to know where you belong. However, most large-cap stocks seem to be highly volatile and good for swing trading.

2. Volatile & Sedate Stocks

Ideally, you have the choice to either trade volatile stocks where there is enough market volatility to make a profit in the market. If you choose to trade on sedate stocks that move occasionally, you need to have the technical indicators to confirm that trade. Remember that the game in swing trading is to make short term profits through little price swings in the market. This will enable to ensure you dealing with the right stocks.

3. Low Price & High Price Stocks

What are you thinking about? Cheap prices stocks or high priced stocks? You can decide to make money on penny stocks if that's your trading plan. But before you consider trading low priced stocks consider several factors that surround the trading volume, volatility and price history of the stock.

4. Bear & Bull Market

Another indicator to help you choose the right market for your trade is to look at the status of the market: is it a bull market or bear market? The condition of the market is also critical to know which stock to pick, and that also impact your trading strategies. Check the pattern of movement of financial security before trading.

Finding the Right Entry & Exit Points for Swing Trading

After choosing your security and determining the amount of money you want to trade, you have to look for the opportunity. In swing trading, opportunity and timing are everything. You are looking for the right exit and entry point that will most likely guarantee a profit for the trade.

Remember that due to the short-term nature of swing trading, you have to use technical analysis and then watch out for fundamental news when trading. Thus, you need to be aware and learn of the basic technical indicators for swing trading. The following entails some of those indicators to use and keep watch over:

1. Simple Moving Average (SMA)
2. Exponential Moving Average (EMA)
3. Support and resistance levels
4. The Fibonacci retracement

Small Moving Average (EMA)

This is probably one of the easiest and fattest technical indicators to use for swing trading. A small moving average helps to determine buy and sell signals by analyzing related average daily prices of a security over a specified period of time.

A 10-day SMA is calculated by summing up the daily closing prices of a particular financial instrument for the last ten (10) days and then dividing it by ten (10) again. It helps you to forecast the next average range of price if the market is moving in the same direction.

A 20-day SMA will be calculated in the same way, but in this case, the number of days will be twenty (20), divided by twenty (20). When the average moving averages are determined, the next step will be to plot the figures and join with a smooth line.

When the 10-day SMA crosses the 20-day SMA, a buy signal is determined, showing signs of an uptrend. The reverse will indicate a buy signal, showing signs of a downward trend. It is very important to note that the shorter the small moving average, the quicker it will respond to price changes in the market.

Exponential Moving Average

The simple moving average (SMA) and the exponential moving average (EMA) are close and similar. The only thing to take note is a slight variation in the usage and calculation of both. But both are used to determine to buy (entry) and sell (exit) signals of the market.

The crossing of two EMAs helps to determine the trend of the market as well as forecast the which exit strategy to use. The simplest among them is to the 9, 13 and the 50 exponential moving average. When the price breaks of the EMA occurs above the starting point, it indicates an upward trend, showing signs of a bullish market.

Generally, a buy signal is triggered when your 9-day EMA crosses the 13-day EMA. The same thing will happen if the 13-day EMA crosses or is above the 50-day EMA. These two indicators a buy signal. But you need to check other fundamental news before making your move.

Conversely, when price breaks of the EMA take place below the starting point, it shows a sign of bearish market, a downward trend. This is expressed by the 9-day EMA breaking the 13-day EMA and the 13-day EMA being below or crossing below the 50-day EMA. By looking at the time frames of both the bearish and bullish market, you can be on your way to make the right trading decision.

Support and Resistance Levels

When you're using support and resistance levels for swing trading, what you need to remember is that support level is the point where the buying forces of the market outweigh the selling. When this happens, the price of the underlying security drops and a bearish market sets in. To capitalize on the market changes, you will have to buy at the point of the support bounces and then place your stop loss below the support line.

On the flip side, the resistance level is the place where the selling forces of the market outweigh the buying. When this happens, the prices of financial instruments fall below their actual market value, creating a bullish market and then finally turns back again. To leverage this in your swing trading, you have to sell at the bounce of level and place your stop loss above the resistance level.

Fibonacci Retracement Patterns

The Fibonacci Retracement pattern can be used to figure out support and resistance triggers in order to know when the price of financial securities will reverse back to a certain level again to stabilize a moving trend in the market. How do you determine the resistance and support levels with Fibonacci Retracement in the swing trading market?

There are two main Fibonacci ratios to keep in mind: 23.6% and 61.8% reversal levels.

Now, when the price of underlying security retraces to 61.8% Fibonacci level and then bounces off, it indicates a resistance trigger, which sends the sign of to enter and buy. On the other side, when the price of the underlying security fluctuates to the 23.6% Fibonacci level and the moves back again, it will create a support and sends a sign to sell and exit the market.

How Much Profit to Make in Swing Trading

The amount of profit you make in swing trading depends on a number of factors, but most importantly the trader. Your trading plan, preparation, strategies, capital investment, and the system will determine how much you make per trader and over a period of time. Under most circumstances, you might earn between 2% to 15% per trade and then compound the profit over time.

Sometimes too, it depends on which type of assets you are trading. Some assets have better and higher yields than others. It is important that you stay within your "circle of competence." Stay within the asset class that you find that you are most comfortable at and then aim for consistent profits by using strategic trading processes.

After trading for a period of months, you will be able to finalize on your trading profits and returns. Keep track of all your earnings so that you can regularly evaluate them and make better financial projections that will enhance your monetary trading insight.

Tips for Successful Swing Trading

Here are some few tips that you must keep in mind as you practice swing trading. These tips will enable you to reduce making mistakes and increase your profit margins over a period of time. The key is to focus, be patient and emotionally stabled over your trading period.

1. *Choose the right swing trading broker*

Your broker is more or less your partner. To be successful in swing trading, you need to choose the right broker. Analyze your swing trading needs and focus on looking for the kind of trader that will most likely serve you better with the tools, techniques, platforms, and commissions to excel in your swing trading.

There are some brokers that cater to a particular market. To excel in swing trading, you have to watch out and look for those brokers that support your trading niche. You can use a demo account to examine and see how the platform works before trading live. Also, build a portfolio of financial securities to keep watch of and trade in the future.

2. *Stay close with the financial news of the market*

To be a professional swing trader, you have to stay close to the financial news of the market. If you simply jump in and out of the game because you perceive some trends in the market, you're going to be wiped out. Remember what Larry Hite said, *"I have two basic rules about winning in trading as well as in life: (1) If you don't bet, you can't win. (2) If you lose all your chips, you can't bet"*

To remain in the game, you need to regularly know what is going on. Listen to market news reports, commentaries, stock corrections, company reports, weekly charts, price patterns, industry performance news and so forth. The key is to stay up to date with the market so that you can make intelligent buying and selling swing-trading decisions.

3. Develop a Learning Edge

The most important to a successful swing trading is to develop a learning habit. You need to stay focus and keep learning if you want to do well in the market. Learn across markets, financial securities, trading strategies, and techniques.

Always remember the quote from Paul Tudor Jones, "The secret to being successful from a trading perspective is to have an indefatigable and an undying and unquenchable thirst for information and knowledge." Use books, podcasts, video tutorials, and many others to keep learning and growing.

Chapter 7: Guide to Position Trading

If you want to have a better performance than the crowd, you must do things differently from the crowd.
 Sir John Templeton

The game of trading has different approaches. You don't have to follow the crowd, you have to analyze yourself and find out what will work best for you. Just because your friends are making a lot of profit in day trading or swing trading, does not mean you should also do so. You can take your time to explore other trading styles that are suitable for your personality.

In trading, what works for one person may not necessarily work for the other party. And this is the reason you have to take your mind off envying someone because of his or her success. You need to believe that you can succeed and then chart your own course. When you do what you love, as opposed to doing what other people are doing, you'll make enough profits and also enjoy the ride.

Always keep in mind what Sir John Templeton, one of the brightest minds in investing and trading said, "If you want to have a better performance than the crowd, you must do things differently from the crowd." This does not mean you should learn from other people, you should, but make sure you do not veer away from what will work for you.

Whilst day trading and swing trading has become so popular in recent times, position traders have been used by many highly successful traders to grow their investment portfolio. People, who use position trading, seem to care less about the day-to-day noise of the market. They have a long term approach to trading and they do not allow the noise of the market to affect their trading strategy.

If you are the type which doesn't wait to place fewer traders per year and still make a good profit margin from your trading activities, then position trading might be good for you. Well, it might even be that you love this trading thing, but you do not have the time to be following the market every single minute. Position trading might best suit your needs.

You can explore the world of position trading even if you have limited time to trade. As opposed to day trading where you have to be worrying about the market, your trade, strategies, and ways to make money by the close of every single trading day, you do not have to fret when you are using position-trading style. But to be successful as a position trader, you need to understand how to play the game to win.

The Basics of Position Trading

You've got to get down to the basics and be brilliant with it. When you grasp the fundamentals of position trading, you'll know how to trade, when to trade and how to leverage it to grow your portfolio. To get started, let us look at the meaning of what position trading entails.

Investopedia defines position trading simply the method of taking a long-term position on a financial instrument and then waiting for a major trend to cause a great move in the pricing in order to reap a huge profit from the trade. It takes a long-term for a financial instrument to have a significant price change, as compared to slight daily and weekly changes.

A position trader focuses on how to use trend trading to be able to make a profit from the market when financial security makes a huge move. This means exercising patience and having a long-term view of the market. It means to monitor and track a particular asset for the long term and then makes a profit from it, rather than running after many others.

Investopedia defines a position trader as *"Position trader refers to an individual who holds an investment for an extended period of time with the expectation that it will appreciate in value. The average time frames for holding positions can be measured in weeks to months. They are less concerned with short-term fluctuations and the news of the day unless it impacts the long-term view of their position. Position traders do not trade actively, with most placing less than 10 trades a year."*

Does that mean a position trader is also an investor? No! Just because someone holds, an investment for a long period of time does not make them an investor. An investor is quite passive about the investment and generally invests for cash flow through dividends as opposed to earning profit through capital gains.

Apart from that, investors usually buy and hold their investment positions longer than position trader. Position traders may hold their positions for about four (4) months and then sell off their position to make a huge profit when the market has moved to an expected level they want. While a position trade sells the underlying asset, takes the profit and goes on the next thing, the investor still holds on to the position.

The main differentiating feature about the position trader is the ability to avoid daily market fluctuations and seek a long-term view of financial security. Instead of capturing just a little from the start of a trend, they hold the position a bit longer than swing traders os that they can "capture the bulk of the trend", as experts would say.

You should also notice that the position trader places a few traders per year. Generally, a swing trader will place about 25 to 100 trades in a single year, but the position trader may just place five or six based on the movement of the trend. This makes the position trading style unique and different from scalping, day trading, and swing trading.

The Pros & Cons of Position Trading

Wait a minute! Don't think position trading looks so good with profit prospects. What you want to do is to, first of all, understand what the advantages and disadvantages of position trading and then figure out if you will want to go ahead with it.

The Pros of Position Trading

- The ability to capture a major trend

This is the cool part of position trading. Instead of a day trader or swing trader that simply jumps in and out of the market to make little profits, you can follow a major trend and then finally maximize the trend to make big profits. Profit margins may vary based on your alertness and the kind of stock you are looking to trade.

- Huge saving in time and asset monitoring

As a position trader, you can afford to take your eye off the screen for minutes and days. Instead of being hooked up to the screen like a scalper or day trader, you can save time. Once you have done your analysis and placed your stop-loss order, you just have to relax and check the market from time to time to ensure that everything is on track.

- Huge savings on commission and fees

The challenge with day traders is that they trade a lot and pay a lot in commission and fees. Sometimes, you will realize that much of their profit is sucked by taxes, trading fees, and commissions. But as a trader, you can earn more and pay less in commissions, since you place a few trades and get to earn huge profits per trade placed.

- Invest time in other revenue-generating activities

Since a position trader saves a lot of trading time, it can be invested in other revenue-generating projects and activities. You don't need any high-speed monitoring. You can travel the world or possibly be running a business while engaging in position trading. These activities can generate money that can offset the risks related to position trading.

The Cons of Position Trading

- Require a large trend move

To be successful in position trading, you have to be on the lookout for stocks with a huge trend move direction. You have to look at the direction of the trend. But in markets where everything seems stable and sedate, position trading will not work. Ideally, position trading is good for an up moving bullish market.

- Illiquid due to tied-up capital

A day trader might be considered liquid than a position trader. Here, your trading capital will be locked up or tied up to investment positions that you are trading on. You may not get access to those funds as long as they've been invested in the stock market or any other financial instrument. This can create financial stress if you are having current money problems.

- High level of patience to succeed

As a position trader, you need a lot of patience to succeed. You can't just be moved by daily news reports and alerts. You need a high level of patience if you're going to reap the profits that you are looking for in the market. And that means you'll have to check your personality style and see if position trading works well for you. If very active and long to be in the market, all the time, then you will find position trading challenging.

- Slow learning curve

A day trader might learn a lot about the market faster than a position trader because he or she is always present, and trading. As a position trader, your learning curve will not be steep. You place a few trades per year, you gain less experience and learn a few trading strategies as compared to other traders. As a result, you might take a long time to be confident and experienced in all kinds of trading strategies.

Position Trading Strategies

Just like a day trader, you need to have a system of trading that will yield consistent profits over a period of time. The aim is to make sure you winning much more than you are losing, by developing a plan that will maximize your gains and minimize your losses. To do well in position trading, you need to a well-defined strategy for entry, exit and controlling risk.

Entry Strategy

How will you enter the market? When will you enter the market? Which trades will you consider entering? All these questions will have to be answered through your entry strategy. Your entry strategy should be able to help you know the best trade to enter in order to capture the profit you are seeking. To do this, there are a couple of measures to take.

- *A strong bullish trend*: Position trading works well in a strong bullish trend. Before you place a trade, you need to analyze the market conditions before trading. What kind of market there is? What is the direction of the trend? Where is the trend moving to?

- *The direction of the trend*: If you notice a bear market movement, you should not execute a position trading. Also, check whether the market is moving sideways or simply flat. These market conditions are not typically, favorable for position trading. It might work well if you are also using a position trading style.

- *Range/channel breakout*: The goal of position trading is to look for a stock or financial security that is just about to start moving and then monitor it to make a catch. Usually, the trend begins to start after the breakout of a channel or range. The price will normally be held by the range, and when the range breaks, the price begins to trend for some time. This is where you should consider initiating a position trading. Technical indicators of trend breakout include triangles, head & shoulders.

Exit Strategy

You need to have a planned exit strategy to enable you to mitigate the risks of position trading. By developing a good exit trading strategy, you can capture your profits without having your money drowned in the market. The key is to enter the trade when a major trend move is underway and then place a stop-loss order at below the moving average will help to avoid any negative effect.

HQ Trader, a leading trading and investment firm advice: "When the trade is initially placed, a stop loss is used to cap the amount that is lost should it immediately move in an unfavorable direction. Where this is placed depends on the volatility of the asset and the time frame of the trader. Setting a stop loss 5% below the moving average will serve to protect capital but still allow for upside potential."

You need to make sure you stop loss is placed at the area where the trend move will begin to subside. This will ensure that you do not make any huge losses when a trend reversal takes you by surprise. While you need to be patient, you have to evaluate the technical and fundamental factors surrounding the moving trend in order to take your profit before the trend reverses to generate a loss on your trade.

Controlling Risk

You need to develop a strategy to control the risks associated with position trading. Risk control involves fundamental analysis, technical analysis and using stop-loss orders. These three measures can help you avoid terrible losses that come with position trading.

Sometimes, you can see a trend of moving very strong. You think that the trend will continue and you will finally reap the profits you require over a period of time. But before you realize there is a trend reversal that causes you to lose on the trade placed. This is the reason to keep watch over your trade from time to time and not leave everything to chance.

Another risk to consider before trading is the fact that you can accumulate huge profits on trade without it being compounded. A day or swing trader will close their position on trading, collect their profits and move on to the next thing. But as position trader, you might earn profits on a trade, but until you close the trade, you won't have access to those funds. This might create an opportunity risk for trading other stocks or securities.

You need to leverage fundamental and technical analysis to find winning stocks that will earn the right amount of profits over time. That means looking at industry news, company earnings reports, macroeconomics and the financials of the underlying company. If the company is beginning to have a lot of problems, it might lead to a sharp trend reversal.

Technical analysis is also needed to identifying moving trends, when the trend started and when you supposed it might reverse. Consider using technical indicators like simple moving average, headers, and shoulders to safeguard your funds from any unheeded trend reversal.

Final Thoughts

For traders with long term view, position trading can be the best place. Make sure you do your homework and analyze your position and market before trading. Make your trading decision after careful fundamental and technical analysis. Both day trading and swing trading involve making short-term profits, but here, you have to discipline yourself to stay in the market for a while into to accumulate high profit.

But that also doesn't mean you should forget watching your position. If you do, a full trend reversal might overtake you and crash your profits into powder. While position trading is considered less research-intensive, you still need to monitor your position to maximize and get the highest possible profit from the strong bullish trend.

Chapter 8: Guide to Scalping

"Volatility is greatest at turning points, diminishing as a new trend becomes established."
 George Soros

If you're the type that wants a very short term form of trading, then scalping might be the best for you. While day trading involves placing trades with a holding session within one trading day, scalping is much shorter than that. When you're scalping, you run through several times in a day than the day trader, which helps you to make all your profit for the day in some few minutes.

Many people are jumping on the day trading bandwagon! And that's right! But what if you want something shorter and easier than day trading? What if you are just looking to catch small and little prices of profits in the market several times in the day? What if you're the type that loves the game and want to keep your eye on the screen every minute?

Well, you don't have to worry yourself with doing what people are doing with other trading styles. What you need to do is to select a trading style that will work for you. In this case, scalping might be a perfect fit for you! But if you are a position trader, looking for another way to earn money, scalping might not be very good for you.

The Basics of Scalping

Always remember that personality determines the trading style. You don't do what others are doing. You do what will match your trading personality, style, and approach. When you're a position trader, your system is designed to take a long term view of assets. When you switch to a scalping trading, your system might be suitable with that mode of trading.

However, a day trader can use scalping several times in a day. Generally, day trading involves holding positions for about thirty minutes or more. But scalping involves holding positions from seconds to even five minutes. That is why many scalpers love reading and analyzing five-minute stock charts. It helps them to make good scalping decisions.

A scalper cannot wait for several days before trading. He or she is an active trader, looking to make the most amount of profit in the market in the shortest possible time. Thus, a scalper engages in more trades than all the others of traders in a single trading session. To get started with scalping, you need to understand the basics and how it works.

Investopedia defines scalping as "a trading style that specializes in profiting off small price changes, generally after a trade is executed and becomes profitable. It requires a trader to have a strict exit strategy because one large loss could eliminate the many small gains the trader worked to obtain. Having the right tools such as a live feed, a direct-access broker and the stamina to place many trades is required for this strategy to be successful."

Based on this definition, there are few things you have to know: one, scalping focuses on "profiting off small price changes" and the second is that the seasoned scalers simply focus on "a trade that has been executed and becomes profitable." They do not worry about huge price changes in the market. A scalper makes trading easy because they lavage profitable trades to make profits.

Types of Scalping

Volatility, pricing, and volume are the three main factors that influenced how scalp trades are being placed. Before you proceed and start using scalping, you might as well learn a lot from about these critical elements of successful scalping. Not only do they affect scalping, but they also help to create the different types of scalping that exit in the financial market.

1. "Less Volatile Security" Approach

These type of scalping focuses on trading less volatile stocks with no real price changes, but they have high trading volume. Once there is a large trading volume, scalpers will then focus on capitalizing the spread to trade and make profits. This type of scalping is known as "market-making."

In this approach, a scalper is trying to bet against the "market makers." It is executed by posting a bid and an offer on the same financial instrument simultaneously. You level price difference between the bid and the offer to quickly make money in the market. Analyzing the direction of the stock and volume is critical for success.

2. "Highly Volatile Security" Approach

When the stock or a financial instrument is quickly moving, you can consider a trading approach that will tally with the volatility of the market. When the market is volatile, pricing will obviously be changing quickly creating a perfect environment for scalp trading.

The idea here is to buy a large number of shares and the bet against price movement. When the price moves slightly, the scalp will generate a profit and you will win. The stock must be liquid and you need to evaluate and time the market well before trading. The focus is to wait for a small movement to make a profit.

3. "Close at Exit" Approach

In the third trading approach, you use the same or similar trading as the second one. You try to make profits by waiting for a small change in prices of stocks or financial securities to make money. But here, you're more focused on your exit. Once the trade hits your exit strategy, you close the trade, take your profits and get out of the position.

With this approach, you need to analyze and develop an exit strategy that allows you to make the maximum from the scalp as well as reduce losses from market reversals. Ideally, the risk/reward ratio for this kind of trade will be set at 1:1.

Trading Psychology for Scalpers

A scalper operates with the belief that it is easy to capture profit from small prices changes in the financial market rather than wait for a large price moves to make a profit. The accumulated profits from the small profits are what give scalpers the winning edge over long-term traders like position traders.

To become a successful scalper, you need to have a specific way of thinking, behaving and acting. If not, you will see yourself giving up before you succeed. No matter the kind of financial instrument you want to engage in through scalping, here are the top three psychological and behavioral patterns you must have.

1. *Consistency*

Scalping can look very easy from the outside, but if you don't follow a trading system consistently, you're not going to make it. As a scalper, you're placing trades every few minutes and second. That means your trading must be carefully planned and organized to avoid disaster. If you do not, you will only waste your trading capital on useless stuff.

2. *Discipline*

The decision-making system of a scalper is quite different from that of a swing trader and a day trader. You need to be brutally hard with yourself to be successful. When you reach a decision about a trading decision, you don't have time to be feeling and rehearsing. You have to learn to independent decisions very quickly to enter and exit a trade.

3. Flexible

While you have to be hard on yourself, rugged and stiff with your trading plan and system, you need to also be flexible. Flexibility is necessary to respond to change that might occur in the market that might not be discussed in your trading plan. When a trade is not going as you expect, just get out of the market and move on to the next trade.

4. Commitment to research

A position trader needs an amount of research to trade, but scalping needs more. If you're scalping, you are placing more trade in a day and that requires you to do your homework on different kinds of securities before scalping. By so doing, you can ensure that all you can construct your trade very well to be successful.

Trading Strategies for Scalpers

Once you have chosen to use scalping to trade the financial market, you must familiarize yourself with the methods, ideas, and techniques required to be successful in the long term. This will ensure that you succeed. There are certain tools required for scalping. Some of them include a direct access broker, five minutes chart and a live news feed and alert. All this is required for trading success. Your scalping will aways begin with preparation and market analysis. Since fundamental news about companies and economics have a bearing on the price, trend, and directions in the market, it will be very important that you get access to a news feed that can provide you with all these information.

Your job is to understand and trade based on the news, that is news trading. Using fundamental ratios about the stock is also key in making good scalping decisions. These rations help you to figure out new supply and demand forces that will likely breakout after a major event.

But, most of the time, your scalping will heavily be dependent on technical analysis. Using short term historic price information to predict small changes in the market with the help of other technical indications such as moving average, candlestick charts, cups and handles, triangles and trend channel. Consider volume and price spread before making the trading decisions. Always make sure volume and trend correlated together.

When you are trading with support and resistant indicators, the key is to look for low volatility and a high trading range. Low productivity helps to keep the market calm, avoid light price fluctuation that might work against your trade. You trading range, support and resistance levels will enable to know here to enter and exit the market to make a profit.

What should be your risk management criteria? Well, you can consider a risk/reward ratio of 1:1. This means you should have a target profit is as equal as the stop loss. You are risking as much as you are earning to make the trade successful because of the price length of the trade. Examining the trade and focusing on the right market indicators is the key.

Unlike position trading which works better in a bull market, you can execute scalp trades in both bull and bear market. The strategy in a bear market is to make a profit as prices go upward and the strategy in a bear market is to maximize profits from financial securities that do better in a bad market. You can use scalp trading for options, stocks, index, futures, and many others. It all depends on your strategy.

The Challenges/Risks of Scalping

The game of scalping is built on the belief that you are can make huge profits by trading several times a day rather than holding unto one security to generate a huge profit in the long term. As a result, scalpers place several trades in a single trading day to make enough money. While this is good, the challenge is paying a lot of money through commissions and taxes.

That is why you need to be aware of the cost implication and analyze how it will impact your trading capital. Constantly paying commissions, trading fees and taxes can drastically cut down the profits you make scalping even though you might be earning small profits per trade that will accumulate. The best approach is to choose the right broker that will offer you trade incentives and discounts to favor the scalping.

The next challenge is to the ability to stick to a single trading day for scalping. When things do not work your way, you are tempted to think that you can hold your position overnight. Nope! This will derail your scalp-trading plan. When you hit a loss in the game, just cuts the losses and move to the next trade. Consider waiting for an amount of time to evaluate and analyze your trade if you keep making trade losses.

Failure to follow your exit strategy can run you into losses. Thus, you need to keep the idea of maintaining a "strick exit strategy" as the experts will say in your trading. When you are ready to enter a trade, define your exit strategy and stay with it to avoid running into losses.

Chapter 9: Deadly Trading Mistakes to Avoid

"Throughout my financial career, I have continually witnessed examples of other people that I have known being ruined by a failure to respect risk. If you don't take a hard look at risk, it will take you."

> *Larry Hite*

As human beings, we are prone to making mistakes. While a certain amount of mistake is tolerated, when you make too many mistakes in trading, you're going to be wiped out. Therefore, while it is important to learn from your mistakes, you'll have to avoid making a lot of mistakes to save your trading capital.

You'll also need to know that any mistakes you make in trading cost you money. The more mistakes you make, the more money goes out of your trading account. When this continues for a long period of time, you'll get disappointed and lose the desire to even trade. You'll become negative, bitter and depressed. This is why it's very important to consider possible mistakes and try as much as possible to avoid them.

Yea, you can memorize all the trading strategies and answers in your head. You can take all the trading courses for scalping, day trading, position trading, and swing trading, but will not immune you from making some amount of mistakes. Real-life trading involves some amount of real-life mistakes. So, the key is not to be fearful and be afraid of taking action.

No, that is not the point. You should be bold and take bold actions. But, please put measures in place in your trading activities to ensure that your trades are successful. If you learn to avoid the trading mistakes that cause many people to lose their capital, you will end up being successful in the long term.

With that said, what are the deadly mistakes you must keep watch of and avoid?

1. Allowing your emotions to control your trade
2. Not paying attention to technical indicators
3. Buying financial securities without an entry and exit plan
4. Not admitting that you're wrong and cutting losses
5. Risking too much capital on one single trade
6. Not preparing before getting into the trade
7. Trading low volume securities with unclear patterns

Allowing your emotions to control your trade

There are two main negative emotions that control trading and investing: fear and greed. These two negative emotions contribute to a lot of losses in the trade. That's why institutional traders like using computers. You see, as for computers, they don't have emotions. They care and feel nothing about the market. They indicate entry and exit signals based on market indications.

That does not mean you should become a robot. Of course, human beings are more intelligent than computers. Computers do not really think and see if things are not going well. For instance, computers can know if bad things are happening that might impact supply and demand. Yet, you need to stay in check and in control of your emotions. The key is not to let your emotions outsmart your logical, critical and analytical thinking about the market. Analyze the market and take the right actions, forget your feelings!

Not paying attention to technical indicators

The purpose of technical indicators is to help you minimize your risk and maximize your gains. It has to help you give you a clear vision of the market before trading. The technical indicators help you to know when to trade and when not to. If you are not paying attention to the technical indicators, you will be exposing yourself to doom and destruction.

Many people think that they have experienced so that do not have to pay attention to the market too much. This is where the problems come. No matter how experienced you are, if do not stay close to the market; it will take a nosedive before you realize it, and it will be too late before you know. When the indicators tell you a trend is about to reverse, swallow your pride, close the trade, take your profits and just get out!

Buying financial securities without an entry and exit plan

It's really amazing how many people trade. Actually, they're not trading, they're just gambling in the market and no wonder they keep on losing on most of their trades. Before you enter the market, you need to have your exit and entry plan in place. Your exit plan should always come before your entry plan because you can earn profits and still lose it.

What are the odds of the trade? What is your risk/reward ration? What is your price target? Which indicators are you basing your trade on? Which markets are you trading? What is the trend and pattern of the market? Ask as many questions you can and make sure you develop your entry and exit strategy. Do not just enter a trade and then hope the market moves to ensure you earn a profit. You cannot control the market, what you can control is your trading decisions.

Not admitting that you're wrong and cutting losses

It's amazing how some traders are stubborn and egotistical. They're losing, instead of them to recognize and cut their losses, they simply refuse and get burnt in the trade. Don't this happen to you! If you're going to do well in trading, you must learn to admit that you're wrong when you recognize that you have placed and made a bad trade. That will not kill you, but rather save you!

When you make a mistake in a trade, cuts your losses and then move on to the next thing. You should not complain and grumble about the market. Always know that the market has no-fault. It is your fault. Never fight against the market. Know your trade. Know your risk. Know your stop-loss levels. Be conservative and try hard to avoid blowing your account through reckless mistakes.

Risking too much capital on one single trade

Some people sort of believe one single trade to the extent that they commit their entire profit to it. Taking too much risk in the trade is dangerous and can create a big hole in your trading account. Always learn to remain calm and don't let your feelings get ahead of your thinking. You need to remember that greed and inpatient kill faster.

The rule of trading is that you should never invest what you cannot afford to lose. If you cannot afford to lose that amount of money in the trade, then reduce your investment or completely avoid the trade. If you use this principle in your trading system, you will adhere to good risk management practices that lead to successful trading.

Not preparing before getting into the trade

The challenge in trading is not what do before you trade. But what to do when you're not actively trading. When you get in a trade is a reflection of the use of the time far before the trade was initiated. How you use your spare time and how you prepare ahead of the game. Many dear folks sleep on their beds, wake up in the morning, watch the TV, look into the screen and start trading.

That is not preparation. What you need to do is to prepare for the trade as though your life depends on it. If you trade with that way of thinking, you will pay the price needed for success. You have to hold your accountable and responsible and be prepared to learn about what you need to do.

Trading low volume securities with unclear patterns

Effective trading involves looking at two main indicators: volume and price. Just looking trading based on price alone, you'll end up in jeopardy. This is a mistake you have to avoid. A strong price move in one direction must be affirmed and validated by a trading volume. As one expert said, "Volume validates the price." Always endeavor to look at the price before trading.

If you take your trading seriously and endeavor to deadly mistakes that might wipe your trading capital, you'll be successful. Avoid being overconfident and sat emotionally stable. If you pick the right securities and do your analysis well before trading, you will increase your odds of success.

Conclusion Part 1

Whether you're looking to trade for a living or simply trade once in a while to build your portfolio, you can start leveraging these principles to achieve success. You can increase your ability to succeed in the financial market by following the secrets of every trading style, instead of playing by chance and accident.

Analyze yourself now. This is the time. Why do you want to become a trader in the financial market? Outline your motivations and clarify your purpose for trading. This should be followed by checking your beliefs and thought system. Do you have the mindset that is required to be successful in trading? Do you have the emotional discipline required to achieve long-term success in the market?

Evaluate yourself to know whether your mind has been set up for success. If you have the mindset of successful and seasoned traders, by applying the right principles and techniques, you will increase your chances for success. But if you have the right strategies and techniques, and your mindset is wrong, it's not going work.

So, start by working on yourself, not the trade or investment. Always remember that there is nothing wrong with the market. You cannot change the market, but you can change your attitude towards the market. And by so doing, you will become a better trader. The way you think, interpret and analyze things will influence your success in the long term.

Which market do you want to focus on? Is it options, forex, stocks, index or bonds? Which area would you most likely succeed at? Decide that and then proceed to choose the trading style that will help you reach your goals. Your trading style should match up with your personality and time commitment to the trading business.

Understand the long-term success is not going to come easily. You will have to pay the price. And this includes studying about the field, funding your trading account, preparing for every trade, analyzing risks before trading, practicing successful trading strategies, creating stop-loss orders, learning from your mistakes, following the market news, keeping a trading journal, evaluating your progress and celebrating your wins.

If you realize that you have made a trading mistake, just cut your losses and move on to the next trade. Do not agonize over your past mistakes. Just learn from it and move on to the next trade. If you focus on becoming a better trader every single day, you will be successful in your trading in the long run and achieve the financial freedom that you are dreaming about. Happy and successful trading!

Day Trading for a living Part 2

Introduction Part 2

The stock market can be seen as a place where shares of different companies are publicly owned. In other words, the stock market is involved in trading of shares of public listed companies. This means that you can buy or sell these shares either through the centralized exchanges or through the OTC. The stock market, also known as the equity market, has effectively established itself as a free-market economy offering companies with the ability to access capital an in exchange offer interested outsiders with a portion of the ownership of the company.

As an investor, the stock market offers you the opportunity to increase your income without having the high risks that are usually witnessed when venturing in other businesses. By selling stocks, the company is able to expand itself exponentially. Therefore, as an investor, when you purchase the shares of a company, you have increased the worth of the company. Thus it's a win-win situation for both investor and owner. The negative risk associated with the stock market can be small or large, but all depends on the number of stock shares that you, as an investor, have bought. Therefore, if a company's stock shares lose value, the stocks you have bought also loses value, and if you decide to sell your stocks when the value is low, you will go at a loss.

Why Do Companies Sell Stocks?

The main reason as to why companies sell stocks is for the purpose of obtaining funds to enable then to grow larger. Look at this scenario: When you and your friends want to start your own business, what will you do? In most cases, if you and your friends have no savings or your savings are not enough, you will often go for personal loans or even use your credit cards. Then, you have successfully started the company, and it has grown enough; now, you proceed to get bank loans. At this stage, you can also sell bonds, particularly to individual investors. However, as the company grows, you will want to take it to the next phase. This will require large amounts of money, and this is where you will start selling your first stocks.

This is referred to as an initial public offering. Once your company has made the initial public offering, it is no longer owned by you and your friends, but rather to all the stockholders. Selling of stocks is one way that will enable you to grow very large.

Why Should You Invest In The Stock Shares?

Investing in the stock market is the most appropriate way that you can use to achieve returns that beat inflation over time. Here are the main four other benefits that you will get from investing in the stock market.

i. By investing in the stock market, you will be helping the economy of your country to expand because you will be boosting up the companies wishing to grow very large.

ii. The stock market differs from other markets like real estate because you can easily buy as well as sell stocks.

iii. Stock market give you the opportunity to make money in two ways; Over time, you can let your stock appreciate in value as time goes by and the sell it. Secondly, by default, you get money by giving the yearly dividend payment as one of the stockholders.

The Advantages and Disadvantages Of Investing In Stocks

The stock market for a long time has given generous returns to investors. However, the stock market today has been seen to go down, presenting both profits and loss. Here is a summary of the benefits and disadvantages that comes with owning stocks.

The Benefits

i. The ownership of stocks takes advantage of a growing economy

The growth of the economy also results in the growth of corporate earnings. Why is this so? When the economy grows, jobs are created, and in turn, income is also created. In the end, the overall result is that sales are created. The fatter the paycheck of people in an economy, the greater to boost to the demands of consumers, and this implies that a company's cash register will have more revenue.

ii. The stock market provides traders with the best opportunity to stay ahead of inflation.

In most of the cases witnessed, the stock market has always given investors an average of 10% annual return. This is far much better than the 3.2% annual inflation rate. However, this means that the time horizon must also be longer. Longer time horizons will enable you to buy and hold despite the temporary drops in stock value.

iii. It is easy to buy stock

It is very easy to buy shares of companies in the stock market. There are many ways with which you can buy stocks as an investor. You can buy online, or through a broker or through a financial planner. Once you have your account set up, it will only take you a few minutes to buy stocks.

iv. Stocks are easy to sell

In the stock market, investors are allowed to sell their stock at any given time. This means that the stock market is very liquid because as an investor, you can quickly turn your stocks into cash.

v. The stock market allows you to make money in two ways

As an investor, you can buy low and sell high. It is advisable to invest in fast-growing companies. This is because fast-growing companies usually appreciate in value. Whether you are a buy-and-hold trader or a day trader, the stock market presents you the opportunity to take advantage of the growth of stock price over time. The second way that you can use to make money is through dividends that companies pay annually to its stockholders.

The Disadvantages

    i.   You can lose your entire investment

This happens when the company does poorly, thereby compelling investors to sell their shares, thus lowering the stock value. You will end up losing the initial investment amount when you sell. If you are afraid of losing your initial investment, you will be made to buy bonds.

    ii.   You will be paid last

In the case where the company goes broke, stockholders are paid last. Only the creditors/bondholders and preferred stockholders are paid first.

    iii. It requires a lot of time

Before entering the stock market and buying a stock, it is appropriate that you do extensive research on each and every company and tries to determine how profitable they will be. You have to learn how annual reports and financial statements are read. You also have to follow the company's developments, be it in the news, the company website, or magazines.

    iv. The stock market can be an emotional roller coaster

This is because stock prices constantly rise and fall each second, and if you have the tendency of buying high and selling low, you can find it hard.

Chapter 1: Understanding the Stocks Market

Before entering the stock market, you have to consider and have an understanding of the various segments of this type of market. First, this market can be simplified into the following sections: the primary stock market, OTC market as well as a secondary market.

a. The Primary Stock Market

This is the initial point where the creation of securities happens. In other words, the primary market is an open stock market where companies offer and directly sell their shares for the first time. This opens doors to investors inviting them to buy shares. Usually, this market is mainly dominated by larger investment institutes like hedge funds, investment banks, etc.

b. Secondary Market

The secondary market provides traders with the opportunity to trade the stocks themselves. Therefore the company that had initially sold the stock, in this case, does not directly participate in the transactions. The investors already own the selling and buying of shares, and this is the typical idea of the stock market. Despite the fact that stocks are also sold on the primary market, this is the stage that they are initially issued from.

c. OTC Market

The OTC market is also known as the off-exchange in the stock market. The OTC market offers a decentralized market opportunity for investors to participate in purchasing and selling of stocks. When we talk of decentralized, we simply mean that a transaction involving buying or selling of a stock will take place between two parties, like between a trader and a broker. Generally, these transactions are not conducted through the local stock exchange but rather are conducted electronically through a trading platform, a telephone, or via an email. However, in most cases, the OTC market has always been for stocks and stock prices and not often listed on the stock exchange.

The Stock Exchange

The stock exchange generally is the traditional medium with which a stockbroker and a trader exchange stock/shares and bonds. The stock exchange provides the facilities for issuing and redeeming financial instruments that includes the means of income and dividends payment. Pooled investment products, unit trusts, derivatives, and bonds are also some of the assets listed on the stock exchange. There are a number of alternative ways with which you can invest in a company's stocks and trading and be able to make a profit. Here are the alternative ways;

i. Value Investing

In this investment strategy, there are certain stocks which trade for a lesser amount for what their actual value should be. When you are a value investor, you should be active in identifying the undervalued stocks that you believe will yield returns. It is not necessarily that you have some deep background in finance, but rather, you should have a basic understanding of finance and trading.

ii. P/E Ration (Price-Earnings)

This is a ration that measures the value of a company based on the share prices the company holds in the current market in relation to the per-share earnings the company has. The Price -Earning E ratio can be obtained as follows;
P/E ratio = (stock price/ per-share earnings)

iii. Dividend-Paying Stock

Companies must reward their shareholders as one way of appreciating you for owning a stock with them. These rewards are what we call dividend. In most cases, dividends are paid in cash and usually on a yearly or quarterly basis. Dividends can become a steady payment, particularly when your investment becomes fruitful, giving you an opportunity as an investor to purchase additional stocks. As a beginner, this can be your long-term investment that has an extremely low risk. As the company you have invested in becomes more financially stable with time, your dividends also rise.

Shares Trading

i. Swing Trading

This is one of the most popular ways with which you can trade stocks in the short-term. Swing trading usually lasts less than one day, but the position of swing traders can last up to 2 weeks. Your goal as a swing trader is to identify the overall market trends and capture the gains. If you choose to be a swing trader, it is appropriate that you learn technical analysis as it will give you an advantage in monitoring and identifying market changes.

ii. Day Trading

This involves buying or selling a particular currency, index, commodity, or share strictly on the same day. Positions are opened right from the second the markets are opened and go throughout the day, and these positions must be closed before the trading day of a market is closed. If you have chosen to be a trader who will use day trading, you are referred to as a day trader. Irrespective of whether you are a long or short-term trader, you have to note that in as much as trading in the short-term will give you more profit; the risks of potential loss involved are as well very high.

Chapter 2: How Stocks Market Works

In general, stock markets provide investors with a regulated and secure environment where they can transact in shares and other right financial instruments with confidence because of the low operational risk. Because the regulators provide the rules with which investors can operate, the stock market can be seen as both primary markets and as secondary markets. Acting as a primary market, the stock market provides companies with the first time opportunity to sell and issue their shares to the common public. This process is referred to as the initial public offerings (IPO). This is an activity that focuses on helping a company raise the capital necessary for its growth from investors. This basically means that when you have a company, you can divide it into a number of shares, for instance, 30 million shares and then sell part of these shares to the common public. For instance, out of the 30 million shares, you can decide to sell 10 million shares at $20 per share.

This process can only be effectively facilitated by having a marketplace where you can sell the shares as a company. This is where the stock market comes in. The stock market will provide a marketplace for you. Suppose everything goes as planned, you will have sold 10 million shares at $20 per share resulting in funds worth $200 million. These investors are allowed to hold these shared for their preferred duration. They get benefits from dividends, and they can also sell their shares when the share price rises. The stock exchange, in other words, can also be seen as a facilitator, particularly for raising capital for a company and, at the same time, also receives a fee for its services.

The stock exchange after the issuance of the first-time share (IPO exercise) does listing, which also serves as a trading platform facilitating regular buying and selling of the shares that of the companies that have listed. The buying of listed shares of listed can be seen as a secondary market, and the stock exchange at this stage now earns a fee for every trade transacted. The stock exchange market, therefore, is given the responsibility of ensuring liquidity, fair trade dealings, price transparency, and price discovery. Today, almost all stock markets in the world operate electronically to effectively maintain trading systems responsible for managing the buy and sell orders in an efficient manner. The stock exchange also performs the role of price matching, which ensures that trade is executed at fair prices both to the sellers and buyers. At some later stage, a listed company is also allowed to provide additional or new shares through a rights issue. Other ways of offering new or additional shares include follow-on offers, buyback, and share delisting.

Chapter 3: Functions of Stock Market

Growth of the Economy

Through the stock market, people who have shared are able to find a market for their shares. There are those who will choose to buy more shares while there are those who sell theirs, especially if the price of shares is favorable. Investors are able to get a platform where they learn about the most productive investments. This enables them to be able to channel their investments in the area that they know that they will get high returns. Through the investments, their capital grows, which, in return, ensures the growth of the economy. Every citizen is in returnable to benefit from the growth of the economy since there will be money circulation. It is through the prices of the market prices that a government will be able to tell whether the economy is doing well or not. The prices of shares normally give a clear picture of the state of the economy. A country is, therefore, able to work on the challenges it's facing in order for the economy to become more stable.

Giving Value of Securities

The stock market is known for giving the value of securities which are normally based on demand and supply. As for the companies which are profitable and growth-oriented, their securities are normally given a higher value since their securities are mostly on high demand. All the investors, the government, and also the creditors are always checking out on the valuation of those securities. The government's interest is on imposing taxes on the securities. The creditors, on the other hand, will be able to tell the creditworthiness on an investor while the investors will be able to assess the value of the investments.

Security of the trades

Through a stock market, investors are sure that their investments are in safe hands. This is because it is only the securities that have been listed that traded. All the companies' names are also included in the list. This means that all the listed companies are legit since they have gone through the whole process of verification. Investors are, therefore, sure that their shares are in the right hands.

Liquidity

The main purpose of a stock market is for it to provide a platform for investors to buy and sell shares. Investors are, therefore, sure that they can change their shares into cash any time they require cash. They will, therefore, be able to make big investments without hesitating since they are sure that they can convert them into cash when need be.

Offering Investors with an Opportunity to Save and Invest

Through the stock market, different securities offer various different opportunities for investors to be able to invest as well as save. This offers great encouragement for investors to invest more and also save, which may benefit them in the future.

Chapter 4: Regulating Stock Markets

How the Stock Market is Regulated

The stock market has very many players who may be from the private or the public sector. The government has to regulate the stock market in order to ensure that all investors are protected. The government's aim is to ensure that there is fair exchange in the stock market. Regulation of the stock market may have a positive or negative impact. Research, however, shows that the positive impacts are, however, more. As a result of the regulations, most companies have been able to make sure that they are accountable for all their actions. The regulations have provided the investors with a safe platform to invest in since risks such as fraud and mismanagement are eliminated. An investor is, therefore, able to have confidence even as they buy and sell shares in the stock market. This is because they are sure that they will be able to have great returns from it without experiencing any kinds of challenges.

Below are some of the ways that the stock market can be regulated.

Day Trading

In the stock market, there is something referred to as day trading. Day trading is the act of buying and selling shares on a particular day. Day trading has very strict regulations as compared to any other form of investment in shares. It is meant to protect traders from this risky business where one can lose lots of money if they engage in it without proper guidance. Even though investors can purchase stock for sale at a later day, day trading has strict limitations. The restrictions protect investors from losing money in the stock market to gamblers.

There are many brokers who are aware that most traders do not know the tricks involved when it comes to trading. They may prey on them, which would result in the traders making great losses which can be avoided through regulating the stock market. Through the regulations, gamblers are eliminated in the stock market since gambling is not allowed. The day traders are restricted to using margin accounts only. These traders are also required to a minimum of $25000 for cash and stocks in their margin accounts whereby these accounts are suspended for failure to maintain the minimum amount of money required. The strict regulations enable investors to be able to follow all the given instructions since they would not want to risk having their accounts suspended. It is a regulation that has worked so well with investors since the investors have to do everything to ensure that they meet all the requirements.

Going Public

The main purpose of stock markets is to ensure that the public invest in shares. Going public ensures that the public gains ownership of the corporation. The public has many potential investors who would grab invest opportunities once they arise. They could have money that they are not sure on where to invest it. Every investor would want an investment that is profitable as well as safe. When companies decide to go public, it would be of great help since the public will heavily invest in the shares. In return, the stock market will be able to experience investment of capital in large numbers. This improves the value of the shares since they will be bought at a better price and by a large number of people.

Registration of Brokers

Brokers are those people who have access to the stock market exchange and will normally act as middlemen to investors who would want to buy or sell shares in the stock market. Brokers are aware of everything about the stock market, so most often, investors prefer buying and selling shares in the stock market through them. Most investors may not be able to buy or sell shares in the stock market exchange. The government has to protect its investors from brokers, however. They have to ensure that the investor is not defrauded through the brokers. In order for fairness to be practiced in the stock market, the government has to regulate the actions of the brokers. The government does that by identifying the best brokers on the market. The best brokers are known since they have been in the business for a long time. The best ones are, however, identified through the way they carry out their dealings.

The best brokers in the market are those that do not exaggerate the prices too much. They get little profit from each exchange, but the profits they make should not make the investors make losses. One of the requirements is that they have to be registered by the Securities and Exchange Commission. They should have evidence in the form of a certificate to show that they are fully registered. This will help in ensuring that the brokers are certified to engage in stock market dealings on behalf of the investors. These regulations are also able to differentiate dealers from brokers. Dealers operate transactions for their own corporate accounts. It is a requirement for investors who are both brokers and dealers to have different accounts.

Trading Business

There are people whose source of livelihood is stock market trading. They do not have any other businesses out there. They depend on the money they make from buying and selling shares in the stock market. This means that fluctuation of prices would make their lives to come to a standstill. The government, therefore, has a responsibility to regulate how their returns are taxed. These investors normally get trader status after trading in the stock market

 For investors who have acquired the trader status, there are no severe limitations on their capital gains limitations. This is because all the capital they get is normally treated as an income. For the trader to qualify for the trader status, they should be able to prove to the government that stock market trading is their only source of income. They should also be able to prove that they fully depend on the profits they get from the stock market. This would mean that if the prices fluctuate, their profits are negatively affected. They should be able to prove that they participate in the stock market all year round through their trading records.

Chapter 5: Participants in the Stock Market

These are entities that are involved with the selling and buying of equities in the stock market. They include individuals, publicly traded corporations, insurance firms, banks, as well as investing institutions. Hedge funds are also contributing participants though to a lesser extent as compared to the rest. About half a century ago, the stock market used to be a preserve for wealthy persons and their associates. It has since evolved to include even more participants, as indicated above. A big chunk of the current investors in the stock market are financial institutions. This new trend has seen a reduction in fixed costs and the elimination of brokers to some a larger degree. Another factor that has led to a reduction of costs in the stock market is the introduction of a computerized asset management system that has cut down on employee-related costs.

Participation in the stock market occurs in a variety of ways as determined by stakeholders and their associates. A major determinant of participants in a financial exchange is the wealth and income of the players and corresponding fixed costs associated with the investment. It has also been determined that the level of participation is closely tied to the amount of information about financial exchange available to the public. The ease with which people process and fully understand how the system of the stock market works determines their participation in it. This means that most of the participants are the educated members of society, while less educated households have shown a much lower interest in the stock market. Participation also varies from time to time, depending on the state of bigger economies. During recess periods, for example, there is a general lack of trust and interest in the stock market compared to periods when those economies are doing well.

Direct and Indirect Participation

Participation in the stock market mostly refers to the number of agents who buy and sell equity-backed securities on behalf of individuals and other financial institutions. The agents do so either directly or indirectly according to agreed terms. Direct participation means those individuals or financial institutions buy and sell securities by themselves while indirect participation refers to the use of representatives, mostly institutionalized investors, to buy and sell them on their behalf. Indirect participation could be in the form of pooled managed financial accounts. The last two decades have seen a steady rise in equity-backed securities to values over 500% in developed countries and market capitalization surging to over $18 trillion by early 2013 in the United States alone. Direct ownership of securities by single entities, on the other hand, increased to 18% in the last quarter of 2007. This translates to about $17.5 trillion in the value of holdings. However, the lack of a harmonized taxing strategy by most governments has seen most entities choose a direct investment.

Participation by Household and Gender

The level of participation in a financial exchange has been found to vary with the nature of the household and partly by gender. Households with an average or low income invest less in the stock market compared to high-income households. Participation from households headed by married couples is slightly above the national average in most countries with most of them participating indirectly through pension accounts. Similarly, participation varies with the racial composition of a country. In the United States, for example, households headed by whites have more participants compared to those headed by other races such as blacks and Hispanics. Households headed by males have a higher participation rate compared to those headed by females. Both genders mostly own stocks indirectly through a retirement account. Women have been found to score low in financial literacy, and this has consequently contributed to their low participation in the stock market. Other factors that inhibit women from participating in the stock market include gender stereotyping, a negative attitude towards stock markets, and personal constraints. Women are generally a little more cautious when it comes to taking risks, the kind of risks associated with the stock market.

Participation by Income and Wealth

Participation rates differ according to the level of income and wealth of the participants. Low-income earners have a participation rate of 5% in the direct stock ownership and 10.5% in indirect stock ownership, all in the form of retirement accounts. Richer participants, on the other hand, have a rate of 47% in the direct stock ownership and 89% in indirect stock ownership in the form of retirement accounts. Low-income households have been reducing their direct and indirect participation in the stock market in the past decade, a reduction rate of about 5% by 2013. This was mostly motivated by the great recession of 2008 that saw a crash in stock markets across the globe. About five years ago, stocks across all classes (low, middle, and upper classes) were valued at $270,000 in the United States alone. Larger accounts do exceptionally well in the stock market as a result of higher returns, while smaller ones do poorly. Similarly, some undiversified portfolios do well while others don't. The money gap and excessive competition have caused a general surge in stock prices, making it unreachable for most low-income households. The stock market is a game of numbers where the level of wealth you put in determines if you will reap big or not. Wealthy individuals and corporations have more resources at their disposal to pump in the market and thus can get high returns within a short period. For those with little to invest, it is an endless struggle before they finally accumulate enough wealth to realize good returns. This can also turn to a disaster in the case of a stock market crash.

Chapter 6: Basic Information About the Stock Market

Financial literacy is quite essential when it comes to participation in the stock market. Overconfidence in financial literacy improves your score in the stock market. Under-confidence, on the other hand, is a major cause of poor performance and possible slow-death of the participant. This difference has become a major motivator for participants to undergo basic financial literacy before throwing all their weight in the stock market. No one wants to end up losing up to 80% of their portfolio value just because they rushed to invest in the stock market without first knowing how it works. What most people cannot tell you is that investing in the stock market comes with many risks. Your best chance against these risks is boosting your scope of knowledge about the market in advance. Then as time goes by, you will accumulate plenty of experience, and within no time, you will count yourself like a pro.

First, a share, also known as stock or equity represents a claim on a company or corporation's assets and earnings when it makes a profit. This claim equals the number of shares and individual or institution has in the company. Buying a company's shares gives you some rights in the company, such as the ability to vote as well as claim earnings corresponding to your share(s) in the form of dividends and capital gains. It is important to note that while buying shares in the stock market, you don't buy them directly from the company. Rather you buy them from existing shareholders. The market is controlled by market makers or specialists charged with maintaining fairness and orderliness. However, market makers don't determine share prices as is determined solely by demand and supply when the participants are placing and taking orders. Lastly, the stock market itself is where institutionalized investors and individuals meet to buy and sell securities. The venue can be a public place or a computerized platform.

Shares are classified as either common or preferred shares. Common shares carry voting rights in the company's corporate meetings while preferred shares carry no voting rights. Companies sell shares to increase their capital base since the more shares sold out, the more access it has to capital. This capital is used to expand the company's operations, thus generating more profit. You need to understand the following terms used in stock exchange before making that decision of investing in it.

Bull Markets vs. Bear Markets

Bull markets are where when prices of commodities, stocks, bonds, and sometimes housing increases over a long period before dropping unexpectedly. This kind of market is very misleading to investors because the extended period where prices consistently go up makes them believe that it will be again. What they don't realize is that this rising bubble going to burst any time and prices will fall. When prices fall by 10% or below, it creates a market correction.

A bear market is a result of stock prices falling to 20% or more. This kills the investors' morale, and they will think the prices will keep falling and see no need for investing in those stocks. Some bear markets have been known to run for close to two years, and this greatly compromises the affected companies' position in the market.

A market bull and market bear are two individuals with contrasting views about existing and future market trends. The bull thinks the prices will go up while the bear thinks that they will fall. The longest bull market was seen from 1990 to 2000 while a bear market can last 18 months.

Stock Market Crash vs. Correction

A stock market crash is an abrupt reduction in prices of stocks that affect a significant part of the stock market resulting in a massive loss of wealth. This situation is normally made worse by panic and speculative market bubbles. The main reason for the stock market to crash is unfavorable and unforeseen economic factors. These are the conditions under which a market crash will seem inevitable.

- A lengthy bull market.
- Too much trust in the economy.

- Pressure from a majority of the participants.
- Price-earnings ratio that is more than the average.
- Participants that use excessive margin debt.
- Wars.
- Cybercrimes targeting large corporations.
- Change in government laws and regulations.
- Natural disasters such as devastating earthquakes, hurricanes, tsunamis, and sometimes wildfires.

Most stock market prices lead to bear markets, especially when struggling firms take advantage of the crash to compete with affected ones. They result in a surge in sales and a corresponding decline in prices. However, not all stock market crashes lead to a bear market. The reason for this is because most crashes last for only some days before the situation is contained.

A correction occurs when the prices of stocks fall by a margin of 10% or more following a peak. This takes place for a shorter period like a few days or in an extended period that may take several months. A correction can affect all types of securities, including bonds, commodities, and several other assets. These corrections are monitored using charts solely generated for that purpose. These charts start by tracking the activities and management styles of many companies before narrowing down to individual companies to predict which ones will likely cause corrections. The best method to manage corrections is by being on the alert all the time because they are always there, what you don't know s where they will appear. Corrections can be quite devastating for short-term investors as compared to long-term investors hence the need to consult an expert before rushing to invest. Similarly, some equities are more vulnerable than others at any given time. For instance, securities that deal with production and processing tend to react less to corrections compared to more volatile ones like insurance.

Chapter 7: How to Find Good Stock to Buy

The Stock Buying Process

For a new stock investor, you cannot just start buying stock from any company. You must do research to choose which company to invest in through reading financial reports of different companies and seeking advice from qualified experts in FOREX trading. You should also look at the financial statements and reading reports on the company you are interested in its stock. The research will help to make a decision that is well informed.

As an investor, you have a company of investment, but you are yet to make a decision on the amount of stock to buy. The amount of stock guides the amount you would want to invest. However, remember that investing in a stock like any other investment has risks, and therefore you should put in an amount that you are ready to lose. However, do not be pessimistic.

When you want to buy a stock, you should understand that the stock market works by transferring ownership of the stock from one person to another. This means that when you want to buy stock, you will have to look for a seller, and you should note that not all sellers are willing to give you the same amount of stock at the price you would like to buy at. The marketplace is the stock markets, which are available online through brokers thanks to computer technology. To access the markets, you must have an account with the broker of your choice because most exchanges are done through brokers. The investors place their orders to sell or buy stock with their brokers, and it is the broker who makes the order available in other available markets.

You should choose a broker wisely from the three kinds of brokers. The deep-discount brokers who only provide order execution to buy or sell and account maintenance. The interaction with the broker can be through the telephone or through the web browser. A full-service type of brokers provides more services besides maintenance of accounts and execution of orders, which includes providing advice regarding investment opportunities, appropriate strategies, and those to avoid. The broker also does research on behalf of the investor. They also have offices where investors can visit them. Discount brokers offer more investment insights compared to the others but charge a fee in the form of a commission. The commission depends on the service you need; if most of the work is done by the broker, the commission fee is high and vice versa.

When you have already chosen a broker that suits your needs, and you want to buy, you can place an order to buy using either of the two types of orders: the market and limit orders. When you give a market order, your broker will immediately buy for you the stock you require at the best price. Conversely, when using a limit order, you specify the maximum price for buying and the broker buys for you the stock at the specified price or at a lower price. Therefore, depending on the order that you give the broker, the broker routes the order to buy in other available markets and executes it. Sometimes the whole process is automated, and the request takes place within seconds. The remaining part is to transfer the stock from the seller to you and the payment made. The payment method is discussed and agreed upon by the seller and the buyer through the broker; the payment should be compatible and flexible. There are many online transaction methods depending on the region; therefore, choose the most popular within the region to allow smooth transfers.

The process of buying repeats itself, but you can maintain your broker if you feel comfortable. But in case you change the broker, there will also be a need to open an account with the new broker. More information can be obtained about the best stock to buy from experts and also analyzing the stocks in terms of the fluctuation in prices.

The buying of stock can also be through dealers, who trade using their own accounts. In this case, you do not involve a broker, and the orders are traded using bids. As an investor, you contact the dealer that you wish from and quote your bid, and the seller quotes the selling price. Negotiations between you and the seller might lead to a deal or no deal. If it is not a deal, you are free to try another dealer, but if it is a deal, mode of payment is discussed, and the transfer of stock from the seller to you is done through the account, payment made and deal closed.

Chapter 8: What Do You Need to Get Started?

Just like any other business, before you start stock marketing, there are several things you need to put in place. No one ever wakes up one day and find themselves perfect in the business world. You need to learn, put yourself together, have a starting point, then grow step by step. There are a lot of risks involved, and as a beginner, you must be ready to take risks.

Stock marketing is a different kind of investment as compared to normal trading. You need to understand and put into practice different techniques related to investment. This chapter specifically tackles the requirements for one to start stock marketing. Below is the detailed information on what you need to get started in this kind of investment.

Know Exactly What You Want

Before you start investing in any kind of business, you need to have an idea of what you really want. Knowing what you want to invest in will help you in carrying out research about the particular business from those who are experienced in the same. It will also help you know the benefits of this stock you are going to market and how to handle it to ensure you attract more gain than loss.

Be Disciplined Emotionally

Being emotionally disciplined means that you learn to accept defeat. Stock marketing is not as easy as the name goes. Once you get yourself in such kind of trading, be ready to face loses. As a beginner, you always lose more because you are still not familiar with it. Emotional discipline will help you accept the lose and get you ready to try it again now in a better way.

Pay Attention to Technical Analysis

Read the flow charts and try to understand better how it works. This will make it easier for you to make a decision about stock marketing and get you ready to try something new. You will have the urge to start trading in this culture as you will be eager to know what awaits for in the future. This is the most important practice that should not be overpassed by anyone who is sure and is convinced that they want to invest in this business.

Take Your Time to Learn

Nothing is easy. Learning how to trade in stock marketing is easy neither. Take your time to learn and understand how it works. This is something that will earn you a lot of money, so be ready to spend your time and effort on knowing how it is done. Without good knowledge, you will end up recording more losses than profits.

Be Patient

Unlike many people who give up on their dreams when things are not going their way, learn them of process. Everything is a process, and every person has their own timing. Don't be the kind that loses hope easily and letting go of what had taken the time and energy to start. Wait patiently for your time to reap what you sow. You can't reap early when you sew late, so act like a wise farmer. Wait for your fruits to ripe then harvest happily.

Develop Passion for What You Are Doing

Be passionate about your business. Be cheerful and work towards making your business more profitable. You chose this because you loved it. You felt that this was the thing for you and that this was the right decision to make so never regret when things become tough. Rather, put a smile on your face, tell yourself, "I'm tougher than the situation" the fightback.

Be Dedicated To the Business

Never give up on what you started. Fight for it to stay. Spend more time trying to make it work and don't compare other people's earnings to what you get because that was their energy, and this is now your time to invest your time and energy. You will reach that level when it is your turn to see the results of your sweat.

Understand the Market Mechanism

Concentrate more on the flow chart of the business. Get to learn how market varies from season to season and get to know when you maximize your profit and make it worth all the sacrifices that you made. You never get what you did not invest in. Be wise.

Be Strategic

Build your own marketing strategies that are different from others. Have your own way of doing your things and dragging success your way. All you need is to put together ideas, compare the ideas and chose which one best fits your interest then apply the idea to your previous plans, and watch yourself going.

Get Familiar With The Market

Get to understand how stock marketing operates before you get started. You can always trade with the demo account until you understand the flow of good. This will help you perfectly on how to do your trading. You should only start trading with cash after you have gathered enough skills and ideas in the demo account. You will realize that when you are much familiar with the market, trading becomes easier.

Unlike other types of investment, stock marketing takes quite a long time before showing interest. As a beginner, you will realize that you are losing more at first instead of gaining. Train your emotions to accept the situation and be patient enough to learn and perfect your skills. Never get angry when you lose because there is no business in the world that does not record a loss. When you read widely on the history of trade, you will get to understand that in every market there's always the gaining side and the losing side and that everything changes with experience. The more you get exposed, the more you learn how to handle different situations.

To become an expert in this sector, you should avoid taking shortcuts like opting for the fastest way. Instead, take everything step by step, starting with the easy ones as you rise slowly. Get to tackle the slightly easy tasks first before moving to more complicated tasks.

If anyone could ask for my opinion on stock trading, I would recommend they read the books on marketing psychology and research deeply on the best criteria they can apply in their trading. This will help them gather all the information they need and how to balance the ideas they have to get going.

I can also recommend you to seek guidance on marketing tutors online. They will help you greatly in coming up with the best strategies for your trading. You will realize an easy time handling the changes in the market trend-making trading easier for you.

Chapter 9: How to Buy and Sell Stocks

Buying and Selling Stocks

When you have some cash from savings or have borrowed some, and you want to invest it in stock, you choose a stockbroker and open an account with them. This account is known as a stock trading account, and it is like opening a bank account where you give personal information, during the process of opening the account, you will be required to sign an agreement that supplies you with information about the obligations of the broker and your obligations as a customer. The agreement also gives the rights of both the broker and the customer. After signing the agreement you are now ready, and because you are using a broker, it is better to give instruction on the amount of stock to buy, and when you want to sell, you still give the instructions to the broker. Instructions are mostly done through a form that contains details on the type of stock, amount to be bought and when to be bought. When placing orders, there are two basic orders, which are limit and market orders. The market order is a sell or purchase order of the stock, usually using the offered price. When this order is given it is executed immediately, but remember that stock prices fluctuate in seconds or minutes, and therefore, it is not a guarantee that the price at the time of order will be the buying or selling price of the stock.

A limit order, in contrast, is an order given by the buyer or the seller to sell or purchase stock at a better-offered price. The limit order, however, can only be completed at a lower price or at the limit price in the case of buying, and when selling, the limit order can simply be completed at a greater or limit price. Therefore, this order is not assured that it will be executed, and the limit order form can only be completed when the stock prices are at the limit price. The fact that it is not a guarantee that a limit order is executed makes it safe for the investor because he or she does not pay more than the price determined at the time of order. For example, if you want to buy stock from HSBC for not more than $20, you put a limit order that ensures that the stock from HSBC will only be purchased when the stock is $20 or less.

In addition to market order and limit order, there are other orders or instructions that you can give regarding buying and selling of your stock. One of these instructions is the stop order instruction, which is also identified as the stop-loss order that is given by the customer to sell or purchase the stock when an indicated price is reached. At the point of the stop price, the order turns into the market order. A stop order when it comes to buying is entered when the stop price is greater when it is compared to the market price of the stock. This is done to limit loss or prevent the loss of profit gained earlier. When selling, the stop order is issued by the investor when it is below the current market price of the specified stock. This order is good, but before using it, the investor should look at market fluctuations in the short-term and the rules that are used to issue a stop order by a particular brokerage company.

The stop-limit order is another instruction that can be used by a stock investor. It has both characteristics of limit and stops orders, whereby once the stop price of the stock is arrived at; it ceases to be a stop order and fit as a limit order, allowing transactions at a stated price or at a better price. The stop-limit order is good for an investor for it helps to control the price at which the stock is bought. Before the use of this order, the investor should look at the fluctuations of the price of the stock in the market in the short-term so as to take advantage of the positive fluctuations. The investor should also look at the rules that apply in a brokerage company one is using to trade.

As an investor, one should also know other terms used to refer to orders in the stock market so as to understand the trade. There is the day order, which is an order to purchase or sell stock that is put up for sale or order to buy on a trading day. The Good-Til-Cancelled (GTC) order is a type of order to sell or purchase a stock that remains on sale up to the time the order is canceled or completed. The time limit for a GTC depends on the brokerage company the investor is trading with. Some companies have a longer time, and others have a shorter time depending on the type of stock. Therefore, before applying to get a GTC order, it is good to contact the brokerage company to find out the time frame for the order.

The Immediate-Or Cancel (IOC) order is a type of order to sell or purchase stock; the order must be completed instantly. If the order contains a portion that cannot be completed immediately, it is canceled. The Fill-Or-Kill (FOK) order is an order that authorizes buying and selling of a stock. The stock must be completed immediately in its entirety, and if not, it is canceled. All-Or-None (AON) order is similar to the FOK; it should be executed fully, and if not, it should not be executed. The AON, however, remains active; it is not canceled like in the case of FOK.

With knowledge of the type of orders placed to sell or buy, an investor can use them to make an order to sell or buy. In addition, some orders can be placed outside the normal trading hours, and such orders can be completed at the opening stock price when the trading day begins. However, opening transactions vary from one brokerage company to another; therefore, an investor should contact his or her broker to get how it works.

Chapter 10: Common Mistakes to Avoid- Entails the Common Mistakes Involved in the Stock Market

A lot of traders who fall throttle in the industry have higher expectations of making profits. However, most of the times, they discover that making money consistently isn`t that easy. For most traders, this reality tends to be discouraging, and they may end up quitting. It is worth noting that the process of making money in the arena of stock often lures many people; however, the reality of losing it tends to be a quick deterrent to many. Although it is hard to maintain the consistency of making money, the mistakes that traders do deters the progress of many. Professional marketers have identified such errors and have been working on avoiding them for their development.

Take a look at some of the mistakes you need to avoid.

Little Preparation or Training

When you start or enter in the marketing arena, you need to be well prepared. However, most traders indulge in business without considering their diligence or rather the aspects that are required for the progress of the same. For instance, if you want to go and swim, you need to have trained well or rather attend some swimming lessons and perfect in them. In case you jump into a swimming pool and you dint have a trainer or someone to train you, you might end up drowning and losing your life as well.

In the same way, when you indulge in the market arena, you need to be well trained and have all the necessary tools that are vital for the progress. However, most traders are lured by the fact that the marketing arena has a lot of ways where one can make money. They, therefore, indulge in such business without considering their level of preparation or instead of their training. Without considering the demerits in there, they end up losing everything.

Being too Emotional about Money

According to several professionals, the reason a lot of traders fail to earn profits consistently is their perception of money. Most of the traders perceive money as a source of power or rather a sense of security. Thus, if they lose it, they react so emotionally. Traders are, therefore, worried about losing the funds. In the long run, they lose control of these funds and end up making drops.

In most cases, they allow the stock to go negative against them as they try to gain control over the funds they have. Thus, you need to avoid being emotional about money. In other words, even if you are making 10,000 in an hour, relax and avoid being emotional. Such aspects will be critical in ensuring that you have no emotional distress and prepared to lose or gain colossal money. If you become successful in the industry, be slow on raising the share size, and avoid raising your blood pressure for nothing. Be considerate and operate at a personal level. Avoid being over-prepared, and you will be able to achieve your goals with ease.

Lack of Records

It is at times understandable why some traders tend to be so emotional when it comes to trading. When you are new in the stock exchange market, it is either you are gaining profits or making losses as well. However, it reaches a time when you have no control over what is happening. According to many experts, the best thing to do is to keep a daily diary of what is happening in your business life. Such records will be critical in the sense that you will be able to avoid cases of being too emotional when you realize you are making a lot of funds or huge loses at a go. However, if you are able to maintain a daily record, you will be in a position to locate the progress and handle it with ease.

In most cases, traders hate having a daily log of their development, especially when they are making huge profits. Most of they end up spending money in inappropriate means, and in the long run, they end up lacking the control of their business. The art of maintaining a daily record is critical in the sense that it allows a trader to have a daily analysis of the flow of the funds, as well as the progress, being made in the marketing arena. The aspect allows the traders to be prepared if the prospects being made and make the necessary adjustments to avoid making huge loses at a go.

Anticipating Profits

In most cases, traders don't acknowledge that a trade can go against them in one way or another. Most of them enter into markets with prospects that they will make profits and become successful at a go. Thus, most of them enter the marketing arena without having a review of what is happening in the industry. The approach is dangerous as such traders are terrified and downcast when they make loses. In other words, even if you need to have plans as well as ambitions of being successful in the industry, it is not wise to be too much prepared. Make a point of being reasonable and learn the marketing trends before making your judgments.

It is good to enter the industry with a neutral mind. That is expected to make profits as you prospect that you might suffer loss at some point. Such approaches will allow you to make necessary adjustments and be ready in case you incur injuries. Also, don't blindly follow the mechanical systems as well as computers without considering the costs involved. Although the technical know-how is vital, you need to be moderate and avoid thinking that a computer will solve all your problems. In other words, there is software that is utilized to analyze the flow of events in the trade market. However, if you replace thinking and analysis with a computer, you might be the toast of losing everything. Thus, you need to avoid following the mechanical support blindly without considering the human inputs availed. Such approaches will help you to tackle any issue that may arise.

Chapter 11: Index Stocks or Individual Stocks

A stock in an index is collected in one place known as the basket. For instance, if you wanted to invest in a particular index, you may have to acquire a minimum of thirty shares in the index basket. In most cases, you would own shares of more than 30 different organizations. The way the index stock is designed is to tract a particular number of assets in a specific market. For instance, an index of gold and copper, among other precious metals may contain different companies that mine these precious metals. Thus, if one buys shares from such an index, will have shares form all these organizations that are listed in this index. One of the merits of buying shares forms the index is that one gains the exposure of having shares from all the organizations without necessarily buying from all the companies. The other merit is that the profits increased tend to be shared. Thus, there are minimal chances of making loses on purchasing these shares.

Index Weighting

The art of index weighting is critical in the sense that one can understand the design of the index he or she is buying from. For instance, the price of a price-weighted index has different amounts of shares that are based on the cost of these shares. It is worth noting a stock worth $20 would have a single share while a stock worth $5 would have four shares so as the total shares would be equal to $20 stock. Also, index stock is weighed using market capitalization. The shares of each weighed index depend on the value of the market as well as the outstanding shares. It is worth noting that the art of measuring these stocks is critical in the sense that it helps in identifying the amount of floated stock as well as the adjustment needed. One of the merits of buying an index stock is that one gets exposure to different sectors without necessarily having to corner all the market stock. It is more comfortable to purchase the commodity index instead of buying individual stock. In other words, one gets exposed to the entire market at a go. However, although there are merits that are associated with index stock, it is not 100 % accurate. In other words, one may be required to survey individual inventory for satisfaction.

Individual Stock

It is worth noting that a stock also known as a share signifies the security as well as the proportionate of ownership of a particular organization. In other words, it entitles the entity that the stock-holder has in a specific object. It is worth noting that the investments can be assessed or be purchased using online means. It is worth noting that an individual stock refers to a type of investment where money from different investors is invested together but in different stocks. It is worth noting that the particular stock offers the merit of diversification as well as convenience. In other words, one is exposed to different stock where one chooses from the one that suits them best. Also, such stock isn't limited to a specific group of organizations. The art of diversification is enhanced hence increase in making profits. In other words, is the stock identified doesn't make earning profits; one can quickly shift and purchase another type of equity and keep earning profits. The other merit of this stock is that it is convenient, and one can buy from different levels of organizations with ease. There are few limitations hence more effective.

In a nutshell, one may prefer an individual stock to an index stock. The aspect is linked to the fact that the former is more flexible and diversified. In other words, one is not limited to the art of buying shares from a list of companies that are listed in the index. However, the individual stock is diversified in the sense that one can select equity that is well paying and one that is commanding a higher profit. It is worth noting that individual stock tends to be convenient in the sense that one buys the shares following his will and efforts. In other words, the stock is listed and priced at a comfortable price that encourages more buying.

The profits made are personalized in the sense that one may not suffer the losses incurred from other organizations that might be listed in the index. In other words, the index stock tends to be disadvantaged by the fact that the losses incurred by a particular firm may affect the pricing of the shares in the index hence the distribution of losses. The art may discourage the buying of shares from a specific index. However, it is good to consider all types of shares as there are situations that index stock does well that individual stock. The art is affected by the type of market involved.

Chapter 12: Protecting Your Stock Investments

Diversify internationally

There can be favorable deals in other countries apart from in your own country. Other countries can have higher yields on investments, and it could be wiser if you consider investing there. Even a 1% positive difference is an assurance that your investment will compound faster. It is not recommendable to put all your money in one pool, and investing in different countries is advisable. You need considering investing in a country that their economy is stable and growing. Some countries outperform others, and so appropriate that you first survey before investing there. When you distribute your portfolio internationally, you tend to catch growth experienced across the world.

It is vital considering commodity exposure

Having real assets will be of help when inflation hits the economy since the value of the asset remains the same. The assets serve as a great idea since they can be a variety of item or as many as you can desire. Real assets help in managing risks in case of specific incidences, and your investment is with no doubt safe as well as secure. Some assets may have good returns at the end of the day. A country having inflation that is too low as well as too high is both worrying. For either stock or bonds to yield reasonably, stable inflation that brings the required balance is essential. It is good to be on the safer end in case there are boom goes up or too low. Having stock in the form of an asset can be better since when inflation goes up, its value is as well likely to go up to reflect a similar amount.

Consider bonds as part of your investment

Bonds given by the government have a guarantee that even when the economy goes down, there will be returns. When the stock falls, bonds may not fall as well and so having them in the same pool with share is an excellent idea. The bond may have a good performance when the stock is falling. Investing only in-stock may be a bit risky, and considering the addition of bonds in the allocation will not be a bad idea after all. When the market decline, that is the moment that you get to see the importance of investing in bonds. You can consider any percentage for the benefits received from diversifying.

Make sure that the cash you have at hand is for spending in a short-term

The money that you will put in your stock should not be of use in a few months or years to come. You can take a risk on your money when you source cash from your investment. Any money that you need to be directed in use shortly should not come from the investment portfolio. It is not a good idea neither a safe place, in the stock market, to keep the money you will need in the short-term. It is because, when the market does down, you still have expenses to handle, and you may be financially down when the market has fallen.

Consider a put option

You can put the options market as a way of risk management to avoid easily frightened about valuation. The value of the put option can increase while there is a fall in the price of the underlying assets. Even when there is a drop in the stock market, you will still make some money out of your option. The put option bought out of money is considered as vital protection which needs consideration.

Avoid the need to Control

Most of the investors are unable to help with panic when the market tanks and losses are incurred. In this case, one may need a financial advisor. However, it is worth noting that a financial advisor may change the approach that one has towards stock with a tiny percentage. Thus, to protect your inventory, you need to avoid the art of controlling the stock exchange market and make a point of allowing the financial advisors to keep your investment portfolio on track at all times. Despite the profits you might have gained, it is critical to consider the market timers that favors your stock. The aspect is crucial in this sense that one can identify the collapse of a stock at a distance and avoid them as well.

Chapter 13: Penny Stocks vs Regular Stocks

When you are new to trading, you may wonder what these terms mean. Penny stocks refer to stocks trading below five dollars. Penny stocks are often shares for companies which are about to go bankrupt, small or new companies or highly over-leveraged businesses. Most of the trade through over-the-counter (OTC) means since they are small hence cannot afford regular exchange listing requirements.

On the other hand, regular stocks are blue-chip stocks. They are shares for blue-chip companies which can afford to offer safety to investors in volatile markets. These companies offer attractive dividends and have promising prospects for growth.

The pros and cons of the two stocks can easily be understood by analyzing their differences. Most of these differences are centered on the risk of investment and their way of operation. With a good knowledge of their differences, and a new trader can make a much more informed decision on buying a share on the different stocks. In this chapter, will focus on the differences between penny stocks and regular stock.

Speculation

Penny stocks thrive based on speculation. This is because there is scanty information on how they operate, little revenues, inadequate or uncertain management, and no established products and specific industry. Speculative buying thrives on the hope of selling without reliable information on how it will be possible. On the other hand, blue-chips stocks have got very little or no speculative value. In these companies, you may not get substantial short-term gains, but you are sure of returns of say 10% or 15% per year.

Predictability and value

Regular stocks have more predictable revenues and earnings because many investors and analysts follow them. Their day to day activities are known and can be easily included in their share price. The stock shows the actual worth. Contrary, the actual value of penny stocks cannot be calculated easily, because some do not have revenue streams, inventories, or proven products. Shares in penny stocks will rise or fall depending on the demand to buy and sell with speculation being the determinant of demand. It is hard to know the price at which a penny stock share trades at since financial ratios and industry comparison are not effective for establishing the actual worth of a penny stock.

Fundamental analysis and availability of information

Penny stocks are poorly analyzed; hence, there is little information about them. They, therefore, have reduced visibility levels and irresponsible reporting on their inner activities; thus, they have no following. On the other hand, there is a lot of information about regular stocks. They are, therefore well known and heavily monitored.

Volatility

Penny stocks are highly volatile, and their prices fluctuate dramatically. You can either win big or lose big. Regular stocks are more secure and stable. They do not experience price swings hence more insulated on making big profits or losses.

Risk and reward ratio

Penny stocks have a high risk. Naïve and unlucky investors have lost money in them quickly. Sometimes the investors lose part of their capital, while other times traders lose everything, especially if the companies stop their operations, or go bankrupt, which is a common thing in penny stocks. It is vital to limit your risk in penny stocks to avoid these common pitfalls. Potential rewards are also higher. Since most of these companies are new start-ups and will grow huge with time into large corporations, a trader could get higher rewards. Regular stocks have less risk of investment and less potential since they are already established companies.

Ease of buying shares

It is possible to buy many shares in penny stocks without having a significant investment capital, but unable to buy the same amount of shares in a blue-chip and large-cap which are highly-traded. If you have just a few dollars, you can spread your risk on several penny stock companies, other than having to buy a few higher-priced shares of blue chips.

Takeover targets

Mostly, big companies acquire penny stocks because their market capitalization is lower. This makes them a ripe target for more prominent companies in the same field. Penny stocks also combine to increase sales and revenues and compete with the more notable players. This benefits the stock prices positively. On the other hand, blue-chip companies are more likely to purchase or take over smaller companies, which is dangerous to the price of the shares.

Dividends

In blue-chip companies, shareholders get a particular portion of the money as dividends because the companies have high cash flow, while in penny stocks, no dividends paid because these companies have no cash flow and are financially unstable.

Revenues and company life cycle,

Most penny stocks are in their initial stage of growth, and all they have is a good story. This means they have the potential for investors since they have good business ideas, business model, and they are trying to implement their operational strategy. They have a great idea but have yet to achieve it. They, therefore, have less or no revenue. Regular stocks are mature companies already in advanced stages. Consequently, they have less growth potential but higher revenue streams.

Industry and sector influences

Penny stocks undergo massive price changes when there is a change in the market. They are highly exposed to sector influences. This can work for the benefit or detriment of their shares. Regular stocks, on the other hand, are protected from the impacts of the sector and industry, and their stock is not dramatic with sector influence.

Niche marketing and economies of scale

Blue chips have enough capital and resources within their reach; they can also make strong alliances with other stronger players. Their products and services are highly recognized. This makes it hard for penny stock companies to make inroads in the pre-existing market due to the dominant force of these blue-chip companies. In such cases, they resort to niche marketing instead of going one on one with their strong competitors, so that they can perform best.

Opportunities and irrational spikes

Penny stocks rise or fall exceptionally even on slight provocations, by factors of little importance. On the other hand, regular stocks are stable and less volatile.

Driving factors and Fiscal situation

Penny stocks operate on huge debts, low or no revenue, and usually, their balance sheets are not pleasing. You can be frightened if you pay close attention to the fiscal outcomes, but investors overlook these basics about the companies and focus on the assumed returns on their shares if the company catches on. Their share price is, therefore, not connected to their basic results and balance sheet. On the other hand, for regular stocks, the most crucial factor to the share price is their fundamental results and the balance sheet.

Chapter 14: Beginners Strategies

It is important to seek knowledge before you venture into any investment — stock trading is not an exception. There are several strategies that you can use as an investor to maximize your gains, and minimize loses or balance both gains and losses in the stock market. In this chapter, we are going to look at some tips that will give you the proper start that you need so that you can become profitable while trading in the stock market.

Know the kind of a trader you are
Before you invest your money, you need to know the type of an investor you are, the goals on investment, and the risk you are prepared to take. You need to know whether you want to be actively involved in the management of your money and growth, or you want to invest it and forget it. Online brokers will ask your investment goals when you open your brokerage account. You will be able to invest in exchange-traded funds, index funds, mutual funds, stocks, and bonds.

Choose a system with a proven edge
Before even writing your plan to trade, you need to be sure that the system you are aiming at has a proven record. It makes no sense to buy in a system that loses money time, and again, it has to have a positive outcome over a particular period. You need to carry out a backtest either manually or with an automated system, but it is always good to be critical while carrying out your backtest. It will be fool handy of you if you don't carry it out thoroughly and correctly. You do not expect to plot Stochastic on your chart and then believe you can make money

Set long-term goals
Your goals should be clear as to why you want to invest in stock markets. You need to know whether you will need your money back in a few months or whether

you will need it after several years. You need to see if you are saving for retirement, for your children's education, to buy a house or whether you want to build an estate. If you need your money back soon, it is good to consider investing it elsewhere, because the stock market is volatile and may not guarantee your capital back in a short time. Knowing the possible time in the future when you will need your money will help you calculate how much to invest now to produce the desired results and meet your goals. You can calculate this by using free financial calculators available over the internet.

Understand the things that affect the growth of your portfolio

The growth of your portfolio will be affected by the initial capital that you invest, annual earnings on capital, and the period of your investment in terms of years. Start your investment plan without delays to maximize your savings and receive high returns.

Understand your risk tolerance

Understanding your anxiety and feelings towards the risk you want to take is vital to success as a stock trader. When you know your level of tolerance, you can avoid investing in stocks that make you anxious. There is no need for you to have an asset that will deny you sleep at night.

Choose your online brokers

They operate either on full-service or discount terms. Full- services brokers offer a full range of brokerage services such as retirement financial advice, health care, and any other money-related service. They charge substantial fees, and most of the times they deal with net-worthy clients on as a percentage of your transactions, assets, and yearly membership fee. In exchange, they give you detailed advice on your needs. It is, therefore, suitable to understand how you react to different types of stock market risks and choose an investment that gives you peace of mind Discount brokers used not to be very much preferred, but today, they have become the norm for most people. They provide you with the tools to select and place your transactions and offer advisory service focusing on long-term investment that doesn't need you to be actively involved in the stocks. As the scope of financial services progresses, online brokers continue to add more features such as educational materials on their sites and mobile applications. There are some discount brokers with no minimum balance requirements, but there may be other fees and charges associated with such accounts. These are all the factors you need to take into consideration while investing in stocks and deciding on your online broker.

Control your emotions

Your emotions can be an obstacle to stock market profits if you are unable to control yourself and make more informed decisions. The stock prices of a company may reflect the emotions of the investors combined in the short-term. When a good number of investors begin to worry about the company, the prices of stock are more likely to dip. When a large number of them feel optimistic, the stock price will often rise. When stock prices move contrary to what the investors' expected, it creates tensions and insecurity. They begin to wonder whether they should sell their position to avoid loss, keep the stock, and remain hopeful that the price will rise again, or by more stock.

Even with better price and better performance, that favors investor's expectations, there are questions on the part of the investors. They get caught in the weather to take the profits before the price drops, keep it and wait for the amount to continue rising or weather to buy more stock and earn more profit. You need to be able to balance yourself depending on what is happing to prices in the stock market.

Make a regular investment plan

Making new investments at regular intervals is a better investment strategy according to experts, than racing to by low and sell high. To create successful ventures, it has to be less about timing but giving your investment portfolio the time to establish itself. Best brokers waiver their requirements on the minimum balance if you make long-term deposits monthly. So do not get into the frenzied race of buying and selling during high times. Taking a slow and steady approach will make you win the race of investment in the long run.

Avoid the dreaded-wash-sale-rule

If you are a regular stock trader, you may find that you have violated the dreaded-wash-sale-rule. According to this rule, you are not supposed to sell shares of stock and buy the same shares after a short time. If you do this, you will be slapped with tax penalties, which are usually huge. By planning well, you can steer clear around such pitfalls and avoid suffering this fate while still enjoying your stock trade. Planning well is good to avoid such a trap if you are a regular trader.

Know how stocks can affect your Tax Bill

Knowing the regulations that govern your positions is essential if you want to trade actively in stock markets. Holding your stock in short-term attracts high IRS taxes. These regulations aim at discouraging short-term guessing and encouraging long-term investment. It will be useful for you to play by the rules as an active trader.

Harness the benefits of passive stock market strategies

As a beginner, you want to minimize cost and create a balanced portfolio. You can achieve this with mutual funds, index funds, and exchange-traded funds, which is also a strategy used by most investors. This is a better strategy to pool multiple stocks together and balance the losers and winners in the market, rather than betting on one company stock. Unlike active investment strategies which outperform the market through buying and selling shares frequently, these funds are built on passive management strategies, which reach for broader market gains to void unnecessary expenses

As a new trader, unnecessary expenses can crush you. Trading expenses are an enemy worthy considering if you are to succeed in stock trading. They come in the form of monies that you lose in terms of commission fees, capital gains tax, fictional expenses in mutual funds, spreads, and fees that do not benefit you. Learning to avoid unnecessary costs will be added advantage to you.

Strive to know

Some traders think that they can make money by opening a brokerage account. This is a misconception. Opening a trading account marks the first step of a long journey. You have to study the stock markets and understand them. Educate yourself with books and articles, look at charts for hours and try to make out what is happening, find a mentor, and attend seminars on stock markets. Many people overlook education, but it is crucial for a new trader who wants to succeed in stock market trading.

Learn from your mistakes and grow

As a new trader, you need to keep records of your trades. You may overlook this since you don't have anyone asking you of reports and updates. Keeping a journal helps you to discipline yourself and remain focused on profitability. By keeping a journal of your activities, you can later see what went wrong and how you can correct it. Otherwise, you will continue to trade still emotional of your previous loss and make more mistakes.

Chapter 15: Right Mindset and Psychology for Stock Market Transactions

In the business world, people engage in businesses with the sole aim of making a profit. This is why the corporate world is crowded with tricksters. In order to trade carefully and smart, one needs to equip themselves with some guidelines. People trade, some make profits and some encounter losses, but it is not always the end of the world since one way or another you will have to stay on your game. An attitude that the business world is a safe place is one that is misguided. In order to succeed in making profits, there are a number of things that need to be in place. For instance, your thinking process should be one that is business-oriented. You need prior planning and consultation. You can consider reviewing some business journals in order to find out what is happening in the business world.

Failing to plan is like going to a match without prior training and practice. Planning should be on top of your to-do list. You should consider planning before engaging in anything else. Your planning should be wide enough to cover the scope of what you want but limited only to the aspects that relate to the subject matter of your business. Through the whole process of planning, you should employ a mindset that will enable you to be successful. The success of a business comes with toil and sweat. The skills and habits that one develops over time are what makes a trader successful.

There are a number of things that makes someone succeed in trading. They include the following.

Having an inward push

For one to succeed in whatever field, one needs to be guided by an inward voice that he is bigger than any task before him or her. This will then push you to strain towards what you want to achieve. The whole process of sharpening your skills through continuous engagement in the field of business transactions. Your mind will be obliged to operate in a manner that focuses on the success of your business.

Keeping the fire burning

The success of many business enterprises did not happen over-night. A trader needs to understand that it is the continuous making of profit that will help enhance his or her business. The road is one that is full of bumps and thorns, but at the end of the day, the ones who survive through sheer agony are the ones that emerge victoriously.

Knowing your inner self

The only way to make it is to understand that challenges need to be a part of you. For instance, you should be ready to acknowledge a mistake, own it, and learn from it. Do not let it define you. Every individual has strengths and weaknesses. Learning to capitalize on your strengths and learning from your weaknesses makes you a bolder individual. In the face of trouble, learn to device new methods that will be of aid to you throughout your struggle. Push yourself and always believe that you can achieve.

Chapter 16: Money Management, Investing Wisely Within Your Scope

Investing is key in the business world because this is the only way that your money can actually grow. Consider investing your money instead of channeling it into wishful spending and impulse buying. A business' greatest asset is its money. Money is directly related to the business in the sense that an increase in money brings about a direct growth to the business. The way a business handles money will determine how fast it grows. Most businesses consider re-investing their initial profits at their early stages. This is the only way to ensure that the business picks up.

There are some guidelines for investing wisely.

Plow back profits

Re-investing in your business refers to the process of channeling your first profits towards improving your business. It can be through increasing some stock, buying an asset, or even replacing one that is worn out. Any move that ensures the business continues running smoothly is a smart move because the business will only thrive in an increment of profit.

Prioritize your moves

Starting a business is like taking care of an infant. You need to devote your utmost attention and thoughts towards it. The business goes through various stages before it becomes fully mature. As a business owner, you need to be equipped enough with market trends. Your expenditure should be geared towards the growth of the business. This means that you need to know when to invest and how much to invest. The business needs to have some deficit to manage the day to day running and thus during spending, spend only what falls within your scope. You need not over-spend and leave your business bankrupt.

Investing proper

An apt businessperson will always thrive on learning from the success of other businesspersons who have made it in the business world. You should also thrive where they made mistakes. This businessperson needs to be a quick learner and one who processes information with the agency it deserves. A slight sense of lackadaisical approach in the business world will land you in many debts. You need not shy away from taxes because this will be the onset of bad business ethics. Invest little by little. Do not invest all your profits at once; make sure that you have an actual strategy. It should be noted that Rome was not built in a single day.

Top-notch timing

The business world is made up of shifts in tides. The market trend change from time to time. Research has it that timing is the best way to attack the market and hit the road running. An entrepreneur should always be in constant anticipation of the business tides to change in his or her favor. He or she should always thrive on understanding the market trends and the various causes of these shifts. With this in mind, he or she will know when to re-invest, increase stock, and also make bold moves towards business success.

Chapter 17: Risks Involved in Stock Market

Investing in stock is risky; one can lose all their money or more than they invested in. Any investment is risky. The stock market involves stocks and bonds. Some risks in the stock market can be managed or controlled, while others are almost impossible to control. Understanding the risks involved before investing will help an investor decide if the risk is worth taking. Having a well thought of investment can keep stocks and bond risks at an acceptable level. Most of the risks affect the market and require investors to adjust the equities. Learning about your investment risks by thorough research can help one meet their financial goals.

Investment returns are not always guaranteed. One cannot for sure say that stock investment will give them money at a particular time. One can be guaranteed that they will stay in business or if the prices will favor them or if they will make to pay their dividends. Stock prices may change completely, turning around investment and even cause them more than they bargained for.

Here are some main types of risks that investors go through, and some of the strategies they used to overcome or minimize the risks.

Risks Faced by Investors

- Economy risks – this is the major risk an investor should be aware of. The economy can go bad at any time, and this is always an inevitable risk. When the market is affected, it may take years to stabilize it. For new investors, increasing positions at the firm and stable companies are the best strategy during this period so that they can overcome the downturns. Foreign markets work great after good research when domestic markets are down. Globalization has enabled most U.S companies to make the majority of their profits from overseas investment. For investors who are almost going into retirement, a downturn in stocks can be a great downfall if one hasn't shifted important assets to bonds or fixed-income securities.

- Inflation risk – sometimes investors think that inflation is under their control. Immense borrowing of the government to fund stimulus packages may force the return of inflation. Since time immemorial, investors have resolved to invest in assets like real estates and precious metals during inflations. Inflation, on the other hand, hits such investors hard since it wears away the value of their income flow. Stocks are the best investments to curb inflation since investors can always adjust prices to the inflation of rate. Old investors are encouraged to retain some of their assets stock because; a global recession may mean an extended period of time before the market can handle high prices.

- Market Risk – sometimes, the market may turn against your investment. This could be as a result of the collapse in the market. Investors may flee out of the market-leading to the suffering of both good and bad stocks. Some investors may take advantage of this situation by accumulating their stocks when the market is not dictating for the prices to go down. However, sometimes, it is heartbreaking to watch other markets go up while your investments are flat month after month. It is therefore important to not put all your investments in one market. Spreading of investments is advantageous in that while one market is still, the other markets may be bringing you huge profits.

- Conservative – being a too conservative investor may not be a good idea. This does not mean that being a careful investor is bad. However, taking risks is one of the ways to make one meet their financial goals.

It may take years for your investments to yield, but in the long run, one may greatly enjoy their decisions. Those who focus on just savings may not find this a wise decision after their retirement.

The changes in the market may lead to volatility. This means that if you expected or hoped for return in a short period of time, you could lose more. This is because of the fast changes in stock markets which make the stock riskier. There are ways to determine volatility:

- Standard deviation – this determines the variation of prices in stock from the past. The up and downs will give the average price from the past.

- Beta – this determines how a stock is doing compared to a certain benchmark.

Ways to Manage the Stock Market Risks:
- Portfolio – it is essential to invest in a diversified portfolio. Before buying a stock, one should try to see how the portfolio stocks match the other investments they have.
- Long-term investments – short-term investments usually are riskier than long-term investments. This is because if one buys with money they may urgently need in a short period, they may be forced to sell at low prices, therefore, making a loss.
- Timing the market – this may be risky because one may invest at a time when the market is doing well but soon after the market may fall. Some other investors, on the other hand, make the mistake of selling when the stock price goes down. Holding on a little longer may see the return of prices back up. This is because stocks are long-term investments with short-term ranges in prices.
- Seeking advice – this is a good strategy because it means you are investing in a market you are well familiar with. A qualified advisor may be a great help. The advisor will help you know everything, including what makes the prices rise and fall and how the investment strategy works.
- Avoiding private stock - private stock may be a bad idea because it may be a scam. You may also be unable to sell or buy when you want to. Private stock sometimes also means large investment, especially if you are not an employee of the company.
- Being widely aware of the risk – It is important to know the risks involved and how well you are protected by the law if it's an overseas investment. If you are not too sure about everything, it is better not to invest there.

Chapter 18: Mutual Funds

Mutual funds are investments that involve pooling money from different investors so as to buy shares of stocks, bonds, and other securities which one may be unable to do on their own. Net asset value (NAV) which is the price of the mutual fund is calculated by dividing the total value of securities into the portfolio and funds outstanding shares. The prices change depending on the value of securities in the portfolio by the end of the day. Investors, however, only own the shares and not the securities they fund. The decision to buy or sell securities of an active and well-managed fund is made by one or several portfolio managers. The portfolio managers may be assisted by researchers. The role of a portfolio manager is to ensure that they get investment opportunities that help the fund outdo its benchmark. By looking at the fund's return compared to its benchmark, one can easily know how the portfolio manager is performing. To determine this, it is best to look at the long-term performance as opposed to the short-term performance.

How It Works

Mutual funds are a smart way of investing for beginners because it may help an individual to be diverse in their investments. This is because most mutual funds hold a various number of securities. For an individual doing this kind of investment alone may be very expensive, impractical, and impossible.

Management

As an investor in the mutual fund, you are privileged to have a professional keep track of the portfolio regularly. Professionals are well equipped with the knowledge and resources that greatly assist in the research of companies before an investment decision is made. The professional deal with the stress of assessing where to and where not to invest, therefore saving time. Professional managers are maybe a little too expensive to an individual.

Liquidity

Mutual funds are very convenient because they allow one to purchase and sell their fund shares at least once a day at the close of the market's net asset value. One is also allowed to reinvest returns got from the dividends and capital gain. One may also decide to make additional investments any time they chose to. More stock funds in a mutual fund may cause you less than it would have cost you to invest as an individual.

Taxing

Securities within the portfolio pay dividends and interests. After a rise in value, a portfolio manager may sell the securities. By law, incomes by funds are to be paid to investors. All the income made to investors of the fund is taxed to them. However, income from generated from investments of a municipal are exempted from taxation by the federal and in some instances state taxes.

Charges

Mutual funds come with a number of charges. Some of the funds have fees for purchase and sale of commissions which is called loads. Some funds also charge sale of shares one has only owned for a short time which is called redemption fee. When figuring out a potential fund, it is important to know that charges determine a fund's performance over time.

Pool Investment Funds

This is where money from many people is put into one big fund with many widespread investments and managed by a professional. This is less risky and way easier than when one opts to purchase shares directly to a company.

How It Works

Many people get together, sum up their money, and give a portfolio manager the task of management. The professional manager invests the money in assets like bonds, shares, and properties. Different funds invest in different areas using different strategies such as income and capital growth.

Why It Is Important To Invest In A Fund:

- Spread of risk: no matter how little amount of money you have to invest, you can invest in a variety of assets. This means that poor performance from one of the fund's investment will not affect you so much since the other investments within the fund may be doing great.
- Sharing of costs: you are sharing the cost with other investors within the fund. Therefore, not using as much as you would have in a personal investment.
- Less stress: the management hired by the fund deals with the stress of buying, selling finding investments, and collecting dividends. Therefore this saves you time and workload.

Before joining a fund, one should be aware of crucial information regarding the fund so that they know what they are going to deal with. The information includes:

- The risk description
- How the fund intends to work
- Charges within the fund
- The fund's investment strategy

Your rights as an investor which include details of opting out, how to go about it, and the duration it may cost to cancel fully.

- The compensations the fund offers.
- The communication strategy within the fund. This includes who to talk to, complain to, and your right to access financial ombudsman service.

Ways of Investing in a Fund

One may choose to invest in a fund directly or chose to buy them as an investment product. This may come as listed below:

- Pension
- Stocks
- Endowment policy
- Stocks and assets investments

Stocks are an equity investment that involves owning shares in a corporation so that one is entitled to the corporation's profits and assets. Although common stocks do not guarantee payment of dividends, shareholders are assured of voting rights. Preferred stocks, on the other hand, do not provide voting rights, but they guarantee payment of dividends.

Assets Allocation Funds

An asset allocation fund is a fund that allows investors an opportunity to invest in a diverse portfolio of various assets. An asset allocation fund can be fixed or variable. Fixed meaning that it can be held to various fixed percentages of assets. Variable meaning that depending on the conditions of the market, it may be allowed to go up.

A fund will go through various asset allocations to see which to choose from. After determining their asset allocation, a fund can manage its investment in different ways. Some funds may choose to invest in different exchange-traded funds to gain different market exposures. Other funds, however, may choose to use the fundamental analysis where they select the best performing securities in every asset class. Most if not all funds will, however, do the monitoring, give or rebalance securities depending on how the market is changing and how the overall economic environment is operating.

Knowing the complete details about assets under management is very important for investors seeking to invest in a fund. When not understood, they can become a reason for a fund's underperformance since it becomes difficult to manage. The number of net assets can help determine the category of asset allocation a fund may settle on. Large investments in small corporations can greatly affect the share price of the company in question. Small capitalized stock funds with high net assets, on the other hand, buy stocks of large capitalized companies. This can make a fund reach the middle capitalization stock fund. This can shift the fund's initial focus when it gets to this level. This style is called the style drift. It is important to note, however, that the index fund's net assets do not affect its performance.

Chapter 19: Initial Public Offering

Initial Public Offering is a process where a company or an issuer makes a proposal to the public in the form of ordinary shares of stock. This means that the Initial Public Offering can be seen as the first sale that a private company makes to the public regarding its stock. Initial Public Offering is usually offered by new and medium-sized companies looking for funds for their own growth and expansion. We can also refer to IPO as a public offering.

Basics of Private and Public

As we understand, companies can either be private or public. A company falling under the private category as the name suggests is privately owned. This means that this type of company has fewer shareholders, and much of its information is not disclosed to the public. In most cases, small businesses are owned privately. However, there are also larger companies that are owned privately, for example, Cargill. In a private company, the shares can only be reached through the owners. Companies falling under the public category, on the other hand, usually have a portion of their business shares already sold to the investors in the public domain. When a company is doing an IPO, the company is said to be going public.

Why Should A Company Go Public?

The main reason as to why a company can choose to go public is for the purpose of raising a reasonable amount of cash for its growth and expansion.

Besides raising funds, the other reasons are;

i. Better rates; Public companies most of the times get better rates when issuing debts as a result of the increased scrutiny.

ii. Public companies usually have the ability to issue more stocks as long as there is market demand.

iii. Being publics presents many opportunities for a company. For instance, in the stock market, only public companies are allowed to implement employee stock ownership plans. As we understand, implementing employee stock ownership plans attracts top talents, and this is a win-win situation.

iv. Liquidity is driven by trading in the open market.

Factors to Consider Before Applying for an IPO

Before a company's IPO is approved, the following must be looked into;

i. The company's historical records

ii. Who are the company's promoters, is the company reliable? And are there any negative past records?

iii. Has the company entered into a collaboration with any other technological firm?

iv. What products or services are offered by the company? Do these products have the potential of going forward?

v. What are the project values and the different techniques put in place to the growth plan into execution?

vi. What the risk aspects are of involved in the plan execution?

The General Terminologies used in IPO

i. Primary market

This is the initial point where creations of securities happen. In other words, the primary market is an open stock market where companies offer and directly sell their shares for the first time. This opens doors to investors inviting them to buy shares. Usually, this market is mainly dominated by larger investment institutes like hedge funds, investment banks, etc.

ii. Prospectus

This refers to a formal legal document that describes the company creating the proposed IPO. This document is important in ensuring that investors are made aware of the risks involved with an investment. Sometimes this document is referred to as offer document.

iii. Book building

This is the process describing the attempt determining the price with which securities can be offered.

   iv. Price band

This refers to the band within which investors are allowed to bid. Usually, there is no regulatory approval used to determine the IPO price. The band price can only be decided by the merchant bankers and the company itself.

   v. Listing

The shares that companies offer in IPOs must be listed on stock exchanges so as to enable trading to take place. When your shares are listed on the stock exchange, it simply means that these stocks are available and can be traded in the secondary market.

   v. Flipping

This simply refers to the reselling of a hot IPO stock just for a few days after offering shares with the goal of earning a quick profit. This is the reason as to why most companies want long-term investors and not traders.

The IPO Process

An IPO basically consists of two main parts. The first part of the IPO is the pre-marketing phase, and the second part is the IPO itself. If you have a company and you are interested in an IPO, the first step will involve an advertisement to the underwriters in the attempt of soliciting private bids. This advertisement can also be used as a way of generating interest by making a public statement. In most cases, a company will have several underwriters who will be responsible for managing the different parts of the IPO processes in a collaborative manner. These underwriters will be involved in each and every aspect of the IPO, including IPO's due diligence, issuance, and preparation of the necessary documents, marketing, and filing. Below is a summary of the IPO process;

Selection of an investment bank

The issuing company must first begin by choosing an investment bank that will advise it on IPO as well as provide underwriting services. A company selecting an investment bank must keenly research on the bank's reputation, bank's expertise in the banking industry, distribution means (ways with which this bank can issue securities to investors) and a history of its relationship with the investment bank.

i.   Due diligence and regulatory filings

An investment bank (underwriter) selected will act as a broker between the public and the company. It is responsible for selling then initial shares of the company to the investing public. The issuing company should choose the underwriting services that best fit them. The underwriting services include firm commitment, a syndicate of underwriters, and best efforts agreement.

ii.   Pricing

After the approval of an IPO, a decision is made to determine the effective date. Just a day to the effective day reaches, the price offer and the precise number of shares are decided. This is done by the issuing company and the underwriter. The offering price is offered by the company's goal and market economic conditions.

iii. Stabilization

After the stock shares have been brought to the market, an analyst recommendation is provided by the underwriter, and after the market has stabilized, a market for the stock issued is created.

iv. Transition to market competition

This is the final stage of the IPO market. It starts twenty-five days after the IPO. Investors move from just relying on the mandated disclosures to market forces in regard to the information on their shares.

Chapter 20: Where to Buy and Sell Stocks-Explains the Platforms for Buying and Selling Stocks

When we talk about buying and selling of shares what comes to mind is the fact this is the sale and buying of a part of a business or company. This selling and buying happen every day. When one buys shares, it means that they own a certain part of the company and may even get some dividends at the end of the financial year. One can be able to collect a good amount of money from the dividends. The selling of the shares meaning you are giving up your ownership rights to the company or business.

Shares are traded in many ways, but the most common is the online trading platform which most people call the forex trade. The forex trade is mostly an online form of buying and selling shares. Forex uses the net to connect people from all parts of the world to buy and sell shares from companies registered under the stock exchange market. The companies which are mostly registered in the stock exchange market are the public entities. Private entities are also involved in the stock and shares trade, but they are done privately. That means their sales and buying is done on private announcements, unlike the public entities.

Forex then deals with brokers. This is the people who connect the buyers and sellers. They are the ones that facilitate the buying and selling of stocks and shares. They guide the buy to the right kind of shares and stocks. They also help a seller to sell the shares or stocks he or she wants to get rid of. The broker is online in this case of forex trade. The broker gives advice to both the buyer and the seller on shares and stock matters. They connect buyers and seller from all around the globe in terms of buying and selling.

One can also use a face to face broker. This avoids someone who works online. This does not use forex trade but the benefits of the broker are all the same when it comes to the face to face broker just like the online broker. They will connect the seller to the buyer so that the seller can be able to sell his or her stocks to the buyer. In the long process, the broker gets commissions if they sell pushes through.

There also others who prefer things such as no broker. They take themselves to the company that is for the buyers and for the sellers is that they take themselves to the buyers. This is an uncommon way to buy and sell shares of stock. This method also is less expensive compared to where a broker is present. This method is mostly used by people who have trust issues and like doing things straight and without hesitation. In this method, the mediator is kindly removed out of the sales picture. This is another way to ensure a trade happens.

All said and done there so many platforms to do selling and buying of shares and stocks. Most of these platforms are online ones. They range in variety, and one has to choose according to his or her liking. One of these platforms includes Ameritrade. It is said to be the best platform in any kind of shares and stock transaction. They have affordable prices for both the buyers and sellers. They ensure that both the buyers and sellers are satisfied at the end of the day. Also, brokers get a good amount in their commissions in the line of work.

The other is known as Robinhood, and most of the people call it practically free. This is due to no entrance free. Each trading platform is categorized differently. In terms of commissions, entrance fee, and many more factors. There many platforms that one can trade-in and enjoy. The better the options, the more people that join. Robinhood does not offer any sort of education about the stock exchange market. It also does not have commissions for sales that make it cheaper for the buyers and sellers. The brokers really avoid this platform because of this small hitch.

Another is the ally invest. It is said to have low costs and also has zero minimum. In this platform, one invests. This is putting a certain amount in which you use to trade, and it grows if the sale happens. The growth of the first installment happens in percentage; it is called a bonus. It may be 20, 30, or even up to 80 percent. They help one to make money which he or she can withdrawal at any time. They also host competitions in which members participate to earn a certain amount of cash adding up to someone's deposit in the platform.

Lastly, there is Olymp trade, this one I have used personally. When one opens up the account with them, one is given a trial account in which one train on ways of how to trade. Mostly one learns how to predict the chart of rising and falling of currency. They also educate someone on ways to become an excellent trader. The other thing is that they host competitions called the webinar where different traders compete against each other. They are traders from different parts of the world. Once, one has topped up their account and uses their own cash after trade one gets bonuses too.

The trading platforms are so many ones just find where you fit right. You have to look at what is think is best with you and work with it. Trading platforms are mostly online; they are so digitalized to fit the era we are in. They make stock market trading so easy to do. They are organized to everyone's taste and preferences, and every man should know the existence of this trading platform. If you want to trade, research on more of them. I have only mentioned a few to keep you informed.

Chapter 21: Indicators to Look Before Investing

There are several factors which can make the price of a stock to drop or rise. This can be anything from certain news about the change in the earnings of a company to the mood on investors about the stock market. Investors consider several factors which they use to make prospects on the returns on their investment before they buy stock. In this chapter, we are going to discuss these factors and how they affect the rise and fall of stock prices.

The company's earnings per share (EPS)
Take the gross profit of the company and divide it by all the shares in that company. You would get the amount that each stock is worth if all the profit was to be paid to the shareholders. You can use EPS to compare different companies in the same industry. Those with streamlined EPS will most likely perform better than those with unsteady earnings over time.

Price to earnings ratio (P/E)
To arrive at this, divide the company's current price of each share with the earnings of each share. Use this number to measure the link between the stock prices of the company with its earnings. This ratio indicates a low stock price or high stock price, in comparison with the company earnings. Companies with high P/E are likely to do better in the future.

Company's earnings ratio to growth ratio (PEG)
It projects the company's growth in terms of profits. Use this to know if a stock will have to be a good or poor value. When it is a low number, it means that you will pay less to benefit out of the company's earnings that are projected to rise in the future.

Price to book value ratio (P/B)

It is the comparison of the value that is recorded on the company's books, with the value that the market indicates about the company. Divide each share's current price by the value of each stock, as stated in the books, to arrive at the P/B. To get the book value of a company, look at the current equity listed on the annual report. You pay less for book value when the P/B is low. You can use P/B to estimate stock picks and end up getting well-priced stock that has excellent growth potential.

Dividend payout ratio (DPR)

To arrive at DRP divide the yearly dividends each share has by earnings for each share. This shows the amount the investors receive from the company in comparison with the earnings of their stock. You can use this figure to get an idea of dividend payment that is being supported by the earnings of the company. The DRP of established companies is usually higher. They use their profits to pay more dividends, which is good for their shareholders and the firm. Growing companies will have low DPR because they have little or no earnings and rarely pay dividends.

Dividend yield

To calculate this, divide the yearly earning of each share by the current price of each share. Use this to measure the returns you are getting on dividends in relation to the price of the stock. It indicates the cash flow that you get for your money.

Investor sentiments

Investor's sentiments have an impact on the market and may make it go up or down, making the stock price to drop or rise. "Bull" is when investors are optimistic and have confidence in the market, and it often leads to rising stock prices. Usually, it is good economic prospects that inspire confidence to investors. "Bear" market shows a lock of optimism on the part of investors due to downtimes in the economy hence dwindling confidence on investors. It often makes the stock prices to fall. This happens when there is an economic recession, unemployment, and rising prices of goods.

Industry performance

Stock prices for companies in the same field move together because they all face the same market conditions. But in case there is bad news about one of them, the other's stock price will benefit from such news because they are competing in the same market.

Management

The management profile of a company has an impact on the company's success and stock prices. If a company has robust control buy experienced professionals, share prices are likely to be higher, but poor management that lacks integrity will make prices of shares to fall.

The political climate of a country

When there are peace and tranquility in the country, with good government policies, the economy thrives hence high stock prices. On the other hand, when poor government policies rock country, the stock prices will fall.

The political profile of a company

Companies which are being politically targeted either directly or by association can suffer, especially if they are not in a popular industry. Companies which draw the attention of politicians such as cigarette companies and breweries may struggle to stabilize in the stock market. Holding stock in such a company which draws undue attention may be risky. It will be better to choose a company with a low political profile.

Whether the stock is optionable

Optionable stock means that you have additional ways to profit for it, hence minimize potential losses and enhance gains or yield additional revenue. It means that you can earn more from the same stock

Profit levels of the company

The essence of being in business is to make a profit. So before you buy stock in the company, you want to know whether it is making losses of it is profitable. Profit is the essential financial element of a company the shows how good the company is doing. If a company is making losses, it means that it may soon or later go out of business. If a company closes its doors, jobs are lost, and the government losses taxes, this means that the government many do not function well when so many companies are closing. This may make the stock price to fall. Investing in a company that is losing money is like making a debt, and it is not a good bargain at all.

Liability levels

Investors will prefer investing in a company with low debt than the one with high debt. High level of debt will render a company bankrupt. A company with limited liability has more borrowing power and can benefit from opportunities such as taking over another company, which will help grow the company further. This will lead to more benefits to the firm and its shareholders.

Company sales

For a new investor who wants to buy stock, he can use the sales of a company to gauge its performance. Looking at three or four years of company sales, you can know whether the company will survive in the coming future because more sales mean a robust customers base. If the sales are dwindling, you need to be wary, regardless of whether the company is making a profit.

Other economic factors

1. **Interest rates**

    When there is a change in monetary policies, and a company takes a loan to grow and expand its activities, the company's cost of the debt may be affected by high-interest rates. This leads to a reduction in dividends paid to shareholders as a result of low profits, hence dropping its stock prices. During high-interest rates, other investments may pay more bonuses and will be attractive to investors than stocks. When interest rates are lower, the demand for funds goes high, and the demand for shares also increases subsequently. High-interest rate lowers demand for funds and demand for shares goes down too.

2. Economic outlook

Expanding economy leads to rising stock prices, and investors may buy more stocks in the hope that they realize more profit later making the stock prices to rise. If the economy is unpredictable or shrinking, investors may stop to buy or start to sell.

3. Inflation

Inflation leads to rising prices of consumer goods, hence reducing sales, which drive to low profits. High prices may also lead to increased interest rates, in the case where the Canadian bank raises interest rates to mitigate the rate of inflation. Such changes tend to make stock prices to drop. Others areas of the economy may do well with inflation shifting the focus of investors to them.

4. Deflation

Deflation means lower prices for goods; thus, companies will not make a lot of profit from the sale of their products. Investors may opt to sell their shares and invest in other areas such as bonds which offer fixed income. During these times, interests get lowered to have people borrow more. The net effect of this will be increased economic activities. Due to low-interest rates, this can cause stock prices to fall.

5. Political and economic shocks

Rising energy costs will lead to the increased cost of production hence low profits for companies and hard economic times for consumers. If there are activities of terrorism in a country, it will harm the economy. Such changes will lead to a fall in stock prices.

6. If there is a change in economic policy

New governments coming to power tend to come with new economic policies. These changes can either be good or bad for business. Such changes can impact negatively on the price of goods, causing inflation, or they may cause interest rates to rise. These changes can either have a negative or positive impact of stock prices.

7. Canadian dollar Value

Most buyers from other countries by goods from companies in Canada. That means, when the value of their dollar rises, Customers consuming products from these companies will have to part with more money to buy them. The rise in prices will result in low sales and lead to a fall in the stock prices. On the other hand, when the value of their dollar falls, prices of these goods will fall hence more sales and rise in stock prices.

Chapter 22: Minimizing Losses Through Diversification

Diversification can be referred to as the process by which individual ventures in different asset classes. When an individual invests in something, their expectations are usually that the returns would be profitable. However, this is not the case because various areas of investment react differently towards investment. The tides in the business world are never predictable. In order to prevent the encounter of losses and make sure that your returns are up to the maximum, you need to diversify. Diversification does not necessarily act as a shield to losses, but I enable continuity of the business towards achieving their long-term set objectives.

The proverbial adage of putting all your eggs in one basket can be best be described by lack of diversification. The importance of diversification can be expressed by the following scenario. Take, for instance, you own a portfolio of shares in a particular service providing industry says Safaricom. Safaricom workers go on strike due to their various grievances going unheard. The value of your shares will drop since customers will revert back to other service providers, for instance, Airtel. Take, for instance, you had balanced your investment shares between Acxiom and Datalogix, as the values of the shares would be dropping in firm A, Firm B will be hitting sky high. Diversification can go further and is not limited by the number of investment stocks.

An apt business mind would want to cut across companies and firms. Focusing on the discrepancy, the more differentiated your stock is, the wider the market is covered, and the safer you are as an investor. Investing in different asset classes is key in the business world because different asset classes react differently to the adverse changing tides in the market. The only way to minimize loss during adverse events is having a group of unrelated assets. The issue of bonds and equity are a clear example of why diversification is key. Generally, in a market structure, bonds and equities tend to counter-cross each other. An increase in one variable, for instance, would see a drop in the other. This way, your equilibrium is maintained. Thus losses are minimized.

Geographical jurisdiction should not be your limit when diversifying. It is key that you always be on the look-out for investment opportunities, especially beyond your boundaries as a businessperson. The harsh conditions of the market trends say in Kenya may not be the same in the United States. You may also find that the market heir is more favorable as compared to the situation at home. With various investments in a different part of the world, you are ensured of continuity since the losses encountered in one aspect say the stock will be absorbed by other assets. This ensures that you stay on course.

It is key to acknowledge the bag of goodies that come with diversification. It is also key to note some demerits that come as a result. For instance, managing various portfolios in different parts of the world can be cumbersome, and it may even eat up into your profits because you will have to delegate some managerial duties. Diversification acts as a method of reducing the impact of loss and not eradicating the loss completely. When investing in a company, for instance, your expectations need to be two way in that the best companies have always thrived in misrepresenting investor a then landing them into losses.

The number of stocks a business that a businessperson owns will always determine how much profit they make. Owning a larger number of stocks will always be advantageous. However, there reaches a time when the stocks are at saturation, and no matter how many stocks you add, no difference is experienced whatsoever. A heated discussion has ensued on the number of stocks that a businessperson needs to maintain in order to keep the high profits coming in and also absorb the various losses that might occur. Research has it that an individual can achieve this by owning not more than 20 stocks across various companies. Diversification helps minimize the risk associated with the stocks of an individual. Market risks take a toll on every stock, and thus, diversifying in the asset classes is key.

Chapter 23: Stock Types and How to Choose. Discusses the Type of Stock and How One May Choose

Stocks that are traded are so many in numbers. They are categorized into groups that have specific features. There are so many groups, but there two main ones. They have their difference, advantages, and disadvantages. They make it easy to know them from both sides. They are both important, but the buyer or seller has to choose between the two of them. Thus, I will cover in-depth writing on the types of stocks and how they both work at the end of it all.

These types of stocks are learned in school for those who take business as a subject or major. They fall under the category of business as they look at the company as a large scale operation. The first type of stock is common stock. When one has these common stocks, then they have voting rights to the company. They also earn the profit of the company that is informed of dividends and is given after the financial year. The dividends are not guaranteed and are not necessarily given to the stock owners. The profit hence is undependable.

The other is the preferred stock. This is the opposite of the common stock. Their similarities to bonds are uncanny. Bonds are loans that are given to a company or institution or even the government. It has a fixed dividend, unlike the common stock in which one is given a certain amount of money at the end of a profitable financial year in the company. They also have the advantage to have their dividends are paid before the ones with common stock holding. This applies even in liquidation or bankruptcy of the company. They are good for someone willing to invest in long-term situations.

Pros and Cons of Preferred Stock and Common Stock

This pros and cons help one to decide on which one is the best type of stock is the best to invest in. They act as a guide for every investor to take while they consider bidding their money in the world of stock exchange. They must do research to know to look at the weighing factors that they have to know about what they are getting themselves into. There is so much the pros and cons give to the investor, and thus, they are good to know.

Both the common and preferred stock they offer dividends at the end of a profitable financial year. Their only difference is that in preferred stock, the dividends are fixed and are very assured. For the common stock, on the other hand, its dividends are not fixed or even assured. The preferred stock is good in long-term investments, which are to say the common stock is not that good in long-term investment. It's unstable or unfixed, making it not such a good choice for long-term investments. They both are good in terms of dividends since they receive each their share.

The common stock has voting rights. This means that they are able to make decisions in the company that they partly own through the shares. This says that every decision made is passed through the people members who own the company. This makes the common shares very good to own. They make you a decision-maker. The preferred stock does not have any voting privileges; hence, one with them does not make decisions at any point the company decisions are made. They are just like a silent partner in terms of the business. They provide capital and gain some share in the profit.

Apart from the common and the preferred stock, there other categories of stock types. These are not major like the two but are still as important as them. I am only going to discuss four of them for now. They are many more, and this just acts as an eye-opener for all those who want to invest in the stock exchange. It is worth to know not all companies have this kind of stock they are just there for some companies, unlike the two types of shares. So here they are and what they consist of the following.

The first is company size. It may not necessarily be the size in square feet but the size in investments and profits that come into the company. This helps to classify the kind of shares to be used in the company. The size of the company small or big determines a lot of things like the profit margin, the number of investors the other also is the shares to be sold to the public. Public entities and private entities vary in this case in the case of public entities; the investment is made by the government while private the funding comes privately from its founders.

The other is the industry factor stocks. This refers to things that relate to coming together, like petroleum and energy. They call themselves the energy industry. They then sell their shares together to get more investors in the industry. They do this to make investing easy and also allow the expanding of the industry in the long run. They work towards a larger goal than just the company goals. They like to merge many companies in this type of stock. They help in most of the public entities in a certain country to improve the economy.

There is also the factor of location. Stocks can also be grouped according to where the company is found. This means like a company having many branches all over the world. One can diversify where they can invest the cash in. They can invest in so many far areas without worrying. One has to make a location to be nothing since the benefits will obviously come through thereafter. This is done by people investing in companies that are all over the world. They get to experience the world of both the local and international business standing as an investor.

Finally, there is the style, as a type of stock. They are said to be value or growth. This is what people refer to stock as in local term. They are categorized in terms of those growing quickly and those that are not. One obviously looks at the companies growing so that they can invest in. No one wants to invest somewhere where the company is not growing — the bigger the growth, the higher the investment. The more you look at it, the better it becomes for you to use at any point when you want to invest in stocks and shares.

The most important thing to look at during choosing where to invest in stock is not really the type of stock you invest in but the funds one provides. The most important and useful fund is the index fund. This kind of fund allows one to buy many stocks at a go. There is also the means of looking for a broker and setting up an account for them to reduce their expense during a transaction in buying and selling of shares. Brokers and even the index have been discussed in certain sections of the book, and more information is depicted.

Chapter 24: Technical Analysis- Discuses the Technical Analysis as a Strategy for Investing Stocks

Technical analysis is a strategy used in the stock market in which one looks at the past charts of the markets so he or she can be able to predict the future charts. This method is mainly used by incoming investors. It helps them to master the tricks of the trade that they are going to join. It is a good way to show them the ropes around the stock exchange market. They are very visual, so they help one understand how they work in an easy and effective way.

Technical analysis is not the only kind of strategy used in the stock market trade; there is fundamental analysis too. This analysis, fundamental analysis, is where one focuses on the economic factors. One looks at the upside and downside of the place of investment by looking at the financial or economic records. This helps one to understand the level of profit and loss and whether the investment will be long-term. Fundamental analysis is believed to work long-term compared to technical, which is very short-term. Technical analysis is cheaper than fundamental analysis since it requires for economic research.

There are two assumptions that make up the technical analysis. The first is the market has values that represent factors that affect the stock prices. The hypothesis of the market gives the stock prices at any given point. They make it easy to predict what comes next just by looking at the past. It also works where the market is uncertain. It is also done to a market that is low and not high since it is not easy to predict if at all, it is that way. It is an interesting assumption to work with at all.

The other assumption is that the market price movements are not just random but move patterns that are easy to identify. The patterns also tend to repeat themselves over time, of course. Technical analysis works with prediction. This is easy if the pattern repeats itself. The more one can notice this then the easy it will be for them to trade. The repeat of the pattern makes things easy and the prediction easier since one can tell where the curve will be heading to. This type of analysis is unlike fundamental analysis because this is just observing the charts. So technical analysis has some pros for itself. Since it is merely observing the charts on gets a clear view and understanding. The only thing one has to do is look at the price movement in the market. One is able to look at the chart by understanding what it means, and that is easy to do. All you have to do is go back to the past and observe. Ensure you get the whole concept so that when you predict the future pattern, it will be easy. The future patterns are clearly affected by the past patterns that were there.

The other advantage is that it is not that expensive. The charts are found online on trading platforms hence easy to acquire without requiring a lot of cash. This is unlike fundamental analysis in which where one has to do very extensive research. That means the amount of information needed is very much big, and the bigger the search for information, the bigger the amount of cash needed for the research. This makes technical analysis likable to the people. It is cheap and can be used by everyone. The only thing needed is a device to connect to the internet, and you get your charts.

Where there are advantages, then the disadvantages are not far off at all. There may be too many indicators on the charts. What does this mean? It means every trader can mark his charts to his or her like for more understanding of the trade. If then the person researching on the former charts finds charts that have been marked fully, then he or she can get confused. The charts have so many indicators already; if there added ones, then the person may get bored or tired of trying to understand the whole chart full of writings.

Finally, one may read the technical information wrong. This is possible since one is looking just at the graphs. The way of learning is observation is what is used in the long run. The eyes can cheat someone in many cases. And since we are dealing with graphs, a person than one may not understand the information that is shown by these graphs. These graphs need someone who knows and understands these graphs. This then limits the number of people who use this technical analysis. This is such a bad disadvantage which limits the people to learning and understanding the stock exchange market in short.

Chapter 25: Stop-Loss and Take Profit-Enlightens Readers on the Different Aspect of Stop-Loss and Take Profit Strategy in Investing

In the stock exchange market, the possibility of loss and profit is there. It is even said to be 50-50 percent on average. This to say the possibility of both happening on this kind of business is out there. All the investor does is to take the risk, or others might say a leap of faith. This, just like all businesses risk, is possible in the form of loss. There is more to profit and loss in such an investment. So how do we make profit and avoid loss?

One way to ensure massive profits and zero losses is by looking at past investments in the market. That means looking at all the charts and curves to identify the downside and the upside of the business. Looking into the past helps one to look to the future ahead. The more one is able to know the curve in the investment charts, the better he or she can garner profit from the investment. This is an easy and simple way to lead yourself to more profit and long-term success of any investor.

The next thing is that one has to invest their money in small amounts. If at all, your plan is to invest in something, then the best thing is to do it slowly by slowly. That might be called by others, tasting the waters. This is just a simple meaning of this tip. Use a certain amount and try the business. If the results come as a profit to you, then dive in a little more, but if the results come like a loss, then it is advisable to look for another option. This clearly helps you to avoid a bigger loss.

The other thing is to find a good source of income. That means to find someone or an institution that can fully fund you for the investment in one's head. The things to consider include the period one needs to return the money, also the interest that is required during the return of the loan. If the period is short, it is then unsuitable for an investment that may take time to gain profit. The other thing is that if the interest is high, then it is unsuitable for most of the investment's plans. This is important to all investors.

It is always good to know these ways to enhance profit and reduce loss. The tips mentioned are just but some but there is more to gaining profit and reducing losses. All investment should consider profit-building activities to eradicate any losses. The more one learns about investment management then and only then will profit be high. Every starting investor should always consult and avoid rushing into things. It is good advice to give you all readers. Do your homework always on each and every business that you feel the need to invest in it. Take a step.

Chapter 26: Simple Step-By-Step Guide to Make the First Order: A Step-By-Step Guide to a Successful Investment

A successful investment is not only about profit; it is all about planning. The great the investor is at planning, then the better his or her investment is. Planning is something naturally bestowed to man, but how one maintains the ability to plan is all in the man himself or herself. It takes effort and needs for man to be great at planning. Man needs to organize his or her life in all aspects if he or she wants maximum excellence. Investments are how one takes them. They might either be successful or a big failure depending on how they are taken. Investments are like a well-planned game of cards. Gambling is very well similar to investment. How is this the case, you ask? Gambling deals with loss, profits, and risk. All those are factors that bring up the word investment to the table. It is important to focus on all these aspects if they expect success in the near future. If you understand this aspect clearly, then you will be an investment guru for all to acquire.

The first thing is to survey the investment one wants to take. One should keep an eye on what he or she wants to take. This is to know the investment works. This is the first step that one takes to diving into an investment. One cannot just dive in deep to something they know nothing of. This helps someone to know where they will start. It also helps one to choose the right investment for him or her. An investor is advised to dig deep in all investment matters to avoid losses and also getting himself or herself in something unsuitable. The investigation can be in legal terms or even economic terms. That means look at the upside and downside in the legal terms of the investment and also in the economic terms. One may also ask for advice from friends and family. These people are those who are closest to you. They always have an opinion and may also have truly good advice about such matters. This is important since one man cannot do it alone. This is very important in any investment plan. It acts like caution or warning for the investor in case the investment is not good to undertake.

The other thing is to find a good source of income. After one has done his or her research on the investment and is sure they want to invest in, then one should be aware of the income they are to use. The income can come from one's personal savings. This may be through some years of hard work savings or a pension or even someone's basic salary. This is the easiest way to acquire the money one needs. It is easy, and there is no paying back unless in terms of the profit of the investment. Another way of acquiring income for investments may be through friends and family. Family and friends are to help someone get through any kind of times like both hard and good. One may have to refund the cashback this may be with or without interest. They may also not have to give back the cash or even may make the friend or family member a partner in their business or investment. The other form is taking a loan. This may be through the bank or SACCOs depending on where it suits you best. This requires refunding with interest, and one must have a guarantee in order to be issued with the loan.

The other thing is taking things slow. Business or investments are not to be rushed. Once you decide to take a step into investments, then one should be good at taking things slow. The business takes longer to build but is easy to destroy. In terms of investments, then an investor is ought to be careful at any point and time. His or her work is to make decisions, provide capital, guide the business, and wait for the results that one is ought to get at the end of it all. Patience is a very important virtue for every investor. An investor must be able to take thing slow and wait for things to go on smoothly. The investor has to put in so much work in so that, later, he or she can get his or her profit. To get to the joys of profit, then one has to grow a very long process of business nurturing. They have to work tirelessly since the profit does not just come easily in the first days of the business. Working for a goal to reach it is never easy; the important thing to know is the fruits ahead.

Finally, it is important knowing what you want in the end. The investors should know whether they want their investments to be long-term or short-term. The investor should also know what they want from the investment in the long run. The goals help one work harder to get to where he or she wants. One should set reasonable goals that he or she knows that they can reach. Then, after setting the goals, the investor should work hard to reach them with no issue. The goals are to set someone on the path they want to be in. This is a great way for one to reach to what they may want in life. After profits come in, they make you hungrier for more. That means that an investor works tirelessly to see his or her dreams come true. Investments keep someone financially stable, but it can also be tragic depending on the results. This is determined by the loss or gain that the investors make in their businesses or investments. This is the greatest things that come from investments: profits and losses. All in all, the above give you a start-up to investments.

Chapter 27: Create a passive income with dividends

Obtaining passive income with dividends, what does that mean? When dealing with securities such as stocks or funds, many people primarily think of their fluctuating prices, i.e. whether the securities rise or fall in value. Another branch that makes securities so interesting and attractive compared to other forms of investment is completely neglected: the dividend.

What are dividends?

Dividends refers to the participation of shareholders or unit holders in the success of the respective security or the underlying companies. Part of the profits are therefore passed on to the owners, also known as distributions. These distributions are then your passive income. In contrast to reinvestment products, the investor receives a passive cash flow from the dividends. Profits are reinvested automatically for reinvesting products, which is why the compound interest effect has a stronger effect there than for distributing products.

But the nice thing about dividends: Despite the current low-interest phase, dividend-oriented stocks and funds can still yield around 5 percent and more without greater risk and reasonably predictable! Dividends are sometimes distributed annually or quarterly. The money then goes directly to your account, from where it can be used at will (or even better: re-invested).

When it comes to finding the best stocks for your own investment portfolio, high-dividend stocks are at the top of the priority list. If you manage to identify stocks with a high dividend, you can benefit twice: once in the form of price increases and once in the form of dividends

The share dividend can also be used to reinvest in shares or other forms of investment. Or you can use it as regular additional income. For example, the reinvestment of the dividend represented 42% of the total return on the Standard & Poor's 500 Index since 1930.

The selection of the best stocks can be overwhelming at first, but there are some guidelines on which you can orientate yourself to facilitate the selection process.

We want to take a look at these below

Dividend stocks offer you money that you can use to pay the rent without having to sell the stock. They provide you with an income. Your money is working for you, so you don't have to. Your share pays you more and more money every year. At least if you have chosen good dividend stocks. Many stocks on the stock exchange have increased their dividends every year for more than 20 years.

Dividends are purely passive income. In my opinion there is no debate about it. You will benefit from dividend income after taking the time in advance to make your investment decision. In addition, you are a minority owner in a business and maintain no controlling-interest decision making. You also don't have to spend a lot of time managing your investment. Just a few efficient readings every few months.
After that, you can take some time to monitor your investments. With the advent of various mobile apps and the speed of information, dividend investments for modern investors will be made now and in the future.

5 Investments steps for passive income with the aim of living off of dividends

If you follow the rules to find the best stocks for dividends, your dividend investment is passive. As you build your portfolio over time, only limited work needs to be done. You just need to make sure that real-time notifications are enabled for your dividend portfolio.

Can you generate passive income from investments? Absolutely, all you need to do is follow these five steps to achieve the ultimate goal of living on dividends.

1. Contribute $200 a month to your dividend portfolio in your first year

Set up an automatic monthly contribution of $200 to your dividend growth portfolio. That should be an easy start. If you want to contribute more, even better! Make your posts automated as much as possible. We want to save our time on other passive sources of income.

2. Increase your monthly contributions by 25% a year

That sounds like a lot, but it can be doable as long as you increase your income from other sources along the way. As long as you are a good saver, you should be able to do this for the first 10 years. After that, the annual increases become much more difficult, but they are certainly achievable.

3. All dividend income you receive should be reinvested in your dividend growth portfolio

Once you receive dividend income, you can use it to buy more stocks in your portfolio. Instead of a dividend reinvestment plan, I like to invest at my own discretion. A dividend reinvestment plan automatically buys shares in that particular share. Without the dividend reinvestment plan, you can invest in a stock if its value goes down, or you can invest in another dividend stock in your portfolio.

4. Invest in high quality stocks that can help you increase 6% of the value of your shares

This point should not be difficult to make. You will have some winners and some There are various other ways to create passive income other than dividends (rental properties, CDs, annuities, and peer-to-peer lending), but I prefer dividends resulting from index funds.

One reason for this belief is because stocks are far more liquid than real estate and other financial assets (easier to sell a stock than a house). Regardless of which method you prefer, you need to start making passive income. I guarantee you won't regret it! Losers, but make sure you have 6-8 winners of every 10 actions each.

5. Repeat steps 1 to 4 over time

Continue with your plan and everything will be fine. I like to build a carefully selected version of dividend stocks, rather than indexed investments. This allows me to focus on certain returns and invest in companies with attractive valuations.

Is it possible to live on dividends?

In the past, dividend investment has been seen as a way for risk-averse investors to invest in the stock market.

Living off of dividends is a marathon. No sprint. However, do not take this marathon lightly. You should have an urgency to both increase your income and save for retirement by getting started right away.

Plant your dividend seeds now by investing in dividend growth stocks. What will it take? With an average dividend yield of ~3.0% in your portfolio, you will need a portfolio of approximately $3.33 million to generate $100,000 a year in dividends.

Is it feasible to live off of dividends right away? No. Can it happen over time? Of course. With a careful plan and strategy, you can achieve the holy grail of passive income. living on dividends ... sooner than you think. I will walk through some steps to help you invest in passive income.

The key to living off of dividends is to focus on dividend growth stocks. Dividend growth stocks increase their dividends annually, which increases our income without doing a single thing.

Important dividend investing calculation to consider

In general, dividend investing is not very complex. In fact, the simpler you keep it the better you'll do. Good investing is boring. However, there are several dividend investing calculations that you should consider as you build and monitor your portfolio.

Here are three essential dividend investing calculations that you need to know:

1. Annual dividend yield: Annual dividend yield is the calculation of the percentage of dividend per share received relative to the stock price. This is a great barometer of the annual income you receive from investing in a stock. For example, if you invest in a $50 stock and it pays $2 per share in dividends. This is equal to a 4% annual dividend yield. If you plan on living off dividends, you want the annual dividend yield based on the cost you invested in shares to be the highest as possible.

2. Dividend growth rate: The dividend growth rate for a dividend stock is very important. You can calculate the dividend growth rate on any annual timeframe. To do so, take the current year's dividend per share divided by last year and subtract 1. This will calculate the dividend growth rate compared to the prior year.

3. Dividend payout ratio: The dividend payout ratio is a measure of how much a dividend stock pays in dividends relative to their earnings. You must consider the payout ratio of a stock because a high payout ratio means the company is retaining limited cash to be reinvested in the business. This can sometimes flash a red flag. If earnings decline, the dividend stock will have to decrease their dividend. That goes completely against our rules. We only want stocks that we know no matter what they will (at a minimum) maintain their dividend or increase it over time.

If you want to live on dividends, you must focus on the income component first. Make sure that the dividend will never decrease in value. You need stability of the income and stock appreciation. Good stocks increase their dividend over time and the stock value appreciates as well. This is since the earnings are likely increasing as well.

Conclusion Part 2

There are various other ways to create passive income other than dividends (rental properties, CDs, annuities, and peer-to-peer lending), but I prefer dividends resulting from index funds.

One reason for this belief is because stocks are far more liquid than real estate and other financial assets (easier to sell a stock than a house). Regardless of which method you prefer, you need to start making passive income. I guarantee you won't regret it!

Glossary

- **Off-exchange market or OTC market** is a market that has a decentralized opportunity for investors to participate in purchasing and selling of stocks to the public. It also involves a definite two parties during a trade.
- **Day trading**. This is the act of buying and selling shares on a particular day. This is usually a method of regulating the stock exchange markets as it runs daily This is to ensure the smooth running of the market.
- **Brokers**. These are people who have access to the stock market and will normally act as middlemen to investors who would like to buy or sell shares in the stock market.
- **Bull markets.** These are markets where when prices of commodities, stocks, bonds, and sometimes, housing increases over a long period of time before dropping unexpectedly.
- **Bear market.** This is when the prices of commodities falling to 20% or more. It kills morale, and they will think the prices will keep falling and see no need for investing in those stocks.
- **Stock market crash.** It is an abrupt reduction in prices of stocks that affect a significant part of the stock market resulting in a massive loss of wealth. This situation is made worse by speculative market bubbles and panic.
- **Index weighting**. This is the art that is critical in the sense that one can understand the design of the index he or she is buying from.
- **Penny stocks.** These refer to stocks trading below five dollars. They are often shares for companies which are about to go bankrupt, small or new companies or highly over-leveraged business.
- **Mutual funds**. These investments are the ones that involve pooling money from different investors so as to buy shares, stocks, bonds, and other securities which one may be unable to do on their own. They ascertain net asset value.

www.ingramcontent.com/pod-product-compliance
Lightning Source LLC
Chambersburg PA
CBHW081801200326
41597CB00023B/4106